GOLF COURSES OF COLORADO

A Guide To Public And Resort Courses

By Don and Jim Gallup

1984 Edition

Colorado Leisure Sports

Publisher:	Colorado Leisure Sports P.O. Box 1953 Estes Park, Colorado Phone (303) 586-6846
Printing:	Publishers Press Salt Lake City, Utah
Editorial Consultant:	James D. Hutchinson Boulder, Colorado
Cover Design and Illustrations:	Henry Schmidt and Terry Orin for Henry Schmidt Design, Boulder, Colorado.
Composition:	Kenton and Associates Denver, Colorado
Photographs:	Don and Margaret Gallup Estes Park, Colorado

Library of Congress Catalog Card Number: 84-70834

ISBN 0-9613458-0-2

Cover photo - View from the Leadville nine-hole golf course with Mt. Massive in the background.

PREFACE

This book provides the golfer with information about all the eighteen and nine-hole public and resort golf courses in Colorado. It tells you how to get to the golf course, gives the phone number of the pro shop, offers information on facilities at both the golf course and clubhouse, and advises you of areas near the golf course where good restaurants and motels are located.

In addition, you will find a general description of every golf course as well as advice and suggestions on how best to play each hole. You will also find ideas on other exciting things to do near many of the courses in addition to playing golf.

An unusually interesting feature is the section on nine-hole golf courses, which the authors claim is Colorado's "best-kept secret". Anyone who is enthusiastic about the game of golf will find the wealth of information contained between the covers of this book invaluable.

INTRODUCTION

Several years ago while visiting Scotland on a sightseeing and golfing vacation, I bought a book entitled *Golf Courses of Scotland.* This book was a directory of all the golf courses in Scotland and included written descriptions of several of the author's favorite courses. As a result of information contained in this book, I was able to play on some out-of-the-way, little known, but fabulous golf courses. Without the benefit of the book I never would have known about them.

The thought occurred to me that a book of this type would be great for residents and visitors to the State of Colorado. Like Scotland, Colorado has thousands of visitors each year, and many of them love to play golf. In addition, Colorado, like Scotland, has some of the finest golf courses in the world.

This book includes a complete directory of all the public and resort golf courses in Colorado, with an informative description of each 18-hole course and a somewhat abbreviated description of the 9-hole courses. Between Jim and me, we have played every golf course described, some of them many times. Because all our handicaps vary, you may find it necessary to make some adjustments in your own game compared to the manner which we have suggested for playing some of the courses.

All distances are measured from the men's regular tees to the center of green.

No information has been included on green fees, because they have a tendency to change from year to year. Neither do we recommend individual restaurants and motels, but merely indicate areas where good ones are located.

Before playing any golf course described in this book, we suggest you read about it or, better yet, take the book with you and read about each hole before playing it. This not only will prove interesting, but also should help your score.

Golf is quite popular in Colorado, and the public courses are all busy during the summer months; so it is best to make inquiries well in advance regarding starting times. Don't overlook playing these golf courses in the fall months because the crowds have thinned out by then, and the fairways and greens are all in excellent condition at that time of year.

If you are a visitor and unfamiliar with the Denver area, then a city map is a must. Between directions given in this book and a map of the city, you should not have any trouble locating the golf course you wish to play.

One thing to remember when playing Colorado's mountain golf courses, bring your umbrella and other rain gear because summer storms can spring up with little warning, although they are usually of short duration.

We hope you will find this book interesting and informative and that you will enjoy playing the many excellent golf courses in colorful Colorado.

SMILE

YOU'RE PLAYING GOLF
IN COLORADO

TABLE OF CONTENTS

SECTION 1

NORTHEAST PLAINS AND FOOTHILLS

COLLINDALE GOLF COURSE

LOCATION:	Ft. Collins, Colorado. One and one-half miles east of South College Avenue on Horsetooth Road.
TELEPHONE:	221-6651
COURSE FACILITIES:	Fully equipped pro shop, riding golf carts, pull carts, club rental, driving range, chipping and putting greens.
CLUBHOUSE FACILITIES:	Excellent snack bar serving hot sandwiches, breakfast, lunch, beer, and soft drinks.
LODGING:	Lots of good motels, located mostly on South and North College Avenue and east of town on Highway 14.
RESTAURANTS:	Ft. Collins has an abundance of fine places to eat. Ask around.

GOLF COURSE:

	Par	Course Rating	Yardage
Championship	71	71.6	6995
Regular	71	69.0	6413
Ladies	73	70.0	5472

Collindale, one of Northern Colorado's several fine courses, combines fertile Poudre Valley farm land with old majestic cottonwoods and many young seedlings. The cottonwoods, clustered around the creek beds, come into play on the par five 6th and 13th holes, as well as the par four 10th and the par three 11th. The fairways are well maintained and yield good lies, while the greens are fast and deceptive. This is an excellent golf course by anyone's standard, lots of fun to play, and easy to walk.

A good drive off the first tee will put you at the corner of the righthand dogleg on the 517-year par five number 3 handicap hole. Be careful of the hidden pond at the right front

Collindale No. 6
541 yards par five

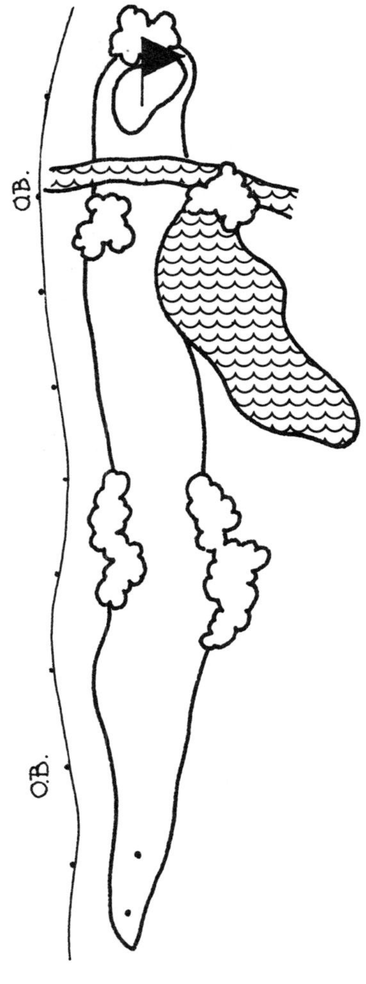

and the sand trap at the left front of the green. Don't expect to reach this green with your second shot. The 382-yard par four No. 2 is straightaway with a wide-open fairway and won't give most golfers any trouble. Hole No. 3 is a little longer at 409 yards, and it bends off to the left a little at a point indicated by a small group of pine trees at the inside corner. Another not so noticeable pond crowds the right front of the green.

The next hole, No. 4, is more uphill than it looks from the tee. Distance is 370 yards, and the par is four. A crescent-shaped lake runs from the left front and along the left side of the green. No. 5 is an uphill par three at 181 yards with a sand trap at the left front of the green. This hole is all carry and usually requires one more club than normally hit for this distance.

The number 1 handicap hole is the 541-yard par five 6th, and rightfully so. Out-of-bounds protects the entire length of the hole on the left, but the larger problem is the irrigation ditch crossing the fairway about 50 yards in front of the green and the two huge cottonwood trees guarding the approach to the green. To further complicate matters, a large lake occupies the right side of the fairway at the 150-yard marker. Most golfers will do best to lay up short of the ditch, and hit a mid-to-short iron onto the green. It takes an almost perfect shot to hit a fairway wood over the ditch and between the cottonwood trees to the green. (see sketch pg. 4)

No. 7 is a short 330-yard par four. A good drive can get you within 110 yards of the green. The small sand trap to the left of the green can protect a tough pin placement and make this hole play a little more difficult. The 135-yard par three 8th hole is guarded by two sand traps, one in front and the other to the right front of the green. The distance here is deceiving, but play it as it says on the card. No. 9 is a tough fitting end to the front nine. It is a long 420-yard par four with the fairway veering off to the left after your drive. A lake on the right which is unreachable for all but the longest of drivers, and trees on the left can reach up and easily grab your ball. To reach this green in regulation will require a solid mid-to-long iron from the fairway, or for the shorter hitter, a fairway wood.

The 10th hole is straightaway, par four and 400 yards long. Two large cottonwood trees guard each side of the fairway about 200 yards off the tee and demand an accurate drive. At 177 yards the par three 11th is one of the better par three holes around. It calls for a straight, all-carry tee shot between two large cottonwood trees a short distance in front of the tee box to a green that is well protected by two menacing sand traps. Take plenty of club here, because the green is a much larger target than it looks from the tee.

The 390-yard par four No. 12 parallels No. 4 and is similar in character. Try to make your second shot end up below the hole; then you should pick up a par. No. 13 is the number 2 handicap hole and is very much like the 6th hole on the front nine. Again, you have the irrigation ditch and cottonwood trees guarding your approach to the green. The lake on the left, which is out about 190 yards from the green, is not easily seen from the fairway. Best to play up short of the ditch, then hit a short-to-medium iron to the green.

One of the very interesting holes on the back nine is the short 344-yard par four 14th. Your tee shot must carry over an irrigation ditch crossing the fairway 175 yards from the tee box. At the end of your drive there is a dogleg left requiring a short iron to the green, which is guarded by a right front sand trap. Don't try to cut the corner from the tee because the left rough can be costly. No. 15 is an uphill 200-yard all-carry shot to a green guarded by a sizeable sand trap at the left front. Not an easy par three in anyone's book. For the 363-yard 16th hole we have a sweeping dogleg right. After a good drive and a medium iron, you should be on this par four in regulation.

The short par four 17th is only 335 yards in length, but is an interesting hole. After a well-hit tee shot the fairway doglegs a little right and calls for a short iron approach to a green protected by a small pond on the right and a sand trap on the left. No. 18 is not an exciting finishing hole. At 381 yards and par four, the only trouble is the lake on the left side of the fairway. At that, it takes a big hit and a pretty good hook to get in the water. The green is elongated and slopes toward the golfer; so it is an opportunity to go for the pin and finish up with a par.

Ft. Collins has an interesting nine hole golf course located in City Park. To get there go west on Mulberry and turn right on Bryan. This was the original course in Ft. Collins; so it has many large mature trees and tight fairways. Facilities include a pro shop, driving range, and putting green. Pull carts and electric golf carts are available for rent. Call 221-6650 for further information.

If you have an extra day and would like to see a part of Colorado that a lot of visitors miss, take a drive west on Highway 14 up the Poudre River Canyon to Walden, Colorado. You can then either return by the same route or go north into Wyoming, over to Laramie, and back down to Ft. Collins. It is a beautiful scenic drive and well worth your time.

EAGLE COUNTRY CLUB

LOCATION: Broomfield, Colorado. From the business section of Broomfield take West Midway Blvd. east to Main Street, turn left and go to East 12th Avenue, turn right and this street will take you to the golf course.

TELEPHONE: 465-1903

COURSE FACILITIES: Fully equipped pro shop, riding golf carts, pull carts, club rental, driving range, and putting green.

CLUBHOUSE FACILITIES: Restaurant serving lunch, sandwiches, dinner, beer, mixed and soft drinks.

LODGING: Denver and Boulder motels.

RESTAURANTS: If you like Italian food, ask directions to Louisville, Colorado. Only a few miles away are some fine Italian restaurants.

GOLF COURSE:

The Eagle Country Club is privately owned and has a private membership, but tee times are also available to the public. This golf course is presently undergoing considerable new and renew construction, with a complete new back nine scheduled for play August 1, 1984, and the changing of several holes on the front nine. When all of this work is completed, Eagle Country Club will be one fine championship golf course.

I am not including a hole-by-hole description of this golf course as it is impossible to do because of the way everything is being changed. A later revision of this book will include a complete description.

When this golf course is complete, it will have over 50 sand traps, plenty of water hazards, and large undulating greens that will very seldom yield a level putt. It will be a super challenge to everyone who plays it. Make a note to give it a shot in 1985.

ESTES PARK GOLF AND COUNTRY CLUB

LOCATION: Approximately one and one-half miles south of the intersection of Highway 34 and 36 on Highway 7 in Estes Park, Colorado.

TELEPHONE: 586-4361

COURSE FACILITIES: Fully equipped pro shop, riding golf carts, pull carts, club rental, driving range, chipping and putting greens.

CLUBHOUSE FACILITIES: Snack bar serving lunch, sandwiches, soft drinks and beer.

LODGING: Estes Park is a resort area and there are many good places to stay. Check with the visitor bureau at the Chamber of Commerce building located east of town on Highway 34. It is best to book in advance during July and August.

RESTAURANTS: Many very good restaurants in and around town. Inquire at the visitor bureau or ask your golfing partner.

GOLF COURSE:

	Par	Course Rating	Yardage
Regular	70	66.4	5833
Ladies	74	71.6	5522

It is a very pleasant and enjoyable experience to play the Estes Park golf course where, at an elevation of 7800 ft., the ball will carry an extra 10 to 15 yards. If this golf course were located in Scotland, it would be called a "Holiday Course." The distance is short, being only slightly more than 5800 yards with five par threes and three par fives. All par fives are possible birdie holes. Of the par threes, the 5th, 10th, and 15th are all testy golf holes, and you will be fortunate indeed to walk away from them with par. Although the course is not long, par is seldom within reach of the majority of golfers who play this course. Putting is always frustrating on mountain courses, and Estes Park is no exception. Find out where Fish Creek is located because your putts will always break in that direction. If you are putting well, this golf course will probably be kind to you, and the good golfer will have an opportunity for a low score.

The first hole is also the number 1 handicap with a fairway that is dead straight and 442 yards in length. Not visible from the tee is a valley crossing the fairway about 140 yards in front of the green. A downhill lie on the tee box side of the valley can be troublesome. Watch out for the grove of trees to the left front of the green and make every effort to be below the hole when putting. The next two holes are relatively easy with the second being 140 yards slightly downhill, while the third is a 384-yard straight-away par four. The 4th hole is a longer par four at 415 yards, and it is best to hit for the left side of the fairway off the tee because your ball will most always kick right. Your putter will get a real test here trying to handle this two-tier green.

Although only a par three, a wood is usually required off the tee for the 241-yard 5th hole. There is out-of-bounds on the right for the slicer, while the rough on the left is composed of thick, fairly tall grass. Above the hole is the wrong place to be for putting. No. 6 is a 136-yard par three. A short iron and two putts should yield a par. The 496-yard No. 7, however, can give the golfer trouble because of the trees along the fairway's right side and the number of putts it can easily take to put the ball in the hole.

The 335-yard short par four 8th hole calls for a good drive to the bottom of the valley, which is about 140 yards from the green. From here a short iron can be hit to the green at the top of the hill. The break is all left (towards Fish Creek) on this green. It may not be apparent to the eye, but believe me, it's there. No. 9 is a short par five at 464 yards and offers a good chance for a birdie. It is reachable in two by the strong golfer, but the grass berm-type bunker immediately in front of the green can cause as much trouble as any sand trap. The average golfer would do well to try to reach the green in regulation three and hope to get it close for a birdie putt.

The back nine is shorter, but is best described as hilly, providing many uneven lies. The holes have also been renumbered, and the old No. 12 is now the 10th hole. With a sand trap on the right and water on the left, the 157-yard par three 10th allows little room for error. This hole, being downhill, plays 10 to 15 yards shorter than the indicated yardage. Again, the best place to putt is from below the hole.

The next four holes are all short par fours, and although interesting to play, they are referred to as "Birdie Alley" and should provide an opportunity to pick up a few strokes.

No. 15 is the second longest par three on the course at 188 yards. Water and a sand trap offer trouble on the right, and if the wind is blowing, it is easy to lose a stroke here. No. 16 is a short dogleg right, par four, which is usually played with a mid-to-long iron off the tee and a short iron to the green. This hole should yield par to most players, but many a match has been lost here with a tee shot that shanked or faded out-of-bounds on the right. Some strong golfers may elect to "go for the green" with a wood or a 1 iron by cutting the corner over the barn, but this is not for the weak of heart or the short of talent.

For the 17th hole we have a sweeping dogleg right, par five, around a right-to-left slope in the terrain and with out-of-bounds on the right all the way to the green. Since the distance here is only 488 yards, it is another good opportunity for a birdie. No. 18 is another story, and a birdie on No. 17 will help a bogey or double bogey on No. 18. The hole is 449 yards in length and, along with the 1st, is one of the most difficult on the course. It is a long par four, and that is the main reason for its difficulty, although a loose approach shot will find trouble on both sides and behind the green. This is a demanding finishing hole to an otherwise rather easy playing but enjoyable golf course.

You will enjoy playing golf in Estes Park. Scenery abounds in this beautiful place, and the personnel in the clubhouse will make you more than welcome. The course is usually open for play from April 15 to October 31, but is in its best playable condition from July 1st to October 15th. Afternoon showers are common during the summer months, so have your rain gear handy.

While visiting in Estes Park, take time to play the nine-hole course located just east of town on Highway 34. Par here is 31, and it is a good test of the golfer's ability. The Big Thompson River winds through the course, and the scenery is even more breathtaking than at the 18-hole course. Facilities include a pro shop and practice putting green. Rental clubs and pull carts are also available.

Estes Park is the eastern gateway to Rocky Mountain National Park. While in the area, take time to visit Bear Lake and hike some of the many mountain trails in the park. A must while in this part of Colorado is to drive west over Trail Ridge Road to Grand Lake. This is the highest and one of the most scenic drives in America. Don't miss it! Allow several hours for the drive and top it all off with a round of golf at the terrific Grand Lake golf course.

FORT MORGAN MUNICIPAL GOLF COURSE

LOCATION: Ft. Morgan, Colorado. From Exit 80 off Interstate-76 go one and one-half miles north and 1 mile west.

TELEPHONE: 867-5990

COURSE FACILITIES: Fully equipped pro shop, riding golf carts, pull carts, club rental, driving range and putting green.

CLUBHOUSE FACILITIES: The clubhouse is private and closed on Mondays. It does serve lunch, sandwiches, dinner, beer, mixed and soft drinks. A swimming pool and tennis courts are also available.

LODGING: Several good modern motels in town all along I-76.

RESTAURANTS: The private Ft. Morgan Country Club reciprocates with other clubs. The motels on I-76 all have good eating facilities. For in-town restaurants it's best to ask local residents.

GOLF COURSE:

	Par	Course Rating	Yardage
Championship	73	69.3	6416
Regular	73	69.3	6416
Ladies	74	75.6	6127

Anyone driving through Colorado on Interstate 76 who doesn't stop and play the Ft. Morgan Municipal Golf Course is missing a real treat! It's just an outstanding golf course with natural terrain that is quite hilly, fairways that are narrow and treelined, and greens that are an absolute pleasure to putt. There are no sand traps or significant water hazards on the course, but the narrow fairways with their hills, valleys, humps, and hollows make up for this deficiency. The course is always in excellent condition with the fairways yielding good lies, however, you will find the rough anything but forgiving. Although a little hilly, this course is still walkable; but, if you ordinarily ride, I would suggest renting an electric golf cart. This is a golf course you would enjoy playing on a regular basis.

The front nine starts off slow and easy, giving the golfer a good chance to warmup. No. 1 is a short 320-yard downhill par four, and the 2nd hole is quite similar at 326 yards, only uphill. The 3rd hole is a little longer at 369 yards, par four, and with a small left-hand dogleg that is enhanced by a grove of large trees at the inside corner. No. 4 is the last of the warm-up holes and is a short 325-yard uphill par four. The only real problem here is out-of-bounds behind the green.

Beginning with No. 5 the golf course achieves real respectability with a 400-yard par four that offers out-of-bounds on the left and a heavily treelined, very narrow fairway. Although the fairway is level, there is not room for a loose shot here. Three troublesome grass mounds rise at the back side of this green, and the lower left part of the green gives this putting surface a two-tier effect.

A good par five in anyone's book is the 575-yard number 1 handicap 6th hole. Out-of-bounds haunts the entire left side of this fairway, which is crossed by two large valleys not visible from the tee. The fairway is heavily treelined on the left, and a thinner line of trees extends along the right side. This is a fine par five that is unreachable in two by all but the very talented.

The 7th hole backs off a bit with a 285-yard slightly downhill par four. Although the fairway is narrow and treelined, there is not a lot of trouble here.

The only par three on the front nine is the 155-yard 8th, and it is a good one. The green is elevated and calls for an all-carry shot over a valley of rough to a putting surface that is not visible from the tee. Although the green is fairly large, it is two-tiered with the front half being lower than the rear. Take plenty of club for this very interesting par three.

No. 9 is quite a hole; you will not find many like it anywhere. This par four is only 323 yards, but it is downhill, treelined, and has a right-hand dogleg with all kinds of trouble in the right rough, making it virtually impossible to cut the corner. Two large trees located in the middle of the fairway just short of the green cause further complications for your approach shot. Play for the left center of this fairway off the tee.

The back nine takes us out among the hills and valleys of the prairie. Not many trees here, but plenty of rough; the hills are more frequent and severe than on the front nine.

The 348-yard 10th fairway doglegs left at the top of the hill, and a strong drive will find your ball at that point. A short iron will get most golfers home in two. Play for the center of this fairway off the tee.

No. 11 is a well-designed par three at 208 yards that is all-carry over unfriendly rough to a point about 20 yards in front of the green, which is located well below the tee. It is another interesting and challenging par three. The 12th hole is the only level fairway on the back nine. It is 522 yards in length, par five, and straightaway. The problem here, other than length, is out-of-bounds along the left side. Be sure and look through the periscope before hitting off the tee because the small hill immediately in front of the tee obscures the view of the group ahead in the fairway.

Although the 13th is short at 348 yards and par four, it calls for an uphill approach shot from the valley below. The surface of the green is not visible from the fairway and therefore presents a club selection problem. Take plenty of club because the green is sizeable. For a par five, 471 yards is rather short, but the 14th hole is very demanding and anything but easy. After a strong drive this fairway doglegs sharply right, but a heavy grove of trees at the inside corner makes it impossible to hit over them. The short hitter off the tee must contend with a left-to-right sloping fairway, but from the dogleg to the green the fairway is quite level. It's important to stay in the fairway on this hole.

At 421 yards the par four 15th is the number 2 handicap hole on the course and rightly so, because the terrain seems to be getting more rugged and hilly all the time. This fairway is quite narrow and requires two well-hit, accurate shots to get home in two.

The short 126-yard par three 16th is an easy one, but it still calls for an accurate and well-placed short iron off the tee to get a par. No. 17 is a medium length par four at 364 yards, quite similar to the 13th hole. It is downhill off the tee, then uphill to a putting surface that cannot be seen from the fairway below. Although not long, it is one of the more difficult holes on the back nine.

The course winds up with a great finishing hole at 530 yards and par five. From the elevated tee it looks much longer, and the very narrow fairway is literally covered with humps and hollows all the way to the green. This 18th hole will require five well-executed shots before yielding to par.

You will enjoy playing this golf course. The "out on the prairie" feeling is different, and the narrow, hilly, treelined fairways guarded by natural rough give this course all the challenge most golfers are looking for. I guarantee you will want to come back and play it again.

FLATIRONS COUNTRY CLUB

LOCATION: Boulder, Colorado. 5706 E. Arapahoe Road. Go three miles east of 28th Street (Highway 36) on Arapahoe Road, and you will see the golf course on your right.

TELEPHONE: 444-3450

COURSE FACILITIES: Fully equipped pro shop, riding golf carts, pull carts, club rental, driving range, chipping and putting greens.

CLUBHOUSE FACILITIES: Snack bar serving sandwiches, beer and soft drinks. Other club facilities are private.

LODGING: Numerous motels are located along Highway 36 on the way into Boulder.

RESTAURANTS: Boulder is fortunate in having an abundance of good places to eat. It's hard to go wrong on any of them, but it probably would be best to ask your golfing partner.

GOLF COURSE:

	Par	Course Rating	Yardage
Championship	70	69.7	6982
Regular	70	68.4	6513
Ladies	72		6009

Flatirons is a municipal golf course attached to a private country club. This situation developed in the middle 1960's when Boulder Country Club members built a new facility 5 miles northeast of Boulder. Flatirons had been the Boulder Country Club for 25 years prior. It is a mature course with many lakes and creeks, treelined fairways, and beautiful greens. From the championship tees the course measures almost 7000 yards, and coupled with all the possibilities for trouble, it provides a very tough test of golf. The name is derived from the mountain formation towering above the town of Boulder to the west. Tee-off times are necessary from April through September, as this is a very popular course.

The first hole is a straightaway 350-yard par four newly constructed in 1971. The driving range is out-of-bounds on the left, and there is an incourse out-of-bounds on the right. The green is elevated and protected in the front right by a large sand trap. No. 2 is a 160-yard par three with large cottonwood trees guarding the left side of the green and a sand trap in front on the right. A small creek in front of the elevated green will grab any ball hit short. Championship tees stretch this hole to an impossible 240 yards. Out-of-bounds protects the left side of the 375-yard par four 3rd hole all the way to the huge green. Trouble lies everywhere you look on the 375-yard par four 4th. You must position the drive in the left center of the fairway to avoid the out-of-bounds left, treelined right side, and the monstrous cottonwood dwelling in the right center of the fairway 250 yards off the tee. The green is two-tiered and oblong with the left-hand lower than the right.

A lake crosses the fairway halfway through the only par five on the front nine, the 520-yard 5th. Another lake begins 175 yards from the green and runs up to the thin, highly contoured carpet. The 206-yard par three 6th is protected on the right by lakes, and on the left and rear by small shrubs and trees. Once again, the green has lots of contour. The 7th hole is a 460-yard nightmare. Favor the right side of the fairway when you steer your drive between the out-of-bounds right and the lakes and trees on the left. The second shot is most often a fairway wood or long iron on this dogleg left par four, and upon reaching the green your troubles may have just begun. The right front of this egg-shaped green is 4 feet higher than the back left, practically insuring a severe downhill or sidehill putt. Be very happy with a bogey five. Eight and nine are parallel 390-yard par fours. They are both straightaway with lakes on the right and relatively easy flat greens. Be thankful for the break at nine as you have just finished three hard par fours, and you have three more to tackle right away. This stretch of six par fours in a row has ruined many a fine round.

No. 10 is a deceptively long 390-yard par four. The second shot is to a small green, and a deep gully on the right has harassed many a golfer. Eleven and twelve are parallel 425-

yard par fours, both demanding long accurate drives, the second to slightly elevated greens. A one-shotter of 200 yards, the 13th has another deep gully on the left of the impeccable two-tiered green. No. 14 is a 390-yard par four requiring a drive with a 175-yard carry over a creek and a precise second to avoid the yawning beach on the left.

Anyone but a very long driver will want to layup short of the lakes on the 360-yard par four 15th. A drive of 230 yards in the air will carry the water, but the smarter shot is a mid-iron. The second is deceiving as the ground in front of the green is raised, distorting the distance and making it appear shorter than it really is. The 555-yard par five 16th is totally unreachable in two, and it is defended on both sides by trees lining the entire length of the rather wide fairway. Again a small creek must be cleared by a 175-yard carry off the tee.

The 17th is a 170-yard par three with a lake in front, sand traps on both sides, and small pines in the back. Play for the middle of the green. I have always had trouble with the 18th hole at Flatirons. Not particularly long at 390 yards, this dogleg left par four calls for a very straight drive avoiding the out-of-bounds left, the trees at the corner of the dogleg, and the lakes strung together along the right side of the fairway. The largest sand trap on the course lies in wait at the right front of this large undulating green.

The first time I played Flatirons I found almost every creek or lake on the course, and only after easing up on my drives and striving for accuracy off the tee was I able to stay out of trouble.

I know you will enjoy the greens as they have long been recognized as some of the truest and best in the state. Boulder is the home of the University of Colorado, one of the most picturesque college campuses in the country, so take a tour and don't forget the Rocky Mountains are only minutes away.

HIGHLAND HILLS MUNICIPAL GOLF COURSE

LOCATION: Greeley, Colorado. Go west of Greeley on Highway 34 by-pass to 35th Avenue. Turn north at this point and go to 20th Street. Turn left on 20th Street and go 1.7 miles west to Clubhouse Road. Turn left here, and the parking lot is straight ahead.

TELEPHONE: 330-7327

COURSE FACILITIES: Fully equipped pro shop, riding golf carts, pull carts, club rental, driving range, chipping and putting greens.

CLUBHOUSE FACILITIES: Complete snack bar serving breakfast, lunch, sandwiches, beer and soft drinks.

LODGING: Most motels are located south of town on Highway 85.

RESTAURANTS: Several good restaurants in the Greeley area. Best to ask your golf partner or at the pro shop.

GOLF COURSE:

	Par	Course Rating	Yardage
Championship	71	71.0	6683
Regular	71	69.8	6459
Ladies	77	73.2	6233

You will find one of Colorado's toughest and most exciting public golf courses in Greeley. The entire course is well maintained, and the greens are lightning fast. As you can see from the course rating of 69.8, a real challenge awaits the golfer after teeing it up at Highland Hills. The front nine is 274 yards longer than the back and is the more difficult of the two nines. Most of the trees have reached maturity, and they must be taken seriously along with the large undulating and fast greens. Walking this course can be enjoyable, so give it a try and get your exercise.

The golf course begins with three testing, parallel, 400-yard par fours, requiring accurate medium iron second shots. Although these holes are anything but easy, I feel the course really starts with the 507-yard par five 4th hole. This fairway is straightaway until about 140 yards from the hole at which point it fades off to the right to an uphill and difficult to see green. The trees along the right side of the fairway and at the bend make it risky to cut the corner. Because of the sand traps in front and at both sides of the green, it is best even for the long hitter not to attempt to reach this hole in two. No. 5 is an excellent par three of 176 yards uphill to an elongated green with a tricky little ridge running from the lower left to the upper right corner.

The 351-yard par four 6th hole, although seemingly a short one, plays longer than indicated because of the lake in front of the green. The lake forces a maximum tee shot of 200 yards, then a very demanding approach over the water to a green closely guarded by a left front sand trap. No. 7 is a long, narrow treelined par five at 511 yards, calling for second and third shots uphill to the green. The main difficulty here is length and the treelined fairway. The 432-yard par four 8th hole is a good one. A long drive and an all-carry long iron are required to reach this green in regulation. The front nine ends with a 167-yard par three to a green that is especially difficult to putt.

The first three holes on the back nine are all short par fours and are somewhat similar in character with doglegs that make it dangerous to cut the corner. Accuracy off the tee will go a long way toward par or possible birdie on these three holes. No. 13 is another dogleg, but much longer at 421 yards and par four. Trees at the corner make it almost impossible to shorten this hole by going over them. A good straight drive and a mid-iron should find your ball on the green.

The par three 14th at 194 yards can be troublesome for anyone leaving the ball out to the right because of the sand trap and lake at that side of the green. The next hole, No. 15 at 494 yards and par four, looks longer than it is, because it is all uphill. Lots of room in the fairway, but the lake in front and out-of-bounds to the left can be worrisome. Two sand traps guard this green, and an accurate approach shot is necessary for par. The 16th hole, at 402 yards and par four, is another interesting one. There doesn't appear to be much trouble from the tee, but it is the second shot that is demanding. With a sand trap at the left front and a lake at the right side of the green, there is little room for error. Even a slight miss to the right of the green will find the water.

At 169 yards, par three, and with no sand traps, the 17th hole should give you little trouble. However, the 373-yard 18th can, if you try to cut the corner over the tall poplar trees on this short but tricky par four. A 4 or 3 wood to the corner and a mid-iron to the green are the clubs for this hole. Two sand traps, one each at the left and right front with very little room between them, guard this green. Although No. 18 is short, it is a fine finishing hole.

Greeley is situated in the heart of some of the richest farm land in America. If you have the time, drive around the countryside and watch things grow. It is an interesting area!

JACKRABBIT TRAIL GOLF COURSE

LOCATION: North of Milliken, Colorado. From Highway 34 by-pass east of Loveland or west of Greeley take Colorado Highway 257 south for 3½ miles, and you will see the entrance to the golf course on the right.

TELEPHONE: 587-4694

COURSE FACILITIES: Fully equipped pro shop, riding golf carts, club rental, driving range, chipping and putting greens.

CLUBHOUSE FACILITIES: Snack bar serving sandwiches, beer and soft drinks. Dining room serving lunch, dinner and mixed drinks. Other facilities include a swimming pool and tennis courts.

LODGING: Greeley or Loveland motels.

RESTAURANTS: Mad Russian Restaurant upstairs in the clubhouse.

GOLF COURSE:

	Par	Course Rating	Yardage
Championship	70	64.4	5026
Regular	70	64.4	5026
Ladies	70	——	——

A unique and interesting experience awaits the golfer at Jackrabbit Trail. Although the course is short at 5026 yards, it is quite sporty and places a premium on accuracy both on and off the tee. This three-year-old course consists of severe slanting fairways, deep and frequent treelined ravines, lakes, and narrow approaches to small, irregularly shaped greens. All of this combines to give the golfer plenty of challenge for any one day! The course is presently undergoing some design change which will add to its playability by improving traffic flow and better definition of the fairways. This "out in the country" golf course offers a great view of the surrounding countryside as well as the back range and snowcapped peaks of the Rocky Mountains to the west.

The course begins with a short par four at 252 yards, calling for a fairway wood or long iron off the tee. Stay to the right here, because there's trouble to the left and behind the green.

The 2nd hole is the number 1 handicap at 393 yards and par four. The fairway is poorly defined, so line up about 20 yards to the right of the sprinkler control box visible from the tee. Use a medium iron or fairway wood off the tee and favor the right side. Two treelined gullies must be negotiated before reaching this small green located in the corner of the course. One must play it safe on this hole, or a double or triple bogey can easily find its way onto your score card.

No. 3 is a short 108-yard par three over another treelined gully to a shallow green that is almost impossible to hold. The 4th hole is a par four at 251 yards with out-of-bounds on the left and a treelined water-filled gully about halfway to the green. No. 5 is another short par four from an elevated tee downhill over a left-to-right sloping fairway to a green 272 yards away. Severe rough and trees guard the right front of this green.

The 6th hole is another par four of similar length at 270 yards. The green cannot be seen from the tee, so line up with the tree in the left rough. This fairway slopes left to right and is further complicated by a sweeping left-hand dogleg. No. 7 is 298 yards, par four, and for a change is straightaway down a well-defined fairway. A water-filled and treelined gully crosses this fairway about 160 yards off the tee and demands a 200 yard all-carry drive to clear it.

For the first time the golfer can get out the heavy timber on the 471-yard par five 8th, with out-of-bounds on the left and a sizeable, deep gully part way down the right side of this downhill fairway. The green is in the valley below at the southeast corner of the course. Don't take as much club as you think you need when approaching this green from the elevated fairway. It is 125 yards from where the fairway drops off to the front of the green, and a small sand trap sits to the green's right side.

The 9th hole is 375 yards, par four, and all uphill. The large gully to the right can spell real trouble. This hole plays much longer than indicated on the score card. No. 10 is downhill, straightaway at 327 yards and par four. The green juts out at the end of the fairway, and a loose approach shot missing the green on either side or to the rear means a nasty uphill chip shot back to the green. The par three 11th is a little uphill, but only 107 yards. Trouble lies to the green's left side, but otherwise a rather simple hole.

No. 12 is another par three, but much longer at 199 yards and very respectable. Water lies all along the right side, the fairway slopes right, and the putting surface is not visible from the tee. Don't be long or to the right, but favor the fairway's left side. The 13th hole is something else! Play a medium iron shot from the tee and aim for the extreme left side of the fairway. If executed properly, your shot will probably end up in the fairway's right side and, hopefully, short of the gully which crosses this fairway diagonally from right to left. From here it is an uphill short-to-medium iron approach to the green.

No. 14 is another short par four at 252 yards, but is very unusual. Line up with the white grain elevators in the distance and hit a medium iron, at the most, off the tee. The green is not visible from the tee box, and the fairway is downhill all the way and narrows sharply at the green which is surrounded by water on three sides and a small gully in front. Being long off this tee spells nothing but trouble.

The 251-yard par four 15th is another troublesome golf hole. Water extends along the right side of this fairway and juts in at the front of the green. Play down the fairway's left side and chip on from there.

A welcome relief is the 476-yard par five 16th. Although there is out-of-bounds on the right, the fairway is level, wide, and inviting with plenty of room for a big hit.

No. 17 is the railroad hole at 154 yards and par three. The green is situated well below the golfer and will require about two less clubs than normally hit for this distance.

The back nine finishes with a short, straightaway 252-yard par four. There is some trouble around the green in the form of a right side sand trap and a sharp drop off into rough at the left. Favor the right side of the fairway, and this should be an easy par.

Golfers will have mixed emotions after playing Jackrabbit. You will probably score very well or very poorly. The big hitter will have more trouble than the short hitter. Accuracy is a must over this natural and difficult terrain.

LAKE VALLEY GOLF CLUB

LOCATION: Four miles north of Boulder on Highway 36 and 1 mile east. Follow the signs.

TELEPHONE: 444-2114

COURSE FACILITIES: Fully equipped pro shop, riding golf carts, pull carts, club rental, driving range, chipping and putting greens.

CLUBHOUSE FACILITIES: Lounge and bar serving sandwiches, beer, mixed and soft drinks.

LODGING: Boulder motels. Most are located along Highway 36.

RESTAURANTS: Plenty of very good restaurants in Boulder. Ask around.

GOLF COURSE:

	Par	Course Rating	Yardage
Championship	70	68.6	6679
Regular	70	66.8	6476
Ladies	72	71.8	5837

Lake Valley for years was one of Colorado's few self-maintaining golf courses. Located out in the country 4 miles north of Boulder at the base of the foothills, it was once called The Foothills Golf Club. Recently, concerned developers bought the property and are making many course and facility improvements. The architect's use of the natural rolling terrain comes as close as I've seen to recreating the feeling one has playing a Scottish links. The layout of the course is one of the most interesting in the state, and coupled with the developers commitment to plant trees and upgrade the playability, this will soon become one of northern Colorado's most enjoyable and challenging courses. The meadowlarks have no manners, they sing constantly, even at the top of your backswing, reminding you that you are truly out in the country.

The 1st hole is a seemingly wide open 355-yard par four. An irrigation ditch runs under the fairway about 220 yards from the tee and can gather in any shot hit in the left or right rough. At the green a small trap guards the left front and another the right rear. Number 2 is a 408-yard dogleg left par four. Beyond the mound on the left are 2 sand traps that cannot be seen from the tee, so favor the right side. Watch out for the irrigation ditch 75 yards short of the green, once again running under the fairway, but emerging in both the right and left rough. This green is nestled against the hillside and slopes severely from back to front resulting in some very touchy putts.

The number 1 handicap hole is the 428-yard 3rd. Another ditch crosses the fairway 125 yards out and runs parallel to the left side up to the dogleg. An almost impossible 2nd shot awaits any golfer who has not favored the left side of the fairway off the tee. The elevated green is protected on the front by a large, some say, magnetic trap. Use at least 1 extra club for your second or it will surely claim another victim.

Position your tee shot short and to the right side on the 308-yard 4th as the fairway slopes right to left. By doing this you will avoid the trap on the left 50 yards from the green and not be bothered by the left and right front greenside traps. This elevated green is oblong and slopes severely towards you again, also hiding the trap in the back right.

The 186-yard uphill par three 5th features a difficult tee shot to this plateau-type green, which is trapped to the right front, left front and left rear. Don't overlook the severe drop-off on the green's left side. The green breaks drastically right to left. The 6th is a 395-yard dogleg right with the dogleg about 250 yards off the tee. A sand trap right and grass mound left narrow the landing area for this fairway which slopes left to right. Most golfers will do best to stay left off the tee and avoid the fairway trap. The strong hitter can clear it, but the right rough is no place to be for your second shot. A right front trap at greenside further complicates this hole.

The 216-yard 7th is downhill with sand in the right front and out-of-bounds along the entire right side. Maybe the smart shot is to lay up on the left side and chip for your par.

A large reservoir will catch a hooked or pulled tee shot on the par four 404-yard 8th. The two large cottonwood trees on the right are 75 yards short of the green, so hit it down the middle. This green also slopes from back to front.

The 9th is a 525-yard par five gradual dogleg left that appears wide open off the tee. However, 250 yards from the tee the landing area narrows, and another irrigation ditch protects the fairway in both the right and left rough. The sand trap on the right is 40 yards from the green, but it is still best to come in from that side for an open 3rd shot, thereby avoiding the sand trap in front.

A downhill par four dogleg right, with the fairway sloping left to right, awaits the golfer after making the turn. The sand trap in the right fairway is about 250 yards from the tee on this 408-yard hole. Favor the left side off the tee and for your approach use 1 less club to avoid the sand trap in the left rear and the small lake behind and to the right of the green.

The 585-yard 11th is one of the longest par fives in the state. It is straight and wide open, but watch out for the irrigation ditch 200 yards from the green, once again protecting both sides of the fairway. The green is elevated, long, and thin. Most golfers are very happy with par. The par three 12th is only 175 yards long, with the irrigation ditch 50 yards in front of the tee winding along the right side of the fairway. This two-tiered green is effectively protected by sand traps in the left front and right rear.

The number 2 handicap 13th is 413 yards long. A small lake guards the entrance 30 yards in front of the green and continues around to the left. Favor the fairway's right side and miss the sand trap at the green's left front. The par four 14th is a 375-yard dogleg left. The ditch in front of the tee comes back into play along the left side on the inside of the dogleg. A tee shot of more than 240 yards will find hard rough on the right, so it may be wise for long hitters to use a long iron or fairway wood to be safe. The sand trap in the left front is 25 yards short of the green.

The 333-yard 15th allows a legitimate chance at a birdie. This is a straightaway hole, with the fairway trap on the right 200 yards off the tee. There is plenty of room between the traps guarding the front right and left of the green. No. 16 is also a relatively easy 1-shotter, 175 yards in length. Difficulty arises when hitting into the wind and falling short into the trap protecting the left front.

The 17th is an excellent par four when played from the championship tees amongst the cottonwoods. Avoid the two fairway traps 200 yards out in the left rough and the traps at the left and right front of the green.

Lake Valley's finishing hole can be deceiving. A large cottonwood and an out-of-bounds driving range come into play on the right. The irrigation ditch in the rough shouldn't bother most golfers as a 150-yard carry or a straight hit will miss it easily. The green is elevated and large, but relatively flat. By now you should have had many long lag putts so it should not be a problem to make a par four on this friendly 18th hole.

LOVELAND GOLF COURSE

LOCATION: Loveland, Colorado. Go west of town on Highway 34, and turn north on Taft Avenue. After going one mile north you will come to West 29th Street. Turn west at this point, and you will soon see the golf course on your right.

TELEPHONE: 667-5256

COURSE FACILITIES: Fully equipped pro shop, riding golf carts, pull carts, club rental, driving range, chipping and putting greens.

CLUBHOUSE FACILITIES: Complete snack bar serving breakfast, lunch, sandwiches, beer and soft drinks.

LODGING: Lots of motels, most of them located east and west of town on Highway 34.

RESTAURANTS: A good number, also located along Highway 34.

GOLF COURSE:

	Par	Course Rating	Yardage
Championship	72	69.0	6762
Regular	72	67.2	6487
Ladies	74	71.9	5899

Loveland is another of Northern Colorado's superb and inviting public golf courses. It is best characterized by an excellent combination of fast greens, water hazards, and plenty of trees. The par five 5th and the par four 14th holes are particularly outstanding, and the entire golf course demands your complete and undivided attention if you hope to score well. Actually this course has a little of everything, and you will probably use all the clubs in your bag before completing 18 holes. You will be asked to make every effort to play your round of golf in four hours.

Although the course starts out slow with four relatively easy holes in succession, there's no room for error beginning with the 5th hole. It is a 526-yard par five dogleg left, with an uphill tee shot and a downhill wood or long iron to a spot short of a small lake in front of the green. Be aware of the out-of-bounds on the right which is in line with the row of poplar trees on that side of the fairway. Anything from a wedge to an 8 iron should clear the water in front, but be careful of the water to the left and behind the green as well. An accurate approach is essential for par on this hole.

The 6th is a 391-yard straightout par four to a fairway that slants left to right. There is a small lake close to the right edge of the green that beckons a second shot if not hit correctly. No. 7 is a 472-yard par five, with the green nestled in behind a lake that can come into play when attempting to reach the green in two. A safe second shot is to play the ball short of the green and to the left of the lake.

The 8th hole is a rather common, short 134-yard par three with a sand trap at the left front of the green. No. 9 is a 379-yard slight dogleg right, with out-of-bounds on that side indicated by the same row of poplar trees that were out-of-bounds on No. 5. It takes a real belt to cut the corner over these trees, so the small hitter shouldn't try it. The green has considerable left-to-right break, and must be taken seriously, or this can be a costly hole.

The back nine starts off with a 376-yard par four that is parallel and similar to No. 1. There is little trouble except for the tree in the middle of the fairway about 20 yards in front of the green. No. 11 is a straightaway 187-yard par three with a shallow green that is hard to hold and tricky to putt.

The 392-yard par four No. 12 is a dogleg left requiring a long straight drive, and a medium iron for a second shot to the green. An irrigation ditch and a gauntlet of trees at the left corner of this fairway advises you not to cut the corner on this hole. No. 13 is a 496-yard par five, with a lake in front of the tee box. The water is a factor here because it takes a pretty good poke to clear the lake. It's tough to reach this green in two. For most golfers, it will take two good wood shots and a short-to-medium iron to get on in regulation.

Next we have the number 1 handicap hole, the 418-yard par four 14th. A long drive here is essential if one expects to reach this green in two. Even with a big tee shot, it will require a medium or long iron to reach this island green. Most players will do best to lay up short of the water and pitch on from there. The 363-yard par four 15th is the number 3 handicap hole and requires a good straight tee shot over an irrigation ditch, but you must stay to the right of the large cottonwood trees on your left. Again, it will usually take a medium iron to the green which is often hard to hold.

The 407-yard par four 16th calls for a long straight drive and a medium iron downhill to the green below. This green has a little of everything — speed, two tiers, valleys, hills, and slopes of all kinds. Getting down in two here is a rarity.

No. 17 is a 516-yard par five, with the fairway veering off mildly to the right. To reach this green in regulation will take three good shots and is another touchy one to putt. Although you don't usually find a par three for a finishing hole, we have one here with the 180-yard 18th. It is however, an excellent golf hole. The two large cottonwood trees guarding both sides of the fairway demand an accurate, well-placed tee shot to a green closely protected by sand traps. This hole is a fitting climax to an exciting and demanding round of golf.

The town of Loveland is located at the foot of the Big Thompson Canyon. Take time to drive up the Big Thompson to Estes Park and return by way of Glen Haven. It is a beautiful drive, and the scenery is inspiring.

RIVERVIEW GOLF COURSE

LOCATION: Sterling, Colorado, 13064 County Road 370 east of town.

TELEPHONE: 522-3035

COURSE FACILITIES: Fully equipped pro shop, riding golf carts, pull carts, club rental, driving range, chipping and putting greens.

CLUBHOUSE FACILITIES: Snack bar serving breakfast, lunch, sandwiches, dinner, beer and soft drinks.

LODGING: Several new motels located close by on Interstate 76.

RESTAURANTS: Best to make local inquiry.

GOLF COURSE:

	Par	Course Rating	Yardage
Championship	71	66.4	6232
Regular	71	66.3	6030
Ladies	72	68	5458

Located east of Sterling and just off Interstate 76, Riverview Golf Course is nestled among the hills and valleys of this eastern Colorado prairie country. Although the course is young and needs time to mature, it is an interesting and challenging design. Most of the trees are newly planted and quite small, so they do not add to the difficulty of the golf course at this time. The only water on the course is the lake in front of the 18th green, but more water hazards are planned over the next several years. The fairways are all quite narrow, and the rough is natural, composed of sandy soil and sparse native prairie grass. A visit to the rough will most likely add several strokes to the golfer's score card. Riverview's natural hilly and open terrain reminds me of some of the well-known Scottish links. If you are in the area, make it a point to play Riverview.

The 510-yard par five 1st hole is level off the tee, then gradually uphill to a rather small green. It will take three good shots over this uneven fairway to reach the green in regulation. No. 2 is a 130-yard par three that is straightaway and a little uphill to an elongated green. It should be an easy par.

At 300 yards and par four the short 3rd hole should yield a lot of pars. It is uphill with a short dogleg left at the end of a well-hit drive. The green is large, but possesses a lot of break and is tricky to putt. The next hole, No. 4, calls for a blind tee shot uphill to a right-hand dogleg in the fairway. From there it is downhill to a medium size green.

The 375-yard par four 5th is very interesting. It is uphill off the tee to the top of a hill at which point the fairway bends sharply left. A sand trap sits in the left rough a little past the inside corner of the dogleg. The green is not visible from the fairway, only the top of the flag. Because this green is below the golfer, take at least one less club than normally hit for the indicated yardage. Check the tops of the sprinkler heads, because many of them will have yards to the green painted on them.

No. 6 at 468 yards and par four is not only the number 2 handicap, but is definitely one of the strong holes on this golf course. It's downhill off the tee to a landing area at the bottom of the valley that is only 35 yards wide. From there it's uphill with a long iron or fairway wood to a slightly elevated green. Out-of-bounds extends along the fairway's left side from tee to green.

The 7th is a rather average 370-yard par four that again is downhill off the tee then uphill to the green. Not a difficult hole. The next two holes, No. 8 and 9, are quite similar, with No. 9 being just a little longer. Both require downhill tee shots and uphill approaches and should yield a lot of pars.

No. 10 is another uncomplicated par three at 190 yards. Although a little uphill, the only real problem here is its 190 yards. The shortest par four on the course is the 282-yard 11th. It is very similar in character to holes No. 8 and 9.

The par five 12th at 515 yards is an excellent par five. It requires a solid drive to the top of the hill and for most of us a well-hit fairway wood to get near the green in two. This number 3 handicap hole is not likely to yield to par easily. No. 13 is a short par four at 328 yards. The green is lower than the tee box, but elevated from the bottom of the valley. Not much trouble here.

At No. 14 we encounter several of the few large trees that are on the golf course. They are located in front of the tee, but are not a problem as most golfers will be able to hit over them. This fairway opens up and is quite roomy at the landing area. The fairway doglegs left after your drive and calls for a short iron approach from that point to the green. The 149-yard par three 15th is a no-trouble hole that most golfers should be able to handle with ease.

The 16th at 499 yards and par five is considerably more demanding, requiring a tee shot that is all uphill and a strong long iron or fairway wood for a second. This fairway slopes a bit left as well as bending gently to the right. It's a very good par five.

No. 17 is the 3rd par three on the back nine. This 157-yard hole goes from an elevated tee over a valley to a green at about the same elevation as the tee box. It's just a good 157-yard par three without any special hazards.

The 18th hole is the number 1 handicap and rightly so. At 434 yards it is already a lengthy par four, and the lake immediately in front of the green makes it play even longer. A strong drive will find your ball at the top of the hill. From that point the fairway doglegs left, and it is about 230 yards to the green. This means that most of us will be forced to lay up short of the water and pitch on from there, hoping to get it close enough for a par putt. This is by far the most difficult hole on the golf course and makes an excellent finishing hole.

Many people driving to Colorado from the east stop in Sterling and play Riverview before driving on to the mountains. This golf course will become even more popular as it improves with age. I enjoyed playing Riverview. I'm sure you will too. Give it a try at your first opportunity.

SOUTH RIDGE GREENS

LOCATION: Ft. Collins, Colorado. Southeast of town. Go about one-half mile south of the junction of Harmony Road and Lemay Avenue.

TELEPHONE: 226-2828

COURSE FACILITIES: Pro shop is presently under construction, and will include a driving range, chipping and putting greens, as well as riding golf carts, pull carts, and club rental.

CLUBHOUSE FACILITIES: Under construction.

LODGING: South College in Ft. Collins.

RESTAURANTS: South College in Ft. Collins.

GOLF COURSE:

	Par	Course Rating	Yardage
Maximum Distance	71	NA	6600
Minimum Distance	71	NA	5185

South Ridge is owned by the City of Ft. Collins and leased back to the developers of the golf course and adjacent property. It is open to the public on a daily fee basis and scheduled for play in early summer of 1984. The two large lakes, hilly terrain, Mall and Fossil Creeks running through the course should offer more than enough natural obstacles for anyone. Trees are being planted now, but it will be several years before they become much of a factor. South Ridge has all the qualifications to become another one of the Northern Colorado's excellent golf courses. Put it on your list of courses to play.

TWIN PEAKS MUNICIPAL GOLF COURSE

LOCATION: Longmont, Colorado. From the intersection of Main Street and Mountain View Avenue go west on Mountain View to Cornell Drive. Turn left at that point and the road will lead you to the parking lot for the golf course.

TELEPHONE: 772-1722

COURSE FACILITIES: Fully equipped pro shop, riding golf carts, pull carts, club rental, driving range, chipping and putting greens.

CLUBHOUSE FACILITIES: Snack bar serving sandwiches, beer and soft drinks.

LODGING: There are very few motels in Longmont, however, if you will check along North Main Street and on I-25 east of town you will find good accommodations.

RESTAURANTS: Longmont has two very fine Mexican restaurants as well as several other excellent places to eat. Inquire locally as to their location.

GOLF COURSE:

	Par	Course Rating	Yardage
Championship	70	70.6	6767
Regular	70	68.1	6237
Ladies	71	71.8	5816

Twin Peaks Municipal Golf Course is relatively new, only a little more than six years old. It is, however, always in excellent condition with good lush grass in both the rough and fairways. The course is quite flat, but has been made more difficult by the use of grass berm-type bunkers placed strategically along the edges of many of the fairways. Most of the greens are elevated and surrounded by large grassy mounds which require very delicate chip shots to extremely fast and irregularly shaped greens. Many trees have been planted recently, but they are all immature and will not come into play for several years. A few small lakes dot the course and, as a result, demand accurate tee shots where they come into play. The panoramic view of the snowcapped Rocky Mountains to the west is spectacular from the entire course, so in case your game isn't the best, you can always enjoy the view. The sand traps on this golf course are extremely difficult to get out of because they are all built into the lower side of the grassy mounds that surround all of the greens. The 150-yard markers are small concrete discs in the center of the fairways. Twin Peaks is another course that is ideal for walking.

The first hole is a short 322-yard par four warm-up hole. No trouble here except for the sand trap at the right front of the green. No. 2, however, is a different story because it is the number 1 handicap hole at 524 yards and par five. Out-of-bounds on the right follows the fairway all the way to the green, and two large grass bunkers guard the fairway about 250 yards off the tee. Of further concern is the lake in the left rough about 100 yards out from the green and another grass bunker in the right rough immediately opposite the lake. A long second shot can easily find this lake which is not noticeable from the fairway. It is best to lay up short of the lake and approach the green from that point because there are no traps and the green slopes conveniently toward the golfer. You can be proud of a par on this hole.

The course relaxes a bit on the next three holes, and although par may escape you, they do not demand the best from most golfers. But an errant tee shot on No. 6 can spell real trouble because of the lakes guarding each side of the fairway. Aim for the grassy mound in the distance. The 157-yard par three 7th is not a difficult golf hole, but the lake in the rough to the right front of the green cannot be ignored.

No. 8 is one of the more difficult and challenging holes on the course. Although not long, at 386 yards, it requires a dead-straight tee shot between two lakes to a narrow landing area. From here the fairway doglegs left, and a long approach shot is needed to hit the green in regulation. Some golfers will hit a mid-iron off the tee to a point short of the lake in the left rough and approach the green from that point. This might very well be the safest shot. Only the very long hitter should attempt to hit over this lake at the left corner of the dogleg. One must know his capabilities and limitations to play this par four hole properly.

At 341 yards and par four, the 9th hole grants an opportunity to pick up a stroke that may have been lost on the previous hole. The two traps guarding the left and right front of this green call for an accurate approach shot and give this hole the respectability it needs.

The back nine begins with two par fours of somewhat equal length and difficulty. The lake in the right rough on No. 10 can be reached by the big hitter, and the grass bunkers on each side of the fairway on No. 11 can catch a long ball off the tee. No. 12 is an excellent par three at 163 yards. The sand trap guarding the front of the green requires an all-carry tee shot, and any putt from above the hole is almost impossible to make.

The next hole, No. 13, is a long straight par four at 422 yards, and is the number 2 handicap hole on the course. Out-of-bounds is on the far left, and the only real trouble here is length and, of course, putting on a slippery green. As on so many of the holes at Twin Peaks, two grass bunkers guard each side of the fairway on the 498-yard par five 14th. The sand trap at the left front of this elevated green is a real hazard, so make every effort to avoid it. Nos. 13 and 14 are two excellent golf holes, and par on either one of them is an accomplishment.

No. 15 is a short 351-yard par four, with the left front sand trap being the only problem. There should be lots of pars on this hole. Accuracy off the tee is a must on the 384-yard par four 16th. Two lakes guard each side of the fairway, and either one can catch a careless tee shot. The fairway doglegs around the lake to the right, but don't try to hit over it from the tee because it is impossible to do so for most golfers. This hole plays much more difficult than indicated on the score card.

The 17th is a good par three at 172 yards and with a small lake perilously close to the left side of the green. The championship tees on this hole play to 234 yards and make it an exceptional challenge for even the best golfer. No. 18, at 398 yards and par four, is not a strong finishing hole. Most golfers will hit their tee shot in the right rough, which shortens the hole considerably. However, when the trees mature, this will be more risky, and the golfer will have to play the hole as originally intended, hitting at least a mid-iron approach shot to the green.

Longmont has an excellent 9-hole golf course. Like the City Park Nine in Ft. Collins, it is an old established course with many large, mature trees. It will provide any golfer with a real challenge and is well worth your time to play it. See the 9-hole section of this book for further details on Sunset Municipal Golf Course.

SECTION II

DENVER METRO AND SUBURBS

APPLEWOOD GOLF COURSE

LOCATION: Golden, Colorado. Go one mile west of the intersection of Interstate 70 and West 32nd Avenue, and you will see the golf course on the right.

TELEPHONE: 279-3003

COURSE FACILITIES: Fully equipped pro shop, riding golf carts, pull carts, club rental, driving range, chipping and putting greens.

CLUBHOUSE FACILITIES: Snack bar serving lunch, sandwiches, beer, mixed and soft drinks.

LODGING: A number of good motels stretch along I-70 back towards Denver.

RESTAURANTS: In addition to the Applewood Inn and the motels, you will find many good places to eat on Wadsworth Blvd. from Arvada to Lakewood.

GOLF COURSE:

	Par	Course Rating	Yardage
Championship	70	68.1	6286
Regular	70	66.5	5934
Ladies	73	72.4	5479

Applewood is best described as a rather flat wide-open course with a sprinkling of trees, lakes, and sand traps. Although not considered difficult to play, it certainly has several very demanding and challenging holes. All of the greens are quite large and rolling. They most definitely will bring out either the best or the worst in you as far as putting is concerned. Putting is the key to scoring well at Applewood.

The course begins with a short 288-yard par four from an elevated tee to a wide-open fairway leading to a green guarded by two sand traps. In addition to these left and right front traps, a further obstacle is a small irrigation ditch running parallel to the fairway in the left rough and extending behind the green. The driving range along the right side of this fairway is not out-of-bounds, but can cause problems in finding your ball if hit in that area.

No. 2 is a short 107-yard par three. Very little trouble here except for the small pond to the right front of the green.

The 363-yard straightaway and level par four 3rd is another warm-up hole. Two traps guard entrance to the green, but otherwise a good drive and a short iron should get most golfers on in regulation.

However, No. 4 is a lengthy one at par four and 460 yards. It plays straight off the tee, then bends gradually to the left. No particular hazards present themselves on this number 1 handicap hole other than its length.

No. 5 is another hole that plays level and straight off the tee, but it doglegs sharply right at the end of a good drive. Again, not a lot of trouble will be encountered here except for the out-of-bounds stakes close to the fairway's right edge.

Although No. 6 is not particularly long at 359 yards, it is quite respectable and offers an opportunity to get in trouble along the left side. The irrigation ditch there is out-of-bounds, and attempting to cut the corner of this par four left-hand dogleg can be dangerous. Of further concern is the left front trap at the green.

The next three holes are all quite interesting with each one requiring accurate shots from tee to green. No. 7 is a 374-yard par four with the fairway curving around a lake on the left side. It takes an exceptionally big hit from the tee to cut this corner, so it is best for most golfers to use a fairway wood and play for the center of the fairway. From that point it is a short-to-medium iron to the green.

The 8th hole is a 327-yard par four that has always been a problem for me. It calls for a 180 to 200 yard tee shot, which should get you to the corner of this 90 degree dogleg left. Then it is a blind approach uphill to a long narrow green guarded by a right front sand trap. Huge cottonwood trees guard and overhang the inside corner of this sharp dogleg, so it is important to get your drive out in the open for any kind of approach to the green. It is almost impossible to cut the corner on this hole and certainly not worth the risk.

No. 9, a 177-yard par three, calls for an all-carry shot over water to a wide but rather shallow green. Very little room for error here.

The back nine begins somewhat like the front nine with a drive from an elevated tee to a wide-open fairway below. However, this 10th hole is much longer at 383 yards and par four. The large lake in the right rough adds further complication to this hole as does the left side sand trap at the green.

No. 11 is 252 yards and par four. It plays level from tee to green, but is severely trapped with two bunkers extending out from the left front and two more extending out from the right front of the green. Only the boldest of hitters should try to reach this green off the tee. Most golfers will do best to play short of the traps or to the right of the green.

The 12th hole is 373 yards, par four, with a fairway that sweeps around to the left. Trees line the fairway's left side, and the wide, thin, two-level green is raised considerably on the right. Watch out for the right front bunker that is not noticeable from the fairway as well as another small trap to the green's left front.

Another good long par four is the 415-yard 13th. The fairway bends slightly right adjacent to a lake that is not noticeable from the tee. Stay away from the right side on this hole. The green is protected by right and left front sand traps, and it takes a well-executed approach shot to avoid them. Par here is an accomplishment.

The par three 149-yard 14th is not difficult, but the pond in front of the tee box and the two sand traps to the left of the green can be a problem.

From an elevated tee we view the number 2 handicap hole, which looks much longer than its 516 yards. However, this fairway is quite spacious, and if you can avoid the left and right front sand traps you quite likely can write a par five on your card for this 15th hole.

I think the straightaway 488-yard par five 16th is one of the more demanding and challenging holes on the golf course. Although the fairway is level, the green is elevated considerably and cut into the side of a hill. Your approach shot is further complicated by left and right front sand traps, as well as the huge cottonwood tree guarding and hanging over the right front of the green. Once on the green one must contend with a considerable amount of break regardless of the pin placement.

No. 17 is a solid par three at 165 yards. This hole plays a little uphill, and although plenty of room lies up by the green, be aware of the right front sand trap.

No. 18 is not long at 365 yards and par four, but it is an exacting finishing hole requiring an accurate approach shot over the small pond in front of the green. Don't be too long off the tee or you might find your ball in the pond, which cannot be seen from the tee.

If you are a visitor to the area and have some extra time, I would recommend one of the guided tours of Coors Brewery in Golden and a visit to Central City, one of Colorado's historic old mining towns. Better yet, take in both of them. It will be time well spent.

ARROWHEAD GOLF COURSE

LOCATION:	Waterton, Colorado. Take Interstate 25 south and exit west on County Line Road. Continue west until you come to Waterton Road. Go three miles south on Waterton Road and you will come to the golf course.
TELEPHONE:	973-9614
COURSE FACILITIES:	Fully equipped pro shop, riding golf carts, club rental, driving range, chipping and putting green.
CLUBHOUSE FACILITIES:	Complete restaurant serving breakfast, lunch, sandwiches, dinner, beer, mixed and soft drinks.
LODGING:	Several motels on Santa Fe heading north.
RESTAURANTS:	Arrowhead is the only game in town.

GOLF COURSE:

	Par	Course Rating	Yardage
Championship	70	70.7	6662
Regular	70	68.7	6229
Ladies	71	67.5	5501

The Roxborough Park area, where Arrowhead is located, is one of only four places in the world with a backdrop of red rock outcroppings. It was a favorite wintering spot for the Ute and Arapaho Indians. The present day name is obviously derived from this Indian heritage, and arrowheads are to be found in the area today.

The following is a quote from Robert Trent Jones Jr.:

> When I first saw the site of the golf course at Roxborough Park, I was overwhelmed by the magnificent gifts that nature has bestowed on the property. The cathedral-like conglomerate rocks jutting up

from the rolling terrain at the foothills of the Rockies, is a majestic setting in which to establish a unique golf course.

Robert Trent Jones, Jr. designed Arrowhead in 1970 and has listed it among his favorite six in the world. He took complete advantage of the natural terrain, added large sloping greens, 76 traps, and six lakes affecting play on nine holes. It is definitely one of the most interesting tracks in the state. The Colorado Golf Association rates Arrowhead tied with Sheraton-Steamboat and Broadmoor South as the fifth most difficult public and resort course in the state.

The fairway slopes sharply from right to left on the downhill 411-yard par four 1st hole. A 210-yard carry over the trap on the right will leave the golfer with a short-to-middle iron for his second shot. Use enough club to get over the lake on the left as any ball hit short will find the water. This St. Andrews concept green also serves No. 17, and has almost 20,000 sq. ft. of area.

The 2nd hole is an uphill par five playing longer than its 505 yards. Avoid the trap trouble on the right side of the fairway and the huge bunker to the left front of the green.

The true distance of the 3rd hole is 188 yards, though it appears longer. This green is nestled in the rocks, and trouble lurks right of the green in a very sharp drop-off.

Arrowhead's number 1 handicap hole is the 413-yard 4th. The landing area on this dogleg right par four is guarded on the right by three menacing traps. Use one club more for your approach as the steep embankment behind will allow any ball hit long to roll back down to the green.

No. 5, only 333 yards long, doglegs right around a massive red rock. Most players will want to lay up to insure keeping the ball in the fairway. The green is well trapped and slopes back to front.

The 6th hole is a straightforward 416-yard par four. No tricks, just too many traps. The sign on the 7th tee reads "245 yards to the lake" on this downhill 354-yard par four. I suggest anywhere from a 4 wood to a 5 iron off the tee depending on the wind. An accurate short iron is a must here as the green is surrounded by water and sand.

A precise second shot is also necessary on the par four 383-yard 8th as six traps protect this elevated green. Consider hiking back to the championship tee located in the rocks on the 177-yard par three 9th hole. The prevailing winds are usually into the golfer's face here, but the sharply elevated tee allows for the use of at least one less club.

The landing area is very narrow between the three sand traps to the right and the scrub oak to the left on the 398-yard 10th. This difficult downhill par four requires a very well-placed drive.

You will find the front half of the 11th green sloping toward you and the back half sloping away on this 141 yard par three. Check the pin placement carefully before selecting a short iron.

Next begins one of my favorite runs of four consecutive holes anywhere. The 399-yard par four 12th doglegs left at 225 yards. Take plenty of club for your approach because the shot is very uphill. The green slopes decidedly right to left and front to back.

The unforgettable 13th is a very picturesque 174-yard par three, and the 95-foot elevation change from tee to green demands one club less then usual.

Leave the slice in your bag on the 356-yard par four 14th. The fairway slopes toward the lake, and the carry is only 150 yards on the left bank, so consider a lay-up shot to the left. Remember though, that the green is protected in front by two traps and is quite narrow, only 52 feet front to back.

The 361-yard par four 15th doglegs right at 215 yards around the 121-foot-high red rock Jackson Photo Site. It is important to position yourself to the left for an easy approach to this well-trapped green.

No. 16 is a straightaway 549-yard par five. Scrub oak creeps close to the fairway near the green, so stay left. Pay particular attention to how the wind blows the flag on the 177-yard 17th because it often changes from tee to green. The lake on the right grabs many balls on this tricky par three.

Direct your tee shot right of the single tree visible from the tee on the 494-yard par five finishing hole. This tree is located at the point of the lake, but you can't see the lake from the tee. The green is trapped on both sides and breaks right to left.

Make a special effort to play this magnificent Robert Trent Jones, Jr. course. The season at Arrowhead is somewhat shorter than the courses located in the city, so you will find it at its best in August and September. Weather permitting, it is open seven days a week. This is one of Denver's most popular courses, so call ahead to make arrangements. Enjoy this thinking man's golf course.

AURORA HILLS GOLF CLUB

LOCATION: Aurora, Colorado. From Highway 225 take Exit No. 9 west for one mile to East Del Mar Circle. Turn left on Del Mar Circle and go to Peoria Street (about one-half mile). Turn left on Peoria and in about one-half a mile you will see the golf course on your left.

TELEPHONE: 364-6111 Pro shop.
364-9401 Starter.

COURSE FACILITIES: Fully equipped pro shop, riding golf carts, pull carts, club rental, driving range, chipping and putting greens.

CLUBHOUSE FACILITIES: Complete snack bar serving breakfast, lunch, sandwiches, dinner, beer, mixed and soft drinks.

LODGING: Lots of motels on East Colfax, north on Peoria, and on I-70, both east and back toward the airport.

RESTAURANTS: Several good restaurants north and south on Peoria.

GOLF COURSE:

	Par	Course Rating	Yardage
Championship	72	69.1	6525
Regular	72	69.1	6525
Ladies	72	71.8	5773

Aurora Hills is a relatively new golf course in the Denver area, with play first commencing in the spring of 1969. It is quite flat and lacks interesting terrain, although the water hazard on No. 10 is spectacular, and the golf course does have 5 par fives, which is a little unusual. Hundreds of 25 ft. to 30 ft. cottonwood trees cover the golf course and line the fairways, but they are still immature and do not adversely affect many golf shots at this time. The fairways and rough are lush and well maintained. You will find the greens large, quite undulating, and all rather similar in character. This course needs a few more years before showing its true colors, but in the meantime it is fun to play, easy to walk, and it will give the majority of golfers a real battle before yielding to par.

The golf course begins with a short 355-yard par four that doglegs right at the 150-yard marker. The line of Russian olive trees all along the right side of the fairway indicates out-of-bounds, and it is risky trying to cut the corner off the tee. Next comes the first of 5 par fives with the 495-yard 2nd. Out-of-bounds on both sides of the fairway and two greenside bunkers are the problems on this hole. No. 3 is a medium length par three at 158 yards. It is level all the way to the green, which is guarded by a right front trap.

For most golfers the number 1 handicap par four 4th hole forces a long iron or fairway wood for a second shot. This 425-yard hole doglegs left early, at about 200 yards off the tee, and although it's possible to cut this corner now with a big tee shot, it won't be in a few years when the trees mature. A left front sand trap guards this large and rolling green.

The next two holes are 380-yard parallel par fours, quite similar and not particularly difficult. The 7th, at 173 yards and par three, has out-of-bounds on the left, a left front trap, and another bunker at the left rear that is not visible from the tee box. Not an easy par three.

No. 8 looks much longer than its 480 yards, and to reach it in two takes a couple of really strong woods. Two greenside bunkers watch over the left side of the green, but lots of pars await on this hole. As with the two previous holes we have out-of-bounds all along the left side of the 367-yard 9th fairway, and a pin placement behind the left front sand trap can put a par four easily out of reach.

No. 10 is one of my favorite holes. It places a premium on accuracy, both on and off the tee. At 537 yards and par five, it follows a lake around to the right all the way to the green. It is possible for some golfers to cut off some of the lake with their drive, but the landing area is quite shallow, and the irrigation ditch beyond creates a further hazard. The fairway continues with the ditch on the left and the lake on the right, leaving no

Aurora Hills No. 10
537 yards par five

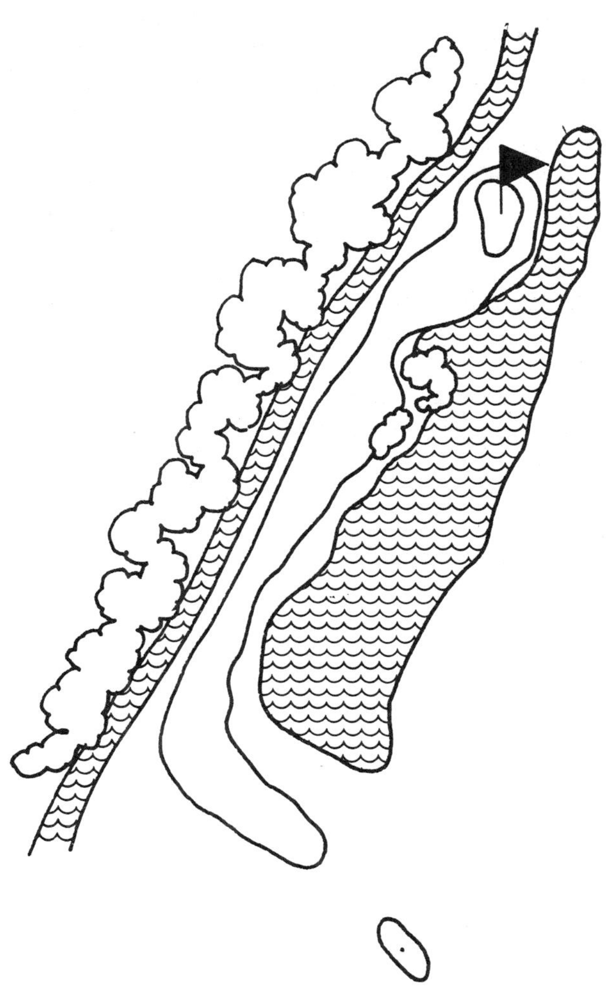

room for anything but a straight ball all the way to the green. Not noticeable from the fairway is an arm of the lake that juts into the fairway about 80 yards in front of the green. There will not be many pars on this hole. (see sketch pg. 55)

The trouble, in the form of a large irrigation ditch and greenside bunker, is all left on the 181-yard par three 11th hole. No. 12 is an uphill 542-yard par five with out-of-bounds on the left. Two traps guard the left and right front of the green. This hole should yield plenty of pars. The green is well trapped on the 158-yard par three 13th hole, otherwise it should give little trouble. No. 14 and 15 are two good long par fours and offer more bogies than pars.

No. 16 is a short 337-yard par four that doglegs left at the 150-yard marker. Too long a shot hit a little to the right off the tee will find a group of pine trees at the outside corner and could prove costly. The sand trap at the right front is of some concern, but this hole ought to yield a lot of pars. No. 17 is a good par three at 160 yards. Take plenty of club and be sure to clear the lake 30 yards in front of the green.

At 455 yards the par four 18th is a respectable finishing hole. The lake near the fairway's right side is the problem here, and the green is protected by two sand traps which add to its difficulty. Along with holes No. 4 and 10, this 18th hole will challenge everyone's ability.

CITY PARK MUNICIPAL GOLF COURSE

LOCATION: Denver, Colorado. Take the York Street Exit from Interstate 70 and go south about 1¾ miles to the intersection of York Street and 26th Avenue. You will see the golf course on your left.

TELEPHONE: 295-2095 Pro Shop.
575-2585 Starter.

COURSE FACILITIES: Fully equipped pro shop, riding golf carts, pull carts, club rental, driving range, chipping and putting greens.

CLUBHOUSE FACILITIES: Restaurant serving breakfast, lunch, sandwiches, dinner, beer, mixed and soft drinks.

LODGING: City Park is located about halfway between the airport and downtown, with plenty of excellent places to stay at either place.

RESTAURANTS: Same as above.

GOLF COURSE:

	Par	Course Rating	Yardage
Championship	72	67.1	6500
Regular	72	67.1	6500
Ladies	77	74.1	6500

City Park Municipal Golf Course is a regulation 18-hole public course located in the heart of Denver. The course was built in 1913, and was originally only nine holes. Prior to that it was a brickyard and apple orchard. Five years later it was expanded to 18 holes as it remains today. With the exception of a few holes, the course design has always been the same. The present clubhouse was originally a one-family mansion owned by the proprietors of the apple orchard.

Huge cottonwood, honey locust, evergreen, and spruce trees seem to be everywhere on this golf course. The greens are excellent and the fairways are good. If you have a tendency to hook the ball, watch out, because ten of the holes have out-of-bounds to the left. Several awe-inspiring views of Denver's skyline and the Rocky Mountains open up to the west.

Take time to enjoy the rest of Denver's City Park to the south of the golf course. In addition to the park itself, you will find a marvelous zoo and the very interesting Museum of Natural History. They are both well worth your time.

The front nine begins in earnest with the 400-yard par four number 1 handicap hole. It plays gradually uphill and straightaway, with out-of-bounds and a line of trees close to the fairway's left side. No fairway bunkers or sand traps at the green come into play. The 2nd hole is another par four, and it plays similar to No. 1, except it is a little shorter at 365 yards.

Continuing in line with the first two holes is the 451-yard straightforward-playing 3rd hole. Again, out-of-bounds crowds the left side of the fairway, but plenty of room extends to the right. Two greenside bunkers guard entry to the green.

No. 4 is a good par three that plays level from tee to green and is 200 yards long. The green is trapped to the right front and right side, and large spruce trees form an attractive backdrop. Out-of-bounds continues along the left side of the fairway.

The 325-yard par four 5th is an interesting hole because it offers a small left-hand dogleg. The hole plays level, and Colorado Blvd. is out-of-bounds to the left. Large evergreens and cottonwoods guard the inside corner of the dogleg, so line up your tee shot a little to the right of these trees. Two bunkers come into play on this hole, one in the left rough shortly past the tall cottonwood sitting behind the evergreens and another to the right front of the green. Large blue spruce, honey locust, and cottonwoods form an attractive setting for this green.

No. 6 is 364 yards, par four, and plays slightly downhill. Twenty-third Avenue to the left is out-of-bounds, although the fairway is actually quite roomy. At the right front of the green the fairway drops off somewhat, leaving an uphill pitch shot if you are short of the green to that side. Large spruce trees again form an attractive backdrop to the green.

The 7th hole is a long par three at 225 yards. This is an interesting hole with sand traps in the right rough short of the green, and another trap close to the green's right side.

The No. 8 hole is at the high point on the golf course, and a fabulous view of the Denver skyline and Rocky Mountains spreads to the west. Don't forget to look. This 325-yard par four plays gradually downhill, and it is the first hole that doesn't have out-of-bounds to the left. Two fairway bunkers, not visible from the tee, sit about 30 yards in front of the green. The big hitter can easily find them, so judge accordingly.

No. 9 at 410 yards and par four is the number 3 handicap. It plays slightly downhill, and a sand trap crowds the left front of the green. Also a little short of the green on the left side is a line of sizeable spruce trees.

The back nine starts out with two long and rather difficult par fives. No. 10 is 565 yards long and is the number 2 handicap. A well-hit drive will get the good golfer even with the large cottonwood tree on the right side of this uphill fairway. Your second shot is a fairway wood continuing uphill and straightaway to a green that is trapped to the left side, right side, and to the rear. Pars will not come easy on this hole.

No. 11 is 530 yards and plays straightaway from tee to green. The fairway is a little bumpy and is also sparsely treelined. A small sand trap appears at the green's left front, and a depressed grass bunker to the rear about three feet deep follows the curve of the green from the left side on around to the right side. You will also find a considerable amount of break in this green.

No. 12 is a short 110-yard par three, but the green is trapped right front and left side. The green also slopes up and away, resulting in some sharp breaking putts.

The 335-yard par four 13th plays straightaway and from a slightly elevated tee. A sand trap sits 50 yards out from the green in the center of the fairway. Your approach shot to the green is more uphill than it looks.

Out-of-bounds is left again on the 350-yard downhill-playing par four 14th. Take another look at Denver's skyline and the Rocky Mountains before teeing it up on this hole. Be aware of the wide but shallow sand trap immediately behind the green. This trap is not noticeable from the fairway.

The 15th hole is a 375-yard par four that continues to play downhill. A well-placed tee shot is required here because of the two fairway bunkers, one on each side of the landing area.

Also another trap sits to the left front of the green. Of further concern, is out-of-bounds to the left.

No. 16 is a straight and level 195-yard par three that is trapped to the green's left side. York Street behind the green is out-of-bounds, so don't be too long. Four huge cottonwoods make an interesting backdrop for this 16th green.

No. 17 is the third par five on the back nine. This 470-yard hole plays level and straight off the tee, but the green is located at the top of a medium size hill which is a little different from the other holes on the course. A troublesome sand trap is cut into the lower right front side of the green. Another narrow trap follows the shape of the green from its left side around to the rear. This trap to the side and rear cannot be seen from the fairway.

At 420 yards and par four, No. 18 is a very respectable finishing hole. Several large cottonwood trees guard the inside corner of this mild left-hand dogleg, so stay to the right of them if at all possible. Two depressed grass bunkers guard the green's right side, and two more guard the green's left side. It will take two well-hit shots to get on this green in regulation, and No. 18 is anything but an easy par four.

It's always enjoyable to play these older golf courses, and City Park is one of Denver's oldest. It is conveniently located to downtown Denver and might be a little easier to get on than some of the other public courses. You will always find it in good condition, so put it on your list of courses to play.

ENGLEWOOD MUNICIPAL GOLF COURSE

LOCATION: Exit off Interstate 25 onto Santa Fe Drive going south. Continue on Santa Fe Drive until you come to West Oxford. Turn right on West Oxford and in a very short distance you will see the golf course on your right. West Oxford is the first stop light after you pass Hampden Avenue.

TELEPHONE: 761-0848

COURSE FACILITIES: Fully equipped pro shop, riding golf carts, pull carts, club rental, driving range, chipping green, putting green, and practice sand traps.

CLUBHOUSE FACILITIES: Full service restaurant serving breakfast, lunch, sandwiches, dinner, beer, mixed and soft drinks.

LODGING: Several good motels are located in the I-25 and Hampden Ave. area.

RESTAURANTS: The Duffer's restaurant at the clubhouse is very good. Other good ones are in the general area. Ask your golfing partners.

GOLF COURSE:

	Par	Course Rating	Yardage
Championship	72	69.4	6708
Regular	72	68.1	6426
Ladies	72	73.0	5991

In a few years, after the front nine has matured a bit more, Englewood Municipal will be one of Colorado's premier public golf courses. It possesses all of the necessary ingredients: hilly and flat terrain, large undulating greens, plenty of fairway and greenside sand traps, and more than enough water hazards (seven lakes) to give any golfer a run for his money. The only thing lacking are large mature trees, and time alone will take care of this situation.

Englewood is two different golf courses, with the front nine being hilly, new, and possessing more sand traps, while the back nine is flatter, mature, and seems to offer more difficulty because of the way its many water hazards come into play. Lots of opportunity for trouble on this golf course, and par will not find its way onto many score cards.

Englewood Municipal offers very good practice facilities. It possesses one of the largest driving ranges in the area, fine chipping and putting greens, and two large sand traps. In addition, the clubhouse facilities are excellent, and the Duffer's Restaurant is a great place to eat.

You will enjoy playing this golf course, and it will do nothing but get better with each succeeding year. Make a special effort to play it soon.

The course begins with a rather easy starter hole at 346 yards and par four. It plays over an undulating, narrow, right-to-left sloping fairway, and a quite large elongated bunker sits about 50 yards past the 150-yard marker in the right rough. The green is unprotected, so par should come easy for many golfers.

At 571 yards and par five, the 2nd hole is also the number 1 handicap. It plays straightforward off the tee, then uphill for your second shot. At the top of the hill the fairway begins to sweep around to the right, and two large bunkers guard this inside corner. The green is trapped to the right front and left side, with the one on the left covering the entire left side. No trees or water hazards plague this hole, but the bumpy fairway, its length, and the large well-placed sand traps provide plenty of trouble and demand accurate shots from tee to green.

Take a look at the panoramic view of the snow-capped Rocky Mountains to the west before teeing it up on the 376-yard par four 3rd. This fairway doglegs a little left near the 150-yard marker and slopes left to right. A sizeable bunker protects the inside corner, and a little beyond another bunker guards the outside corner. Not a lot of room between these two traps. Best to play short of the traps and approach the green from 150 yards out. This green possesses all kinds of character and is well trapped to the right front.

Englewood Municipal No. 6
489 yards par five

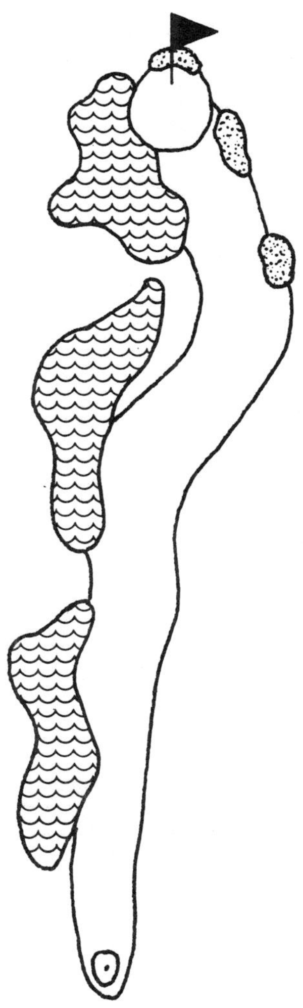

The short 140-yard par three 4th is not difficult, but the right front bunker and breaking putts on the green make it anything but a routine par.

Target the left edge of the fairway off the tee on the 376-yard par four 5th. This hole plays straightaway, slants a little right, and two bunkers guard the landing area at both sides near the 150-yard marker. A huge trap protects the green's left front and another one sits to the left rear.

In my opinion, the 489-yard par five 6th is an outstanding golf hole. For the first time, water comes into play in the form of three large lakes crowding and extending along the entire left side of the fairway. To further complicate matters, out-of-bounds is right, and the fairway possesses two doglegs, the first one right and the second one left. A fairway bunker lies at the end of the first dogleg, another guards the green's right front, and another sits to the rear. Protecting the left front and left side of the green is the third lake. Getting on this green in two is possible for the strong hitter, but it will require an all-carry approach shot over water and is quite risky.

The 188-yard par three 7th is another fine golf hole, because a large lake protects the green's left front and left side, and an unseen sand trap nestles among the grassy mounds to the right side of the green. Take plenty of club to this up-and-away sloping green.

The next two holes play on the other side of the four lakes we've had to contend with on the previous two holes. They continue to be on the left side, and the one guarding the left front of the 8th green is reachable off the tee. A small pot-hole type bunker sits between the lake and the green, and par four on this 334-yard hole is anything but sure.

Water continues to haunt the left side of the fairway on the 380-yard par four 9th all the way to the 150-yard marker, and two fairway bunkers are cut into the side of the hill to the right opposite the last lake. This all makes for a quite small landing area. If you haven't found the water or sand, your second shot is uphill to a green heavily trapped to the left front, right front and right rear. Favor the right side of this right-to-left sloping fairway with your tee shot, but the water on the left is reachable so be careful.

The back nine starts off easy with a short par three at 129 yards. It plays level to a green well trapped to the right, left front and left rear. You are on the older part of the golf course now, which is evident by the thicker grass in the fairway and rough.

No. 11 is a 395-yard slightly downhill-playing par four with a gentle bend to the right. Several small evergreens line the right side of this fairway. The open, unprotected green is inviting, but it is long and quite undulating and getting down in two will not always be easy.

Water crowds the fairway's left side for the 361-yard par four 12th. A fairway bunker lurks in the right rough at the 150-yard marker and tightens up the landing area considerably. You will find this green heavily trapped to the left front, right front, and left side, and the second lake on the left comes to within about 40 yards of the green. Not an easy hole by any means.

The 519-yard par five 13th is a dandy. As the number 2 handicap hole it offers plenty of trouble, mostly in the form of water. Two sizeable, long lakes protect the entire left side of this fairway, and another lake guards the fairway's right side shortly past the point where the fairway swings left. The long-ball hitter can hit over the lake at the inside corner, but the landing area beyond is shallow, and you run the risk of rolling into the lake on the fairway's other side. Most golfers will do best to play it safe down the middle to the dogleg. From that point if you can avoid the water on the left, you might have a chance for par.

No. 14, at 358 yards and par four, plays more level than the previous holes. It is straight off the tee, then bends right around another lake that is reachable by the strong hitter. Guarding entry to the green is a gigantic bunker to the front and right front. It's a big one, cut into the side of a grassy mound, and is the main concern when approaching this green.

Another good par five is the 481-yard 15th. It plays straight and level off the tee, then bends left a little, and three medium-size evergreens guard the inside corner. A well-hit drive can clear these trees. About 100 yards in front of the green the fairway doglegs right, and four huge irregularly shaped sand traps guard this entire corner from the point of the dogleg to the green. Any ball hit short, attempting to cut this second dogleg, will surely find one of these traps.

No. 16 is another tough hole with good length at 410 yards and par four. Out-of-bounds is left, and large cottonwoods guard the inside corner of this left-hand dogleg. Line up with the left side of the fairway off the tee, and be careful of the huge, yawning bunker that beckons about 30 yards short of the green. A long approach shot will be required by most golfers on this hole, and par will not come easy.

The medium-length, 165-yard par three 17th is an attractive golf hole that is heavily treelined along the fairway's left side and behind the green. Don't be left here or you will find the long, narrow bunker that hugs the entire left side of the green. In addition, treacherous unplayable rough drops off sharply to the left of the sand trap.

The golf course finishes in style with the long-playing 410-yard par four 18th. Tree trouble left is an early problem, and out-of-bounds extends along the fairway's left side from tee to green. Dominating the hill in the right rough is a large bunker near the 150-yard marker, and your approach to the green from that point is all uphill. This fine finishing hole will fight you all the way before yielding to par.

EVERGREEN GOLF COURSE

LOCATION: Evergreen, Colorado. Take Interstate 70 west of Denver to the El Rancho Exit (#252) and follow Colorado Highway 74 for about 8 miles. Turn right at the lake just before you get to the town of Evergreen and you will see the golf course on your left.

TELEPHONE: 674-4095

COURSE FACILITIES: Fully equipped pro shop, riding golf carts, pull carts, club rental, and putting green.

CLUBHOUSE FACILITIES: The Keys on the Green restaurant at the site serves lunch, sandwiches, dinner, beer, mixed and soft drinks.

LODGING: Not many places to stay in Evergreen, but I-70 is not far away with plenty of motels on the west edge of Denver.

RESTAURANTS: The Keys on the Green is very good and convenient. Other restaurants can be found in town and north on Colorado Highway 74.

GOLF COURSE:

	Par	Course Rating	Yardage
Regular	69	NA	5103
Ladies	72	NA	5103

Evergreen is best described as a Holiday Course. Built in 1924 as a nine-hole sand greens course, it has only in recent years been converted to grass greens. 1983 saw the completion of the back nine, and eighteen holes will be open for play for the first time in early summer of 1984. The course is very tight, tree lined, hilly, with many doglegs and small greens. Accuracy is a must. The city of Denver operates the course.

Evergreen is an interesting and beautiful community, and this recently completed eighteen-hole grass greens golf course makes it even more attractive.

FOOTHILLS GOLF COURSE

LOCATION: Southwest Denver. Take the Frontage Road on the south side of Hampden Avenue from either Wadsworth Blvd. or Kipling Street and go to South Carr Street. Turn south on Carr and you will drive into the parking lot.

TELEPHONE: 989-3901

COURSE FACILITIES: Fully equipped pro shop, riding golf carts, pull carts, club rental, driving range and putting green.

CLUBHOUSE FACILITIES: Snack bar serving breakfast, lunch, sandwiches, beer, mixed and soft drinks.

LODGING: Denver area motels.

RESTAURANTS: Plenty of good places to eat north and south on Wadsworth Blvd.

GOLF COURSE:

	Par	Course Rating	Yardage
Championship	72	70.3	6787
Regular	72	68.3	6465
Ladies	74	73.4	6107

Foothills was built in 1971, and for a golf course so young it is in excellent playing condition. The trees are still rather small and not much of a factor, but a little time will take care of this situation. The rough is composed of thick native and planted grasses that are quite tall and spell nothing but trouble. Most of the fairways are rather flat. They are well maintained, and the ball sits up nicely, yielding good lies. Large, strategically placed sand traps protect huge, well-manicured greens. One must be able to lag putt on this golf course. Holes No. 6 and 16, both par fives, offer more than enough challenge to any golfer, while No. 18 is not far behind. Foothills will not yield to par easily and is interesting enough that you will want to come back for more. Also a short par three course is located here, which will be of interest to golfers not wishing to tackle the regulation 18-hole layout.

The first hole is an easy one at 358 yards and par four. No trouble awaits here except for the small irrigation ditch that hides behind the green. However, No. 2 demands the golfer's best if he expects to par it. This 496-yard par five fairway bends to the left, but it's best to play down the fairway and not cut the corner. The rough is tall, thick, heavy grass and not the place to be, so play it safe. A huge bunker lies about 80 yards out from the green in the left rough, and the green is well trapped along the left side.

The 398-yard par four 3rd hole plays gradually uphill, with the fairway again bending left. The green perches at the top of this long, sloping fairway and is protected by a large bunker to the right front and another one above the green to the left rear. This hole plays longer than indicated.

No. 4 is not a difficult par three, which is true of all the par threes on this golf course. At 158 yards it plays much shorter, because of the elevated tee. But the 406-yard par four 5th is a fine golf hole. From an elevated tee it plays downhill all the way and doglegs right at the 150-yard marker. The big hitter can cut this corner, but most golfers will do best to play for the middle of the fairway. This green is well guarded by a sizeable right front trap as well as another to the left front.

At 530 yards and par five, No. 6 is the number 1 handicap hole. It definitely has a personality of its own, primarily in the form of water. Immediately in front of the tee is a rather lengthy water reservoir, and if you can carry your ball about 240 yards it's okay to hit over it. Most golfers will want to hit to the right of this reservoir down the first of a two-part fairway. Your second shot then is over an irrigation ditch to the second half of the fairway. A good target off the tee is about 20 yards to the left of the refreshment shack seen in the distance. This 6th hole is a good one and rates right up there with the best of them. (see sketch pg. 70)

Although No. 7 is a short one, it is an excellent golf hole. A medium-to-long iron off the tee and a short iron approach should get most golfers home in regulation. Anyway you play it, your second shot will be over the lake which sits im-

Foothills No. 6
530 yards par five

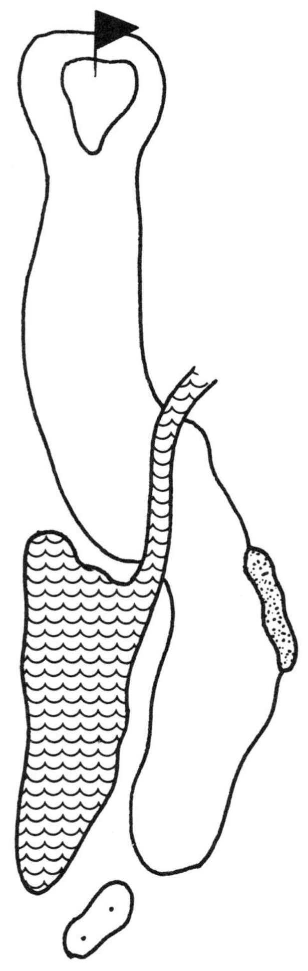

mediately in front of the green. Watch out for the right front bunker.

The large green at the 119-yard par three 8th provides an inviting target. However, it is tightly bunkered to the front, left and rear, so accuracy is essential. No. 9 is a rather uncomplicated hole at 360 yards and par four. It doglegs left, and the green is guarded by two traps, one to the left front another to the left side. Be aware of the water reservoir in the left rough, because it is not easily seen from the tee box.

The back nine starts out very similar to the first hole, but plays more difficult because of the large bunker at the inside corner of this left-hand dogleg. Cutting this corner can be very risky. You will usually come out ahead by playing down the fairway. No. 11 is a short par five at 494 yards that plays slightly uphill and bends gently to the right. Three traps, one to the left, left rear and right front guard this green. Best to come into this green from the fairway's left side.

No. 12 is just a good long par four at 434 yards. Stay out of the rough, and you will have a chance for par. The only long par three on the course is the 193-yard 13th. The trouble is all right here in the form of bunkers to the right and right front. Favor the green's left side a little.

At 383 yards and par four the 14th hole should yield a lot of pars. This fairway slopes a little left to right, so keep your fade under control. No. 15 is another fairway that slopes left to right. It also swings left around the base of a hill, and the green is not noticeable from the tee. Try to cut a little off the corner here, because your ball will definitely kick quite a bit right. Avoid the right rough on this hole if you expect a good score.

No. 16 is another great golf hole. It's the number 2 handicap at 518 yards and par five. We have a two-part fairway with an irrigation ditch cutting diagonally across from left to right about 135 yards from the green. This fairway is straight off the tee for about 200 yards, at which point it swings right. About 150 yards from the green the fairway swings back left, crossing the irrigation ditch. It's very difficult to get over this ditch in two. I would suggest laying up with a medium-to-long iron, then approach the green from that point. Proper club selection is essential here. Watch out for the left front trap by the green.

If you dropped a stroke on No. 16 you should at least pick up a par on the 135-yard par three 17th. This green is tightly bunkered, but it is also quite large, presenting an inviting target.

A fitting climax to an exciting golf course is the 421-yard par four 18th. This is a tough finishing hole, and a lot of matches will be won or lost here. The fairway possesses a huge left-hand dogleg that is heavily bunkered at the inside corner, and out-of-bounds crowds the left side. It's very risky to try to cut the corner here. Most golfers should play it straight down the middle. This green is protected by a lake to the left, a ditch crossing immediately in front, and another lake to the right. The result is a small target for a long iron or fairway-wood approach shot. One should consider laying up short of the ditch and pitching on from there.

Foothills will give everyone a good workout. Practice your lag putts before going to the 1st tee, and you will be richly rewarded.

HYLAND HILLS GOLF COURSE

LOCATION: Westminster, Colorado. Take Highway 36 to the Sheridan Blvd. Exit and go north on Sheridan Blvd. one mile. The golf course will be on your right.

TELEPHONE: 428-6526

COURSE FACILITIES: Fully equipped pro shop, riding golf carts, pull carts, club rental, driving range, chipping and putting greens.

CLUBHOUSE FACILITIES: Restaurant serving breakfast, lunch, sandwiches, dinner, mixed drinks, beer and soft drinks. Other facilities include indoor racquetball courts, sauna, and whirlpool.

LODGING: Denver area motels.

RESTAURANTS: Although it is not our policy to recommend specific restaurants, we are making an exception here, suggesting you try the Hyland Hills Restaurant and Lounge at the clubhouse. Other good places to eat are on Highway 36 between the Sheridan Blvd. Exit and Denver.

GOLF COURSE:

	Par	Course Rating	Yardage
Championship	73	70.6	7107
Regular	73	69.0	6621
Ladies	75	74.0	6185

Hyland Hills is an exceptionally popular golf course. With par at 73, one has the right to expect a number of long and challenging holes, and you will not be disappointed. Nos. 8, 11, 12, and 15 are four holes that belong on everyone's all-time golf course. The fairways and large greens are all well maintained, and although the course is long, it is also an easy one to walk.

The first hole is a straightaway 532-yard par five and demands two long woods and a short iron to the green, then two putts for par, that is if your second shot doesn't find the small pond about 70 yards to the left front of the green. No traps on this number 3 handicap hole, and the main difficulty is its length. No. 2 is a 379-yard par four with a short dogleg left at the end of the fairway. A good drive will carry to the bottom of the valley, but aim for the right side of this fairway and stay away from the group of large cottonwood trees at the corner of the dogleg. A small sand trap guards the left front of the green. The 356-yard wide-open par four third hole, requires a straight tee shot and a short iron. This fairway doglegs right, and too big of a hit off the tee could carry through to the rough and behind a group of weeping willow trees at the outer left edge of the dogleg. Best to hit a 4 or 3 wood off the tee.

A good drive and a very short iron can get most golfers to the green on the 354-yard par four 4th hole. Although not a long one, some problems await with a lake on the left that can catch a long pull or hook shot and a threatening little sand trap at the right front of the green. No. 5 is a 131-yard par three over the edge of a small lake to a green more contoured than necessary. Putting is touchy at best here. A lower left-hand pin placement behind the water can be very menacing.

After teeing off over the arm of a small lake in front of the tee box, the 6th hole veers left and uphill. Par is four on this 324-yard hole, and to reach this elongated two-tier green in two will require a short approach shot for most players. If the pin is placed at the top tier, it will take an extra club. The 7th is a 330-yard par four that is straightaway, but with a line of troublesome trees at about the 150-yard marker on the left. The fairway slopes left to right with a sand trap on the right that could catch a big hit. Another bunker guards the left front of this green, but a short iron for a second shot ought to be the club.

One of the toughest golf holes around is the 526-yard par five 8th. It is the number 1 handicap hole on this golf course, and rightly so. The fairway is wide, but a hook or pull off the tee could find the lake out to the left. Most of the trouble on this hole is a ditch that crosses the fairway about 75 yards in front of the green. The ditch is in the bottom of a small valley

Hyland Hills No. 11
414 yards par four

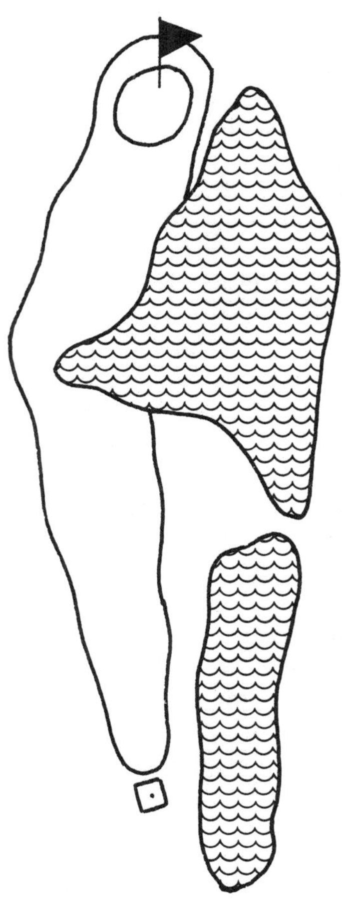

and the grass here yields very poor lies, so it is best to lay up short of this area with your second shot. The two evergreen trees on each side of the fairway indicate 150-yards from the green, and that is a good place to be for a third shot. In case you aren't playing this hole well, take consolation in the fabulous view of the snow-capped Rocky Mountains as you walk down the fairway.

No. 9 is a par four 359-yard dogleg right that is a little uphill. Out-of-bounds runs on the right as well as several trees that have a tendency to attract any shot left out to that side of the fairway. Behind the green is a tall, thick hedge-row that can be expensive if your approach shot is long. This hole should yield a par to most golfers.

No. 10 is a 536-yard par five that calls for two good wood shots and a short iron, very much like the first hole. No sand traps guard the green, and this hole should yield an abundance of pars. No. 11 is a different story because it is very tricky. This 414-yard par four has a lake about 220 yards off the tee that haunts both your first and second shots. To miss the lake one must aim to the left and carry at least 240 yards to a landing area that leaves little room for error. This is risky for most golfers so I would advise a 4 or 5 iron off the tee, then another medium iron or 5 wood over the water to the green. A safer second shot is to play down the left side of the lake then pitch on with a short iron. Accuracy is a necessity on this hole from tee to green. (see sketch pg. 75)

No. 12 is another tough golf hole at 538 yards and par five. Two lakes dominate the right side of this fairway all the way to the green. The fairway actually has two doglegs, both bending right, so it is best to favor the left side, although a strong hitter can cut a small portion off the corner from the tee. The green is protected on the right by a sand trap as well as the lake.

After two difficult par fours, the 146-yard par three No. 13 is a welcome relief. It is slightly uphill and should yield a par. No. 14 is an uphill 323-yard par four with a fairway that slopes right to left. Avoid the cottonwood trees on the left and you can easily come up with another par.

The number 2 handicap hole, No. 15, is a good one. It is 473 yards in length and par four. After a long drive this hole calls for another wood or long iron to reach the green. Out-of-bounds runs along the left side of the fairway, a large cottonwood tree guards the left approach to the green, and an irrigation ditch and greenside bunker spell trouble to the right. If you can't reach this green in two, then lay up short, pitch on with a short iron, and play for a bogey. The 142-yard par three 16th is played from an elevated tee to a green on the other side of an irrigation ditch and is protected by a cluster of willows at the left front of the green. This is not a hard hole, but a left front pin placement is a challenge. No. 17 is a 413-yard par four that doglegs right at the 150-yard marker. The small lake immediately in front of the tee box will not come into play for most golfers. A long ball off the tee will leave a medium iron to a large green protected by two sand traps located along the left side of the green.

At 350 yards and par four, the 18th is not particularly difficult. This hole is straightaway with a left-to-right slope, has small evergreens along the right side, and out-of-bounds and large cottonwoods about 40 yards to the left of the fairway. The green is protected by a bunker at the left front and a small group of evergreen trees at the right rear. Sounds like a lot of trouble, but a good drive and a short iron should find your ball on the green in regulation.

Hyland Hills has a par three course immediately adjacent to the 18-hole course. Par is 27 and you will find it interesting to play and a good way to improve your short game.

A recent addition to the clubhouse facilities here are six indoor handball courts that are available for public use. Call ahead the day before to reserve a court. I must mention again the very fine restaurant located in the clubhouse. It is unusual to find a restaurant of this caliber at many golf courses.

INDIAN TREE GOLF CLUB

LOCATION:	Arvada, Colorado. Go north of Arvada on Wadsworth Blvd. until you see the golf course off to your left. You can also go south of Broomfield on Wadsworth Blvd. until you see the course off to your right.
TELEPHONE:	423-3450
COURSE FACILITIES:	Fully equipped pro shop, riding golf carts, pull carts, club rental, driving range, chipping and putting greens.
CLUBHOUSE FACILITIES:	Snack bar serving breakfast, lunch, sandwiches, beer, mixed and soft drinks.
LODGING:	Most motels near this golf course are back on Interstate 70 both east and west of the I-70 and Wadsworth Blvd. intersection.
RESTAURANTS:	Most of the fast food places as well as a number of very good restaurants are located up and down Wadsworth Blvd.

GOLF COURSE:

	Par	Course Rating	Yardage
Championship	71	69.1	6747
Regular	71	67.5	6386
Ladies	75	73.4	6032

Indian Tree is a friendly and inviting public golf course, with mostly wide open fairways and rough that are well maintained and with good grass. About half of the fairways are doglegs of varying degrees, and in most cases the fairway slopes in the opposite direction of the dogleg. This, of course, toughens up the hole considerably if you have a tendency to hook or slice the ball. Several lakes come into play with the one on No. 12 making it an exceptional golf hole. Although there are lots of trees, most of them are small, except for the large cottonwoods around the lakes. This is a very interesting, enjoyable golf course, and is also somewhat forgiving.

The course begins with two rather average par fours and an uncomplicated medium-length par three. They are good starter holes and hopefully will prepare you for the number 1 handicap hole coming up next.

The 540-yard par five 4th has its share of obstacles to overcome, with the left-to-right slanting fairway off the tee, dogleg left, uphill second shot to a green not visible from that point, two 25 yard long narrow sand traps along the left side of the fairway starting about 30 yards from the green and a rather touchy green to putt. Very few golfers will reach this green in two. No. 5, although not long at 375 yards and par four, is not easy. The fairway slants left, but bends right around a hill that hides the green, and a sand trap awaits in the right rough short of the hill. Be careful of the small cluster of trees at the left front of this green.

The course backs off a bit with the 356-yard short par four 6th. Downhill all the way, if offers a good chance for birdie or par. No. 7 is a demanding 390-yard 90-degree dogleg left at 225 yards off the tee. No way to cut the corner here with trees and water on the left making it impossible. Your second shot is a medium iron from an elevated position in the fairway to a wide-open and inviting green below.

The par three 8th is a versatile and exacting hole with the distance being anywhere from 163 to 215 yards. It is an all-carry one-shotter over a large lake, and how much of the lake you cut off depends on your confidence and the location of the tee markers. This is the only difficult and demanding par three on the course. We finish the front nine with a long downhill par four that has no hazards except for its length, but at 461 yards it's not an easy one to par.

Although No. 10 is a short 321-yard par four that doglegs right, it offers its share of problems. Aim for the willow tree on the far side of the lake which protects this fairway all along the right side. Two large cottonwood trees and a right front sand trap guard the approach to this green. Any loose shot missing the green to the right will kick down into the water. No. 11 is a short par three playing a little uphill and with left and right front bunkers guarding the green.

Indian Tree No. 12
506 yards par five

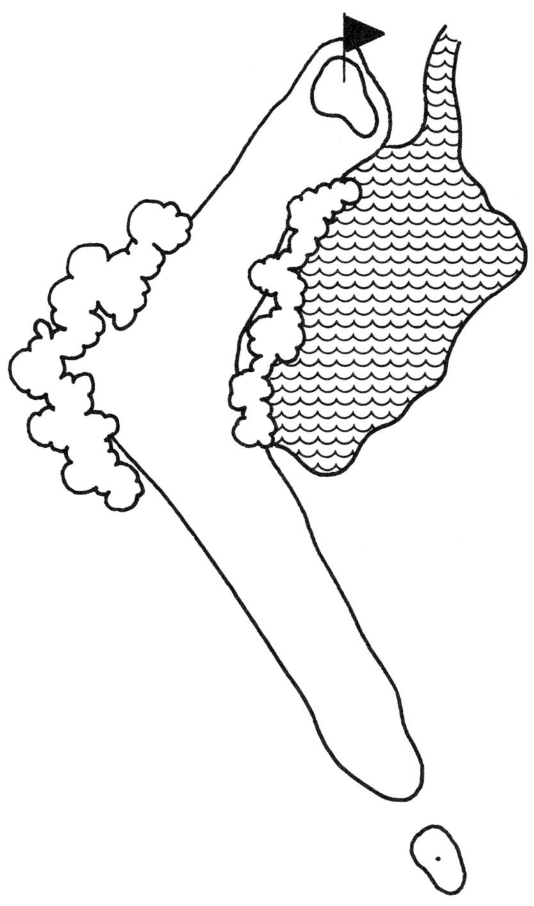

No. 12 is one of my favorite golf holes. It is the number 2 handicap, and could just as well be the number 1. At 506 yards and par five the fairway doglegs right, but it is impossible to hit the ball to the corner off the tee. Even with a long drive, the temptation will be to hit across the lake on the right for your second shot, but this is very risky because of the size of the lake and the large cottonwoods on the far bank. I would suggest hitting a long iron or fairway wood to the corner and a medium iron to the green. (see sketch pg. 80)

The trouble is all on the right for the 340-yard par four 13th, and it is in the form of out-of-bounds and two sand traps, one at the 150-yard marker and the second larger one just beyond. An uphill second shot might require an extra club, but with no trouble around the green this hole should yield par to many golfers. No. 14 is a 506-yard par five that is straightaway with a right-to-left slanting fairway and out-of-bounds on the right. The fairway bends a little right after your tee shot, and the right front sand trap can reach up and grab a long fairway wood without any trouble.

No. 15 and 16 are parallel 400-yard par fours, with the 15th being downhill and the 16th being uphill. Both holes play to about medium difficulty with the 15th the toughest because of the water to the left and behind the green. The easiest hole on the course is the 140-yard par three 17th. The sand trap at the right front of the green is of some concern, but otherwise no problem here.

The 18th is a fine finishing hole at 410 yards and par four. It is downhill, similar to No. 15, but is dominated by a variety of hazards. A trap is positioned in the right rough shortly before the 150-yard marker and another just beyond. In the left rough about 180 yards from the green lurks another long narrow sand trap. If you are short off the tee, a large lake about 100 yards to the left front of the green can easily catch a second shot if you hook or pull your shot over there. Other problems include water to the right and right front of the green, sand trap behind the green, and a large cottonwood tree guarding an approach to the green from the fairway's right side. After a good drive, a second shot calls for a mid-iron, but accuracy is a must for par.

JOHN F. KENNEDY MUNICIPAL GOLF COURSE

LOCATION: Denver, Colorado. Take Exit No. 201 off Interstate 25 onto Hampden Avenue. Continue east for several miles until you see the golf course on your right.

TELEPHONE: 755-0105 Pro shop.
751-0311 Starter.

COURSE FACILITIES: Fully equipped pro shop, riding golf carts, pull carts, club rental, driving range, chipping and putting greens.

CLUBHOUSE FACILITIES: Complete snack bar serving breakfast, lunch, sandwiches, beer, soft and mixed drinks.

LODGING: Several fine motels can be found south on I-25 and east on I-225.

RESTAURANTS: There are plenty of very good restaurants in this part of Denver. Best to ask around.

GOLF COURSE:

	Par	Course Rating	Yardage
Regular	72	69.5	6816
Ladies	80	75.2	6704

At first glance John F. Kennedy appears to be a rather flat, wide-open golf course. However, the many trees, elevated greens and tee boxes, and the long sloping fairways of the back nine soon put this thought to rest. Probably the strongest characteristic of this golf course is its large, fast, and undulating greens. To score well at Kennedy, the golfer must be able to lag putt with consistency and be able to read the breaking putts, which he will have on every green. You will find spruce, Russian olive and cottonwood trees lining most of the fairways, as well as growing in just the wrong places in the rough. The par fours are all lengthy and difficult. Only two of them are less than 400 yards. This is a long golf course, and your fairway woods as well as your putter, will get a real work out.

No. 1 is a 503-yard par five of medium difficulty. It plays level, straightaway, and numerous small-to-medium size trees border each side of the fairway. This is a good warm-up hole and should get you ready for the rest of the golf course.

The 2nd hole is the first of many lengthy par fours. It plays to 443 yards, crosses Cherry Creek early off the tee, and has a good number of spruce trees lining the fairway. This well-contoured and elevated green is typical of more to come and getting down in two putts will require the golfer's best effort.

Not only are most of the par fours lengthy, but the par three 3rd is a long one at 213 yards. It plays level from tee to green and is trapped to the left and right front. No. 4 is the only par four that is under 400 yards, but it plays somewhat longer than indicated because of the elevated green. This 357-yard hole is made more difficult by a sand trap in the fairway's right side at the landing area off the tee, and by two more huge bunkers at the green's lower left front and right front. However, a well-hit drive and a short iron should get most golfers on this large green in regulation.

The 150-yard par three 5th plays from an elevated tee to a green well below the golfer. Use at least one less club here, and be careful of the right front trap. Take a few moments from this tee box to enjoy the view of the entire golf course and the Continental Divide to the west.

No. 6 is the number 1 handicap hole, and it is a good one. Cherry Creek crosses the fairway about 250 to 260 yards off the tee, so most players will have to play short, driving with a lofted wood, then hitting the fairway wood again to the green. The large cottonwood tree to the left and short of Cherry Creek is about 225 yards from the tee. This 440-yard par four will not yield to par easily.

They don't get any easier with the 593-yard par five 7th. It plays level off the tee, is treelined, and bends left and uphill as you approach the green. To further complicate matters this elevated green is heavily trapped with one to the lower left, lower right, and another to the rear and a little above the green. This is anything but an easy hole, and is an excellent par five.

The 400-yard par four 8th is another good one. The only lake on the golf course sits in the left rough and is easily reachable off the tee. Trees line the right side of this fairway and narrow the landing area considerably. Although no traps guard the green, the lake comes to within about 40 yards of the green's left front.

The front nine finishes with another long par four at 410 yards. The same lake from the previous hole sits in the left rough early on, and the fairway which bends a little right is also loosely treelined. This is not a particularly difficult hole, but you still have to putt when you get on the green.

The first three holes on the back nine are somewhat similar, with No. 10 playing uphill at 475 yards and par five, No. 11 playing downhill at 430 yards and par four, and No. 12 playing uphill again at 378 yards and par four. These holes are parallel to each other and are quite heavily treelined.

Although the 165-yard par three 13th is not a long one, it is quite interesting. It plays from an elevated tee, downhill, across a small valley to a large and undulating green that is trapped both left and right front. No. 14 is another long par four at 431 yards. It plays level and straightforward to a huge undulating green resulting in some touchy and interesting putts.

The only short par four on the back nine is the 359-yard 15th. It plays uphill, is treelined, and bends left short of the green. This fairway seems to be crowned in the middle, so if you're not dead center off the tee your ball will kick left or right into the rough.

No. 16 is the last of the long par fours. This 427-yard fairway plays level off the tee, then doglegs left and uphill to the green. Lots of sizeable cottonwoods growing in the left rough at the inside corner prevent most golfers from successfully cutting this corner. The putting surface of this large and undulating green is not visible from the fairway. This is an excellent golf hole, and will usually require a fairway wood or medium-long iron approach to the green.

Another good hole is the 500-yard par five 17th. This fairway also bends left, and a lot of golfers will be able to cut off some distance by hitting over the rather small evergreen trees growing in the rough at the inside corner. A troublesome cottonwood tree sits 40 yards out from the right front of the green, and it can be a real problem if you have to approach the green from that side. The green is trapped to its left and right front.

No shortage of trees line both sides of the fairway on this number 2 handicap hole.

The golf course finishes with the easiest hole on the course, the 142-yard 18th. This is a little disappointing, but a proper pin placement behind one of the two traps guarding the green can make it a challenge.

LAKE ARBOR GOLF COURSE

LOCATION: Arvada, Colorado. At 84th Avenue and Wadsworth Blvd., turn east, and you will see the parking lot and pro shop immediately to your left.

TELEPHONE: 423-1650

COURSE FACILITIES: Fully equipped pro shop, riding golf carts, pull carts, club rental, driving range, and putting green.

CLUBHOUSE FACILITIES: Sandwiches, beer, mixed and soft drinks.

LODGING: Most area motels are south of here on Interstate 70 and west of Wadsworth Blvd.

RESTAURANTS: Plenty of good places to eat are located south on Wadsworth Blvd.

GOLF COURSE:

	Par	Course Rating	Yardage
Championship	70	65.8	5699
Regular	70	65.0	5528
Ladies	73	68.6	5281

Lake Arbor is a rather short golf course, measuring only 5528 yards from the regular tees. However, it is a very tight layout with houses and out-of-bounds closely lining most of the fairways. Several significant water hazards dot the course, and most of the fairways are doglegs of varying degrees. The greens are great and a pleasure to putt, and the fairways are well watered and in good condition. This is a flat course and is an easy one to walk. Keep the ball in the fairway and it might even prove an easy one to play. You will enjoy Lake Arbor — don't overlook it.

No. 1 is a 359-yard par four with a medium left-hand dogleg. A lake sits at the far end of the fairway, where it doglegs, so stay left off the tee and aim over the trees at the inside corner. The lake comes within about 25 yards of the green's right front, but no traps guard the green.

The 506-yard par five 2nd hole is the number 2 handicap. It also doglegs left, and out-of-bounds crowds the entire left side of this fairway. Don't leave your drive out to the right or you can catch the small pond that lies in the rough at the outside corner. A right front bunker guards this quite large green, but if you will favor the fairway's left side a little, this sand trap will not be a problem. A straight drive off the tee is a must on this hole.

Continuing with another left-hand dogleg is the 358-yard par four 3rd. A small lake awaits in the left corner, and a large grouping of mature trees are growing at the outside corner. It takes a big hit to clear the water, so it's best to play down the center of the fairway off the tee. A drive and a short iron will get most golfers on this green, which is a friendly one because no sand traps present themselves.

No. 4 is a 161-yard par three that is trapped to the left front and left rear. Out-of-bounds is left from tee to green. No. 5 is a rather short par five at 481 yards, but it plays a little cozy, especially to the left. A small drainage ditch runs along the left side of the fairway and is played as a hazard. About 10 yards to the left of this ditch is out-of-bounds. Although room spreads to the right, you can easily have tree trouble off the tee. The fairway opens up a bit to the right for your second shot, but be careful of the greenside trap to the right front.

The 144-yard par three 6th plays a little uphill, has out-of-bounds on the right, and a right front trap at the green. Most golfers will need one extra club here. The next hole, No. 7, is a dogleg right, and calls for a lofted wood off the tee. The ideal shot is probably a 3 wood with a little fade hit over the far corner of the tall protective fence. Out-of-bounds is to the right as well as the left on this fairway. A lake protects this green to the right and about halfway across the front. Although it should be a short iron to the green, it must be an accurate one.

The third par three on the front nine is the 160-yard 8th that plays over the edge of a lake to a well-trapped green. A bunker sits to the right front, and another wide thin one lies to the rear. If you get in this rear bunker you will have a nasty little shot downhill to the pin, and it is most likely to prove costly. No. 9 plays straightaway at 330 yards, with the only trouble being out-of-bounds about 15 yards to the right. The fairway is quite roomy otherwise with no hazards around the green.

The 10th hole is another straightforward playing hole at 475 yards and par five. In my opinion this is the best and most difficult hole on the golf course. Very few golfers will be able to reach this green in two, because the lake comes into play in front of the green. Most players will do best to lay up short of the lake with a short-to-medium iron, then approach the green from there. It is very risky to go for the green in two.

No. 11 is another par five at 479 yards, and the fairway has a gentle bend to the left. Aim for the tall right-hand radio tower in the distance. Out-of-bounds to the fairway's right side is of concern here. Right and left front traps guard entry to the green, but plenty of room exists between them.

A wide and inviting fairway greets you at the 365-yard par four 12th. It plays straightaway with no traps at the green. This is a good place to pick up a stroke. Another place to at least get a par is the short 109-yard par three 13th. The only problem is the bunker covering the entire front side of the green.

The 388-yard par four 14th plays somewhat uphill, doglegs right, and has out-of-bounds on the same side. A small grouping of young trees has been planted at the inside corner and will become a factor a few years hence. Another planting of new trees inhabits the outside corner, but is not a problem at this time. No traps at the green, just a good medium-long par four.

The 124-yard par three 15th should be an easy one. With no traps at the green, the only problem is out-of-bounds about 30 yards to the left of the green.

No. 16 is a very respectable par four at 413 yards. It plays straightaway, but if the wind is in your face, this hole will play like a par five. Aim over the grass berms and a little to the right of the large tree up by the green. A right front trap guards this green.

The golf course finishes with two par threes, which is a little unusual. No. 17 is 171 yards and plays to a large deep green that is guarded by a sizeable right front trap. The 18th hole is

163 yards and plays downhill quite a bit. Another good size trap guards the right front of the green. You can probably hit one less club on this hole than you would normally use for the indicated distance.

If you are good at playing par three and par five holes and can keep the ball in the fairway, you ought to score well at Lake Arbor. The City of Arvada now owns and operates this golf course and is continuing to improve the course year after year. Lake Arbor is a much better golf course than I had expected. I'm sure you will enjoy playing it, too.

MEADOW HILLS GOLF CLUB

LOCATION: Aurora, Colorado. From Interstate 225 east of Denver, exit at Parker Road and go south to Hampden Avenue. Turn east on Hampden and the golf course is on your right.

TELEPHONE: 690-2500 Pro-shop
690-2501 Starter

COURSE FACILITIES: Fully equipped pro shop, riding golf carts, pull carts, club rental, driving range, and putting green.

CLUBHOUSE FACILITIES: Restaurant serving breakfast, lunch, sandwiches, dinner, beer, mixed and soft drinks. Additional facilities include tennis courts and a swimming pool.

LODGING: Several new hotels are located along I-225 and Parker Road.

RESTAURANTS: The Fairway Restaurant at the golf course is very good, and many other restaurants abound in the Parker Road-Havana Street area.

GOLF COURSE:

	Par	Course Rating	Yardage
Championship	70	70.4	6717
Regular	70	68.9	6242
Ladies	72	71.5	5670

Meadow Hills was built in 1957 and for 23 years was a private country club. Now it is owned and operated by the city of Aurora, and is one of the finest public golf courses in Colorado.

Although the course is rather flat, all the fairways are heavily treelined, most of the greens are well trapped, and strategically placed water hazards in the form of lakes are a real problem. The excellent well-cared-for greens are of good size with gentle undulations, and the fairways will most always yield clean lies. You will find the last five holes at Meadow Hills a super challenge, with No. 18 one of the best finishing holes in the state. In fact, every hole on this course is different, which is one of the reasons it is so interesting to play.

Greeting the golfer at the 1st tee is a 431-yard straightaway par four, with out-of-bounds left, large trees lining both sides of the fairway, and a sand trap guarding the green's right front. Length and trees are the main problem on this number 1 handicap hole.

In addition to being a par three of adequate challenge, No. 2 offers a great view of the mountains to the west. This 180-yard hole is trapped at the green to the right and left front and very little room extends between them.

Although not as long as the 1st hole, the 422-yard 3rd plays just as difficult. Out of bounds is left, the fairway doglegs right, and only the strongest hitters can cut the corner. Another bunker guards the green's right front. Most golfers will want to play their drive down the middle, then hit a fairway wood or long iron to the green.

No. 4 is a short par three at 145 yards to a green trapped at the right front and left side. Stay out of the sand and this hole should offer little trouble.

Another excellent par four is the 400-yard 5th. The fairway is treelined, out-of-bounds is left, and a lake in the right rough comes to within 20 yards of the right front of the green. Very few golfers will ever reach this lake with their drives.

The 497-yard par five 6th plays uphill a little more than meets the eye from the tee. This roomy but heavily treelined fairway bends slightly left short of the green, which is guarded by three sand traps, one to the right front, one to the front, and another to the left side. These traps are not noticeable from the fairway when hitting your second shot. Best to play short of the sand traps, leaving a short approach to the green.

No. 7 is a routine par four at 338 yards that should not provide much trouble. The only real problems here are the trees lining the fairway and the two sand traps at the green.

The par four 8th offers a number of obstacles, such as 378-yards of length, trees to the right, a long narrow lake to the left, and a green that is trapped left and right front. The lake is reachable off the tee.

Completing the front nine is a 383-yard par four, similar in character to the 8th hole. Again, trees line the fairway's right side and a long narrow lake lurks in the left rough. The strong hitter can clear this lake, but most golfers should favor the fairway to the right. Guarding this rather small green is a right front sand trap.

It takes a long drive to have a shot at the green on the 508-yard dogleg right par five 10th. Large trees guard the inside corner, so it's almost impossible to save any distance here. Play it down the fairway, and if you're past the corner, a long wood might get you near the green. Two traps with very little distance between them guard this 10th green.

No. 11, at 379 yards and par four, is an interesting golf hole that doglegs right near the 150-yard marker. Trees and a lake in the rough at the inside corner create all kinds of problems in that area, so play it down the fairway to the corner and approach the green from that point. The large bunker guarding the green's front side makes for a challenging approach shot.

Two lakes in the left rough are the most serious problem on the 339-yard par four 12th hole. The second lake is not noticeable from the tee. Take a little extra club for your approach shot because it is slightly uphill and the green is trapped left and right front. No. 12 should yield a good number of pars.

The short 125-yard par three 13th is supposed to be the number 18 handicap, but it offers its share of problems. Water comes to within 10 yards of the green's front and a sand trap guards the right front. Accuracy is a must and the green is quite deep, so take plenty of club.

No. 14 is a lengthy par four at 437 yards. Out-of-bounds extends along the fairway's left side, and trees continue to be of concern as they have been on all the previous holes. The green is unprotected, so if you can handle the length, a par is a good possibility.

No. 15, at 183 yards, has good length for a par three and is anything but easy. The green is trapped to the left, and par will be difficult to come by.

The 515-yard par five 16th presents a rather roomy fairway that sweeps gradually to the right. Trees line both sides, but are thicker on the right. The green is trapped left and right front. Out-of-bounds lies to the left, and the green will have some interesting breaking putts.

The most difficult of the par threes on the back nine is the 212-yard 17th. Guarding the fairway's left side and crowding the left side of the green is a large lake, and a sizeable sand trap cuts into the lower right side of the green. You won't find many par threes more difficult than this one. If you miss this green, do so by being short.

I think the 370-yard par four 18th is a great finishing hole. It's certainly anything but a cinch par. Your tee shot plays over a lake and calls for a drive in excess of 200 yards, all carry. A narrow portion of the fairway lies to the right of the water and many golfers will want to play for that part of the fairway. Once over the water the fairway narrows as you approach the green. Trees lie to the left, and out-of-bounds is left, right, and behind the green. Of further concern is the greenside bunker to the right front. I'm sure many a match has been won or lost on this 18th hole.

An interesting bonus offered by Meadow Hill is the abundance of bird and animal life one encounters while playing the course. Its many trees and lakes provide a natural habitat for these creatures. Don't forget to look around.

OVERLAND PARK MUNICIPAL GOLF COURSE

LOCATION: Denver, Colorado. Take the Santa Fe Drive Exit south off Interstate 25 and go to West Jewell Avenue. You will see the golf course on the right side of Santa Fe.

TELEPHONE: 777-7331 Pro shop.
575-2702 Starter.

COURSE FACILITIES: Fully equipped pro shop, riding golf carts, pull carts, club rental, driving range and putting green.

CLUBHOUSE FACILITIES: Restaurant serving breakfast, lunch, sandwiches, dinner, beer, mixed and soft drinks.

LODGING: North and south along I-25.

RESTAURANTS: Best to inquire around, although no shortage of fine restaurants exist in the Denver area.

GOLF COURSE:

	Par	Course Rating	Yardage
Championship	72	69.2	6365
Regular	72	69.2	6365
Ladies	75	73.2	6365

Overland Park, which was originally built for horse racing, occupies a unique place in Denver's history because it was the site of Denver's first golf course. In the early 1890's Senator Walcott, as a means of adding interest to the race track activities held there, had a golf course constructed and introduced the game of golf to Denver. The Overland Park racing association managed the golf course, but the upkeep became quite burdensome, and in about 1895 the Denver Country Club was formed to take care of the golfing end of the park. This original golf course was abandoned when the Denver Country Club moved to its present location early in this century.

In 1932 the present front nine was constructed and opened for play by the public. At the club house you will find an interesting article from a July 10, 1932 issue of the Rocky Mountain News describing the new Overland Park nine-hole golf course. It reads as follows:

> "For a public course Overland Park is certainly a fine layout. There are a number of very sporting holes that would satisfy the most particular golfer, and yet there are a number of holes where there is no particular trouble with wide fairways suitable for public link golfers. The course is such that the maximum pleasure may be derived with the minimum of contention.
>
> The 1st hole has real character. At 382 yards it would be a splendid hole on any golf course. It has a slight dogleg, is lined with trees and rough on both sides and presents the player with the necessity of playing an accurate drive to open the green up properly. Then the green itself is set in a grove of trees that makes a most pictuesque and beautiful setting.
>
> No. 2 is a splendid one-shotter, almost as good as any to be found in any city. It is 187 yards and requires a very accurate shot. The green is guarded well by a trap on the right and a ditch on the left. It is surrounded by mounds covered with good rough so that a par three can only be guaranteed by spotting the shot on the green. Many find this hole deceptive and play short. This is because there is a depression in the fairway not seen from the tee. The player does not see all the terrain between the tee and the green. If I were to criticize this layout, it is that these two splendid holes are the beginning ones and are not farther along. They make splendid finishing holes, although the par five 9th is splendid as it is. Holes with just a little easier start enable the player to get warmed-up to his task before tackling the difficult ones.

The 3rd hole, par five at 512 yards, is a good hole and has the only water hazard on the course. This reservoir, from which the water supply is drawn for sprinkling, is in front of the tee, and although the carry over is not great, many find it is a real mental hazard.

No. 4, 440 yards, is straightaway and presents no special difficulty, but No. 5, 336 yards, is another very picturesque hole. The fairway is a slight dog-leg, and the green lies in the border of a large grove of trees. The green is a two-level one and presents a genuine need for skill in putting.

No. 6 is a par-four hole, 407 yards. It takes a splendid drive and a fine iron shot to get home. A wind nearly always blows in the face of the player on this hole. No. 7 is a good general type of hole, 380 yards with no special difficulties. No. 8 is a good but not hard one-shot hole, and the last one is a par five of 494 yards. Plenty of rough extends along both sides of the 9th fairway, but it is wide enough that the average player should have little difficulty. It is possible to get home with two splendid shots, thus enabling the player to finish his round with a birdie and give him that 'come back feeling'."

Except for the addition of sand traps on all but the par three holes, little has changed at Overland Park since 1932.

The back nine begins with the 154-yard par three 10th that is level and straight. Left and right front traps watch over this green. It has been said that more hole-in-ones have been scored on this hole than any other golf hole in Denver. This is probably true because the hole is not difficult and Overland is quite popular.

No. 11 is the first of two very short par fours, and at 285 yards it should offer a chance to pick up a stroke. The green is well guarded by left and right sand traps. The 364-yard par four 12th offers out-of-bounds on the left and a right-hand dogleg. Again, left and right front sand traps guard this green. A pin placement behind the right front trap will require a best effort approach shot.

At 487 yards, straightaway and par five, the 13th hole gives the golfer a good opportunity to pick up another stroke. Although out-of-bounds is on the left and the green is well trapped, this is not a difficult hole.

No. 14 at 420 yards and par four is the number 2 handicap hole. The fairway is treelined, bends a little right, but is quite roomy. Sand traps guard both the left and right front of the green. Because of its length, this is a very respectable hole.

The 15th is a good medium-length par four at 393 yards with the fairway bending a little left. The green is well protected by two sand traps, but otherwise there is little trouble here. Straightaway and level best describes the 173-yard par three 16th, but don't be long or a tough downhill chip shot back to the green might very well add a stroke to your score.

No. 17 is the other short par four on this back nine. Although only 290 yards it is a very interesting hole. The fairway doglegs left just short of the green, and a good size sand trap lies in the left rough at the edge of the green to discourage the big hitter who wants to get home in one. Large trees along the fairway's left side give further complication to this hole. Best to play for the center of the fairway and pitch on from there.

The 18th at 510 yards and par five is a good long finishing hole. The fairway is wide and inviting, but the green is well trapped. It will be difficult to reach this green in two, but as with the 9th hole, No. 18 should give a lot of players that "come back feeling".

Overland Park is a pleasant and enjoyable course to walk, and as is the case with most of the older courses, it is interesting and challenging to play. It is the kind of golf course you will want to play again.

PARK HILL GOLF CLUB

LOCATION: Denver, Colorado. Northeast of downtown at the intersection of Colorado Blvd. and East 35th Avenue.

TELEPHONE: 333-5411

COURSE FACILITIES: Fully equipped pro shop, riding golf carts, pull carts, club rental, driving range and putting green.

CLUBHOUSE FACILITIES: Restaurant serving breakfast, lunch, sandwiches, beer, mixed and soft drinks.

LODGING: Denver area motels.

RESTAURANTS: The restaurant at Park Hill is excellent for breakfast and lunch. They do not serve dinner except for banquets and special group occasions. Ask your golfing partners for the location of other good places to eat.

GOLF COURSE:

	Par	Course Rating	Yardage
Championship	71	66.5	6325
Regular	71	66.5	6325
Ladies	73	71.2	5814

The game of golf was first played at Park Hill in 1930. Consequently, it has an abundance of large trees as well as many recently planted smaller pine and evergreens. The course is quite level and easy to walk. No sand traps, but the large fast and undulating greens cause enough problems to make up for this shortcoming. Visitors will do best to try for tee times during the week, because Park Hill is a popular weekend course.

The golf course begins with a very respectable 536-yard par five down a fairway that bends a little to the left. This medium-difficulty golf hole will start many a round off with par. No. 2 is a number 1 handicap hole at 429 yards and par four. It is straightaway and quite roomy, but favor the right side of the fairway all the way to the green. Any pin placement on this green will result in a breaking putt. You will find this typical of all the greens on the front nine.

The 3rd hole is a lengthy par three at 206 yards. Out-of-bounds on the left is a problem here as well as its length. No. 4 and 5 are somewhat similar in difficulty. Play for the middle of the fairway on No. 4 and line up with the left edge of the small lake in front of the tee box on No. 5.

The 6th hole is a 521-yard par five with plenty of room in the fairway, but with water problems 150 to 250 yards off the tee in the right rough. Favor the left side of this fairway with your drive, because most any tee shot mishit to the right will find the water. No. 7 and 8 are rather easy golf holes, with the 7th being a 164-yard straightaway par three, and the 8th being a short 317-yard par four. However, both of these greens will challenge the best of putters.

We end the front nine with a 394-yard par four and a fairway that curves a little to the right. The green on this hole is especially interesting because it has a small valley running from the lower left corner to the upper right corner. This can make for some frustrating pin placements.

The back nine begins with the easiest hole on the course, the 313-yard par four 10th. The green here is quite level which is typical of most of the greens on the back nine. No. 11 is an excellent par three at 204 yards and all uphill. Take an extra club because it's all-carry and plays longer than it looks.

Although No. 12 is not long or difficult, it is a very pretty golf hole. The tee is elevated, and the fairway curves right around a small forest of pine trees at the corner. These trees will reach up and grab any ball sliced or hit over in the right rough. Denver's skyline, which is prominent in the distance, is an interesting sight here. Favor the fairway's left side and you should be able to mark a par four on your score card for this 323-yard hole.

Two large cottonwood trees watch over the tee box on the 373-yard par four 13th. This makes for an attractive setting, but does not add to the hole's difficulty. The 14th and 15th holes are both par fours that have a common problem, out-of-bounds on the left all the way to the green. Both of these holes parallel Colorado Blvd., but if you can keep the ball in the fairway, you have a good chance for par.

One of the more interesting holes on the course is the 369-yard par four 16th. It is a dogleg left, and two large cottonwood trees guard the left front approach to the green. Aim down the center of the fairway off the tee. Any approach shot from the left rough must clear the two cottonwoods. Don't try to cut the corner on this hole.

Nothing unusual marks the 170-yard par three 17th. It is a respectable par three, but with no real problems.

I like the 18th at Park Hill. It is a very difficult finishing hole at 540 yards and par five. This hole demands an almost perfect drive because of the five cottonwood trees guarding both sides of the fairway 200 to 250 yards off the tee. After you get through the trees, watch out for the grass bunker adjacent to the left side of the green. Every golf course has its outstanding hole. In my opinion, at Park Hill it's the 18th.

RACCOON CREEK GOLF COURSE

LOCATION: Littleton, Colorado. Go south on Wadsworth to Bowles, then three-fourths mile east, and the golf course is on your left.

TELEPHONE: 973-4653

COURSE FACILITIES: Fully equipped pro shop, riding golf carts, pull carts, club rental, driving range, putting and chipping greens.

CLUBHOUSE FACILITIES: Restaurant serving breakfast, lunch, sandwiches, beer, mixed and soft drinks.

LODGING: Nothing nearby.

RESTAURANTS: North on Wadsworth.

GOLF COURSE:

	Par	Course Rating	Yardage
Championship	72		7000
Regular	72		6600
Ladies	72		5230

Raccoon Creek opens for its first full season of play in May of 1984. You will find it a flatland-type golf course with many sand traps and undulating greens. The rough is maintained, the greens are large, and the sand traps are more than plentiful. Its length is quite adequate, and from my observation it should offer a genuine challenge to all golfers. Give it a try soon.

RIVERDALE GOLF COURSE

LOCATION: Brighton, Colorado. Go 4 miles south of Brighton on Highway 85 and 1 mile west. Follow the signs to the Adams County Fair Grounds.

TELEPHONE: 659-4400

COURSE FACILITIES: Fully equipped pro shop, riding golf carts, club rental, driving range, chipping and putting greens.

CLUBHOUSE FACILITIES: Snack bar serving breakfast, lunch, sandwiches, beer and soft drinks.

LODGING: Denver area motels.

RESTAURANTS: Nothing close.

GOLF COURSE:

	Par	Course Rating	Yardage
Championship	71	70.6	6752
Regular	71	68.7	6464
Ladies	75	74.3	6128

Riverdale is characterized by the myriad of irrigation ditches that cross the golf course. These ditches, some small and some large, come into play on 13 of the 18 holes. Another feature is the excellent condition of the rough, which is the same grass as the fairways only longer. You will find Riverdale a pleasant course to play and an easy one to walk, because for the most part it is quite flat. This course is "in the country", and you will not be bothered by city traffic or homes built too close to the fairways.

The first hole is also the number 1 handicap. It is 552 yards in length, par five, and the fairway is divided into three parts by two irrigation ditches which are the first of many yet to come. The strong golfer can hit a 4 or 3 wood off the tee and another 4 wood to short of the green. Most players however, will do best to hit a wood off the tee, a medium iron to the area between the two ditches, and another medium iron to the green. The fairway doglegs right at the second ditch.

No. 2 is a 179-yard par three with an irrigation ditch crossing the fairway about 100 yards in front of the tee. The 3rd hole is a 413-yard par four that is straightaway, and again we have the already familiar ditch crossing the fairway 100 yards from the tee. Plenty of room in the fairway, but a sand trap lies about 50 yards past the ditch in the right rough. This green is ticklish to putt because of plenty of break, no matter where the pin is placed.

The course eases off a bit with No. 4 and offers a 357-yard par four that is straightaway, uphill, and calls for a short iron second shot to an elevated table-top green. Although not noticeable from the fairway, the green is large and a good one to hit into. No. 5 is a 146-yard par three from an elevated tee to a green that is well bunkered, quite wide, but not too deep.

No. 6 is an attractive golf hole, as well as having its share of difficulty. A good target from the hilltop tee is the large cottonwood at the left side of the fairway. Trouble lurks to the right in the form of two lakes out in the rough. This fairway narrows to about 45 yards at the 150-yard marker, and a loose approach shot can easily find the water at the right of the green.

The 7th hole, although flat and straight, has continuous trouble on the left in the form of our old friend the irrigation ditch. The slightest hook or pull shot can find this ditch. At par four and 393 yards, this fairway narrows to a large flat green guarded by two bunkers, although considerable room extends between them. The 406-yard par four No. 8 has the same irrigation ditch on the left from tee to green, but it is pretty well out of play for all but a big hook. From the fairway it is not easy to see the bunker at the left side of the green, so be aware of this as well as the ditch behind, which can catch too strong of an approach shot. No. 9 is a generous hole, being par four and only 347 yards in length. Avoid the large cottonwood tree on the fairway's right side and this hole should yield a par or better.

The back nine begins with a straightout 402-yard par four, down a wide-open fairway, to a green on the opposite side of another irrigation ditch. This ditch is not noticeable from the fairway and is located about 40 yards in front of a large elongated two-tier green. From an elevated tee to a large green 165 yards away, we find the par three 11th hole. A well-hit ball must avoid the ditch 100 yards in front of the tee box and the trap at the right front of the green. No. 12 is one of the more interesting holes on the course. It is 387 yards long, par four, and doglegs right at the 150-yard marker. The temptation is to cut the corner, but it is best not to do this because of the group of cedar trees and the sand trap in the right rough. This green is bunkered at the left rear and the right front and again is a tricky one to putt.

The par five 13th at 523 yards, looks much longer as you stand on this elevated tee and survey the terrain below. However, the fairway is wide open, and after a good drive over the irrigation ditch 75 yards in front of the tee, another wood and a short iron should find your ball on the green. Par is within reach of most golfers here. No. 14 is a lengthy par three at 192 yards and will require a long iron or 5 wood to a green bunkered at the left front. The golf course takes a rest with the 336-yard par four 15th. It is an uphill fairway with no trouble around the green. Another par.

No. 16, although a little longer than the previous hole, should yield par to most golfers. However this is the calm before the storm at the next hole.

The number 2 handicap 17th could just as well be the number 1 handicap. It is a lengthy 417-yard par four straightforward hole to an elevated plateau-type green, guarded by a trap at the right front. The large irrigation ditch at 385 yards from the tee will not catch many drives, but will gather in lots of second shots if one is short off the tee. Go for the pin when approaching this green. It is large and slopes a little toward the golfer with no chance of hitting short and rolling on.

Although not long, No. 18 is a very good finishing hole. The irrigation ditch crossing the fairway 235 yards from the tee complicates this otherwise amiable and wide-open par five. Most golfers will want to lay up short of the ditch and hit a fairway wood, then a short iron to the green. However, under the right conditions, "going for it" can be justified, and if successful this becomes a rather easy hole.

Note: Another 18 holes are presently under construction at Riverdale. Play is scheduled for sometime in 1985. A new clubhouse is also planned, and when both are completed several of the holes on the original 18 will be renumbered.

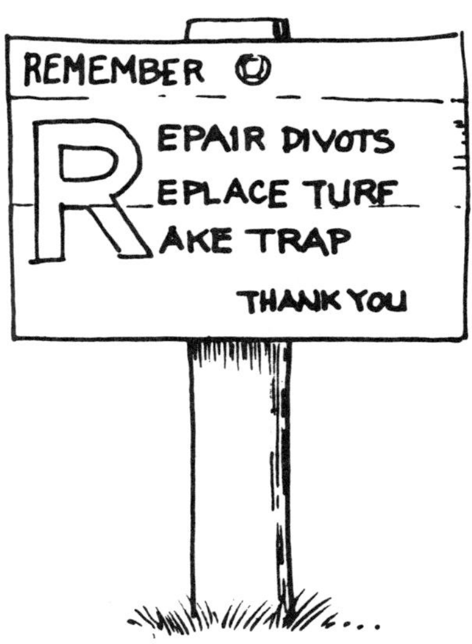

SOUTH SUBURBAN GOLF COURSE

LOCATION: Littleton, Colorado. Take Interstate 25 south of Denver and exit to the west onto County Line Road. Continue west until you come to So. Colorado Blvd. Turn north on So. Colorado Blvd. for about half a mile. The golf course is on your right.

TELEPHONE: 770-5500

COURSE FACILITIES: Fully equipped pro shop, riding golf carts, pull carts, club rental, driving range, chipping and putting greens.

CLUBHOUSE FACILITIES: Very good snack bar serving breakfast, lunch, sandwiches, beer, mixed and soft drinks.

LODGING: The closest motels are on I-25 back towards Denver.

RESTAURANTS: Many good restaurants run along I-25 and in the southeast part of Denver.

GOLF COURSE:

	Par	Course Rating	Yardage
Championship	71	67.8	6410
Regular	71	66.6	6179
Ladies	72	70.8	5649

South Suburban, constructed in 1974, is another one of the several new golf courses built in the Denver area within the last ten years. You will find it in excellent condition with fast, slippery, and very undulating greens. No level putts are to be found at South Suburban. The fairways have had enough years to form a good cushion, and you will usually find your ball sitting up quite nicely. The large sand traps are numerous, and water hazards, in the form of lakes and a water-filled gulch, come into play all too often. You will find this golf course rather hilly, but not a difficult one to walk.

The huge cottonwoods growing in the large gulch running through the course give this golf course a country feeling, and you are not bothered by houses lining the fairways. This fine golf course is a pleasure to play, as well as an excellent challenge to the golfer's ability to play the game. Don't miss this one.

Typical of many of the tee boxes at South Suburban is the elevated 1st tee on the 327-yard par four starter hole. The fairway, which is well below the tee, plays straightaway to the 150-yard marker, then bends right at that point. Any kind of decent drive should leave a short iron approach to the green, but don't be long or to the right because real trouble exists in those areas. A thick clump of bushes and undergrowth guards the green's right front, and a water-filled gulch and sand trap sit below and to the rear. Not a hard hole, but an accurate approach is a must for par.

The golf course presents the number 1 handicap playing hole next with the 479-yard par five 2nd. A water-filled and treelined gully extends along the fairway's left, so favor the right side off the tee. It's your second shot that is the real problem here. At about the landing area for your second shot, the fairway narrows considerably, bends left, and huge cottonwoods guard both corners. Cutting the corner here is virtually impossible. Once you get through this narrow portion of the fairway, you will find your approach to the green wide open. Be aware of the two greenside traps, one to the left and another to the right rear.

No. 3, at 360 yards and par four, is one of my favorites. It consists of a two-part fairway, the first over the gulch and straightaway, and the second a sharp dogleg to the right and over the gulch again. A lofted wood or long iron off the tee is the club to use. This will leave a 150-yard approach shot between an opening in the trees to the green on the other side of the gulch. (see sketch pg. 108)

Another "in control" hole is the 298-yard par four 4th. It plays straightforward off the tee and doglegs left at the 150-yard marker. A huge bunker dominates the rough to the left and is reachable by the strong hitter attempting to cut the corner. Hugging the entire outside bend of this left-to-right sloping fairway is a large lake, and any drive hit too strong can roll into the water. Target the left edge of this fairway off the tee.

South Suburban No. 3
360 yards par four

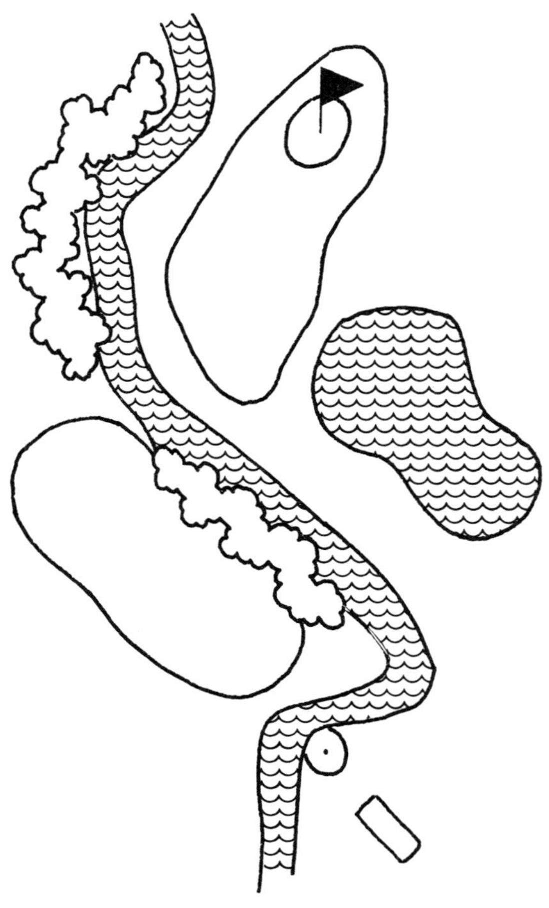

At 130 yards and par three, the 5th hole looks rather easy as you survey the situation from the tee, but it isn't. The lake to the green's right and the bunker to the left give it credibility. No cinch par here.

No. 6 plays straightaway over a fairway that slopes sharply left to right, so favor the left side off the tee. An early bunker to the right shouldn't bother many golfers. Your approach is uphill to a green trapped to the right front and right side. Most golfers should use one extra club when hitting into this green.

Target the 150-yard marker at the fairway's right side on the 407-yard par four 7th. This is the first long par four on the course, and plays even longer than indicated because your second shot is all uphill. This fairway doglegs left at the 150-yard marker, and a reachable bunker sits in the left rough at the inside corner. Take plenty of club when approaching this green, but watch out for the bunker to the green's right.

When you get to the 8th tee, take a moment to look at the fabulous view of the Colorado Rockies to the west. No. 8 plays to a par three at 158 yards to a green trapped at the right front. Not a difficult golf hole.

The 9th hole is a dandy. This 379-yard par four plays from an elevated tee down a fairway that bends right and slopes left to right. A large lake guards the entire inside bend of the fairway and is home for a lot of golf balls. You must favor the fairway's left side on this hole, and most golfers will have a long approach shot to the green. Avoiding the huge bunker to the right front of the green is a must for par on this very demanding hole.

The back nine begins with a medium-length 352-yard par four that plays uphill off the tee, then level to the green from the 150-yard marker. This fairway is quite friendly and roomy with no excuse for missing it. A good drive will go a long way toward par.

No. 11 is a lengthy 526-yard par five that doglegs left. A well-hit drive can clear the dogleg, and from that point it is gradually uphill to the green, which is trapped left front.

The 12th hole bends to the right near the 150-yard marker, and a large mound in the fairway's left side partially blocks your view of the green for your second shot. Another huge sand trap guards the green's right front. Not a hard hole, but neither is it a sure par.

A long, narrow trap guards entry to the green on the 154-yard par three 13th. Take plenty of club here and you should be OK.

The second 547-yard par five on the golf course is No. 14, and it will demand the golfer's best. Actually two bends shape this fairway, the first one to the right and the second to the left. Target the large mound in the left rough with your drive and favor the fairway's left edge for proper direction with your blind second shot. A huge fairway bunker sits about 30 yards to the green's right front, and another large trap locates to the left and above the green. This number 2 handicap hole will give you a real fight before yielding to par.

I like the 368-yard par four 15th. It demands a well-placed drive of about 200 to 220 yards, leaving a medium iron second to the green on the other side of a gully. Favor the fairway's left side off the tee because a large cottonwood growing in the gully can interfere with an approach from the right. Some golfers will do best to lay up short of the gully with their second shot.

No. 16 is a 184-yard par three over the gully to the green on the other side, but getting on this rather large green doesn't automatically insure a par. As you already have discovered, these greens are fast and all have a great deal of break. No. 16 green is no exception.

Take time to enjoy the view again from the tee box of the 358-yard par four 17th. This fairway possesses a lot of small humps and hollows, bends a little left, and a huge bunker guards the inside corner. Favor the right side off the tee because your ball will kick left when it hits the fairway. A sand trap, below and to the left, guards this green.

A well-hit drive will get you to the top of the hill on the 379-yard par four 18th. Avoid the large bunker at the inside corner of this left-hand dogleg and you should have an open approach to the green. Most shots into this 18th green will be medium-to-long irons and must avoid the huge trap guarding the green's left front. The lake in the left rough can be a problem, but if you favor the fairway's right side from tee to green, you might be able to mark a par four on your card. This is an excellent finishing hole.

South Suburban is the type of golf course you will want to come back and play again. No sameness to the course, and that just might be the most interesting thing about it. I played this golf course on the 14th of February, but you can be sure I will be back to play it again in the summer.

In addition to the 18-hole course, South Suburban offers an excellent par three that possesses great terrain and presents a genuine challenge to any golfer. It's an ideal place to work on your short game and is quite exciting to play.

SPRINGHILL GOLF COURSE

LOCATION: Aurora, Colorado. Exit off Interstate 225 east of Denver onto East 6th Avenue, go east for a little over 2 miles, then turn left on Telluride Street. This street will take you to the Paul Beck Recreation Center. The golf course is behind the main building.

TELEPHONE: 343-3963

COURSE FACILITIES: Fully equipped pro shop, riding golf carts, pull carts, club rental, driving range, putting and chipping greens.

CLUBHOUSE FACILITIES: Sandwiches, beer, soft drinks, showers, swimming pool, tennis courts, weight room, sauna, and banquet facilities.

LODGING: Lots of good motels along I-225, I-70, and East Colfax.

RESTAURANTS: Good restaurants abound along Havana and Peoria Streets.

GOLF COURSE:

	Par	Course Rating	Yardage
Regular	64	61.6	4966
Ladies	65		4621

Springhill was originally a private golf course that ran into financial difficulties. It is now owned and operated by the City of Aurora Parks and Recreation Department. Although quite short, at 4966 yards, I found it to be very interesting, with the par fours and fives offering more than enough challenge for anyone. The thick, well-cared-for fairways yield good lies, and you will find your putts rolling true on all the greens. Enough water hazards and sand traps dot the course to be of real concern, but most of the trees are rather small, and it will be several years before they are a problem. Springhill is removed from Aurora's and Denver's heavy population, and a lot of people probably are not aware of it. This interesting and fun course just might be what you are looking for. Give it a try soon.

The front nine begins with a 382-yard par four, followed by a 209-yard par three and another par three at 140 yards. Avoid out-of-bounds to the left and you should score at least two out of three pars.

At 530 yards and par five, No. 4 is a real challenge. This number 1 handicap hole plays straightforward off the tee, then bends slightly left at the 150-yard marker. Two huge cottonwoods guard the inside corner, and a small lake not noticeable from the fairway lurks past these trees. Opposite this lake on the other side of the fairway is another larger lake, and the distance between narrows to only 15 yards as you approach the green. Favor the fairway's right side with your drive, lay up to within about 150 yards of the green with your second, and approach the green from that point. Attempting to reach this green in two is very risky because of these two lakes short of the green. You can be proud of a par on this hole.

No. 5 is a 376-yard par four dogleg right around the same lake that came into play on the previous hole. The strong hitter can cut the corner here, but most golfers should play it down the middle. Take a good look at the snow-capped Rocky Mountains as you tee it up on No. 5. Avoid the lake and a par should not be difficult.

Next we have a 163-yard par three for No. 6. No problems on this hole, another par. No. 7, although not a long par four at 323 yards, is a good golf hole. The fairway bends left about 100 yards from the green, a large bunker in the left rough at the corner says stay away from here, and another bunker to the green's left echos the same sentiments. In other words, don't attempt to cut the corner. Favor the fairway's right side and have a short iron to the green.

Other than its length, No. 8 is a 196-yard no-trouble par three. However, the 9th hole, although shorter at 180 yards and par three, offers some real concern up by the green. Two sand traps, one to the right front and one to the left, watch over this green, and both traps are surrounded by several large grassy mounds. More grassy mounds rise at the rear of the green. An interesting hole to hit into.

The back nine continues the string of par threes with the short 124-yard 10th and the somewhat longer 149-yard 11th. No real problems on either of these holes.

However, No. 12 at 400 yards and par four, will play on anyone's golf course. This slightly downhill-playing fairway swings left near the 150-yard marker, but play your tee shot in the fairway. This will leave most golfers a mid-iron to the green, which is protected by a number of these grassy mounds that we've come to know on some of the previous holes.

At 529 yards and par five, No. 13 is another good one. It's a double dogleg with the first one right and the second one left. The big hitter can cut the corner here, but most golfers should play it safe down the middle of the fairway. At the 150-yard marker the fairway bends left and leaves an interesting approach to a green well protected by grassy mounds and sand traps.

A small pond sits about half way between the tee and the green on the 185 yard par three 14th. Avoid the water and you should have another par.

I like No. 15. It possesses good length for a par four, and the ditch to the left and the cottonwood trees at the inside corner of this left-hand dogleg can be a real problem. You must be in the right side of this fairway to have any kind of shot to the green. At 420 yards No. 15 is the longest par four on the course, and it will require a long approach shot to reach this green in regulation.

No. 16 is another dogleg, this time to the right. Out-of-bounds is left, but the fairway is quite roomy. Play for the middle of the fairway off the tee and you should have a short iron approach on this 353-yard par four hole. Surrounding the green are more grassy mounds as well as two bunkers, one to the left front and another to the right front.

The back nine finishes the same way it started with two rather routine par threes. However, the par fours and the par five on this back nine have all been tough, so maybe it's time for a breather.

You will enjoy playing this golf course, and all of the many other activities here at the center are open to the public. Some good advice might be to drive a little and play a lot at the Paul Beck Recreation Center east of Aurora.

WELLSHIRE MUNICIPAL GOLF COURSE

LOCATION: Denver, Colorado. Take the Colorado Blvd. Exit Off Interstate 25 and go south until you see the golf course on your right.

TELEPHONE: 757-1352 Pro shop.
756-6318 Starter.

COURSE FACILITIES: Fully equipped pro shop, riding golf carts, pull carts, club rental, driving range, and putting green.

CLUBHOUSE FACILITIES: Restaurant and lounge serving breakfast, lunch, sandwiches, dinner, beer, mixed and soft drinks.

LODGING: Most of the motels close to this golf course are back on Interstate 25 or north on Colorado Blvd.

RESTAURANTS: The Wellshire Inn at the golf course is excellent. Other fine restaurants are located on So. Colorado Blvd.

GOLF COURSE:

	Par	Course Rating	Yardage
Mens	72	68.8	6592
Ladies	77	72.4	6142

Wellshire Municipal Golf Course was originally a private club that fell upon hard times and was purchased by the City of Denver in the early 1940's. It is one of Denver's most popular golf courses, as well as one of the oldest in the city. Trees are everywhere at Wellshire, and many new ones are planted every year. The course is always in very good condition for the amount of heavy play it receives. At 6592 yards this is not a short golf course, and the many huge trees lining most of the fairways seem to make it play even longer. You will not only enjoy playing this golf course, but you will also appreciate the view of the mountains to the west from many of the holes. The policy regarding tee times at Wellshire is "first come, first served", so depending on the time of year you will probably have a little wait before getting to play. Use this time to good advantage on the driving range and putting green.

The 510-yard par five 1st hole gives the golfer a chance to loosen up and get ready for the rest of the golf course. Although the fairway is heavily treelined, it is also quite roomy. It plays level off the tee, over a valley, then uphill to the green which is trapped to the left and right sides.

No. 2 is 174 yards and par three. It plays level from tee to green and is trapped to the left and right side. Everything kicks right on this hole, so favor the left side a little. A good target off the tee is the leaning tree behind the green.

No. 3 is a medium-difficulty golf hole that plays straightaway to a green that is guarded by left and right side bunkers. This fairway is wide and inviting off the tee, but huge trees line both sides as you approach the green.

At 423 yards the par four 4th offers a good challenge, mainly due to its length. The landing area off the tee is quite roomy, but watch out for the sand trap to the right of the green. This trap is not visible from the fairway.

The 452-yard 5th is short as par fives go, but the heavy treelined fairway, out-of-bounds left, and left side sand trap at the green make most golfers put up a good fight before it yields to par.

The first dogleg on the course is the 349-yard par four 6th, and it is an interesting golf hole. The fairway slopes mildly left to right, plays slightly uphill, then doglegs left at the large spruce tree growing at the inside corner. A fairway trap sits immediately behind this tree and another bunker occupies the outside corner. Two more bunkers, one to each side, guard the green. The long ball hitter can cut this corner over the spruce tree, but most golfers will do best to play it safe and down the middle.

I like No. 7. It is the number 1 handicap hole at 409 yards and par four. From an elevated tee it plays over a valley to the top of a hill, at which point the fairway bends left a little and plays over another valley to the green. Out-of-bounds is left and the green is trapped to the right front. It will take a medium long iron or fairway wood to reach this green in regulation. A second bunker lies to the left side of this two-level green. You can be proud of making par on this hole, and don't be ashamed of a bogey.

Aim for the opening between the trees in the distance on the 337-yard uphill par four 8th. Not noticeable from the tee are left and right side fairway traps about 50 yards out from the green. Two more traps guard the green's left and right sides. The trap to the right is further complicated by a small cottonwood growing in the middle of it. This short hole is anything but easy.

Completing the front nine is a 162-yard par three that seems to play a little shorter than the indicated yardage. As with most of the previous holes, two sand traps guard the green. Favor the left side with your tee shot, because everything kicks to the right on this hole.

The 475-yard par five 10th parallels the 1st hole and is similar, but not quite as long. This fairway plays downhill to a valley, bends a little left, then heads uphill to the green. The large reservoir to the fairway's left should not bother most players, but the huge cottonwood growing in the left rough at the bottom of the valley can be a problem. Stay to the right of this tree, and you will have an open shot to the green, which is trapped to its right side.

Distance is deceiving on the 143-yard par three 11th, but play it as indicated on the score card. This hole plays a little uphill, over a large irrigation ditch crossing the fairway about 50 yards in front of the green, and the green is bunkered to the left and right sides.

No. 12 is a long par four at 470 yards, but it plays downhill all the way to the green. Aim for the high-rise building seen in the distance and make every effort to stay in the fairway, because the trees lining both sides of this hole can spell real trouble if you stray to either side. You will find a sand trap watching over the right side of the green.

The 435-yard par four 13th is another tough one. It plays from a slightly elevated tee to a fairway that bends right and slopes a little left. At the green two sand traps, one below and to the left and another to the right stand guard. It will take two long hits to get on this green in regulation.

The 226-yard par three 14th is not a difficult hole. However, its length and the left and right side sand traps at the green give it plenty of respectability.

We are now in the southwest corner of the golf course, and the next three holes all parallel Hampden Avenue on the right. It's out of bounds and heavy traffic over there, so avoid the fairway's right side if possible. No. 15 is a 349-yard par four that plays straightaway down a heavily treelined fairway. New tree plantings have narrowed the landing area considerably, and the green is trapped to the lower left front and the right side. This is a demanding golf hole with plenty of opportunity to get in trouble.

No. 16 is another par four at 397 yards, and it plays considerably more uphill than it looks from the tee. A bunker hides in the right rough near the landing area, and it cannot be seen from the tee. Left and right side sand traps guard the green.

A blind tee shot awaits the golfer at the 408-yard 17th. Aim for the center of the fairway, and you should be OK. A good drive will get you past the crest of the hill, leaving a medium iron to the green. Be aware of the bunker in the right rough close to the landing area. Again, left and right side sand traps guard the green.

I like No. 18. It is a fine finishing hole. Although not a long par five at 477 yards, it demands the golfer's best. Your drive must carry about 180 yards to clear the large irrigation ditch crossing the fairway at that point. This ditch continues along the fairway's left side and is of concern all the way to the green. The fairway possesses a good number of sizeable humps and hollows and also slopes a little from right to left. At the green, two sand traps spell further trouble. Be grateful for a par on this 18th hole.

WEST MEADOWS

LOCATION:	Littleton, Colorado. Go south on Wadsworth to Bowles, west on Bowles to Simms, then south on Simms for one-half mile to the golf course.
TELEPHONE:	972-8831 Pro Shop 972-8910 Restaurant
COURSE FACILITIES:	Fully equipped pro shop, riding golf carts, pull carts, club rental, driving range, chipping and putting greens.
CLUBHOUSE FACILITIES:	Fine dining restaurant serving breakfast, lunch, sandwiches, dinner, beer, mixed and soft drinks.
LODGING:	Nothing nearby.
RESTAURANTS:	Try "The Meadows" at the clubhouse. There's nothing else in the area.

GOLF COURSE:

	Par	Course Rating	Yardage
Championship	72	71.9	6959
Regular	72	70.0	6543
Ladies	72	69.9	5439

West Meadows is a new course open for play to the general public in May of 1984. It's not the typical public golf course because it has something like 82 sand traps, some of them quite deep. In addition, three large lakes and an unplayable drainage ditch that meanders the length of the course provide an interesting challenge on almost every hole. The course is laid out lengthwise in the bottom of a valley and winds in and out among the small foothills of the mountains to the west. There are no trees, but the above mentioned hazards and the natural native grass rough will take their toll if you stray from the fairway. West Meadows has the makings of a fine championship golf course. Give it a try at first opportunity.

WILLIS CASE MUNICIPAL GOLF COURSE

LOCATION: Denver, Colorado. Take the Sheridan Blvd. Exit north off Interstate 70 and go north about one-half mile to 52nd Avenue, turn east and go to Tennyson Street, turn right and go to 50th Avenue, turn right again and this road will lead you into the golf course.

TELEPHONE: 455-9801 Pro shop.
575-2112 Starter.

COURSE FACILITIES: Fully equipped pro shop, riding golf carts, pull carts, club rental, putting green, chipping green, and practice area for irons only.

CLUBHOUSE FACILITIES: Snack bar serving breakfast, lunch, hot sandwiches, beer, mixed and soft drinks.

LODGING: Several good motels to the west along I-70.

RESTAURANTS: Try the Wheatridge and Lakewood areas along Wadsworth Blvd. and West Colfax.

GOLF COURSE:

	Par	Course Rating	Yardage
Championship	71	68.6	6364
Regular	71	68.6	6364
Ladies	76	72.8	6364

Willis Case has been in existence for more than 60 years and is one of Denver's oldest golf courses. It was first played in 1922 and was originally a nine hole course called Interlocken Country Club. Later the name was changed to the Berkeley Nine, and in 1932 the name was changed to Willis Case, after the man who donated the land. It is hilly with many trees, yet not difficult to walk, and the view to the west from the elevated 1st tee is spectacular. The entire Continental Divide lies to the west, and you can see at least a hundred miles of mountain range extending north and south. What a way to start off a round of golf on one of Denver's most interesting and exciting courses! The greens at Willis Case are great, and if putting well your score card should show a good number of pars as well as a few birdies!

Along with having an awe-inspiring view, No. 1, 420 yards and downhill, is a good starting hole. The fairway is wide open, friendly, and from atop the first tee box you get the feeling you can almost drive the green. A small trap guards the right front of the green, but this hole should yield par to many golfers. No. 2 is a long and level par three at 240 yards with a sand trap protecting the right side of the green. Any par three of this length can be tough, so hope for par, but be satisfied with bogey. No. 3 is a 390-yard par four that is a little uphill and with a slanting right-to-left fairway bending off to the right. This fairway is lined with many evergreens, and it is best to come into the green from the left. The 145-yard downhill par three 4th plays shorter than indicated, but it is not an easy hole. The green is well bunkered and a little difficult to hold. Don't be long with your tee shot or the trees behind the green will cause trouble.

The number 1 handicap hole is the 573-yard par five 5th. Many trees guard the entire left side of this fairway, and the only water on the golf course lies in waiting about 250 yards off the tee in the right rough. The fairway moves uphill and to the left at the 150-yard marker. Reaching this green in two is beyond the reach of most ordinary mortals. Do not be disheartened with a bogey here. Next we have two long and rather difficult par fours. No. 6 is 443 yards, and the treelined fairway plays gradually uphill and bends off a little to the right. Two greenside bunkers and a bothersome mound in the center of the green give further complication to this hole. The 430-yard 7th is straightaway with out-of-bounds bordering the fairway's right side from tee to green. About 60 yards in front of the green is a small valley, and immediately to its left is the same lake that was mentioned on No. 5. This is a beautiful green to hit into with the grassy mounds on the left, the huge spruce trees behind the green, and mountains beyond all making a spectacular setting.

The 8th is another hole that goes gradually uphill and also has a slight dogleg right. Trees guard the right corner of the dogleg as well as the the left side of the fairway from 150 yards on into the green. This is not a hard par four, but does play somewhat longer than 374 yards. A fitting climax to the front nine is the 367-yard par four 9th. It is level off the tee, but from then on it is all uphill, and a huge trap closely protects the right front of this elevated green.

The back nine is a different golf course than the front nine in that it is 400-yards shorter, has two par fives, and several blind approach shots to the greens. It starts off easy however, with a short 146-yard par three guarded by left and right front sand traps. No. 11 is another short one at 347 yards and par four, but it can be very tricky. This hole has alternate greens and neither of them is visible from the tee so it is best to go down the fairway a little and find out which one is being used. Both greens and fairway are well trapped, with the green on the right being especially difficult because of its two tiers. This green is further complicated by the fact that it seems to slope away from the golfer with the top tier being on the near side, making for some impossible putts. A long hitter off the tee should use a 3 or 4 wood because all fairway traps are reachable. No. 12 is a 480-yard par five that parallels I-70. Berkeley Lake over on the other side of the highway seems to add considerably to this very pleasant environment. Although not a long par five, this hole has its share of obstacles with out-of-bounds on the left, right-to-left sloping fairway, huge left and right greenside traps, and another large two-tier green. Pin placement here can be murder.

The course eases off somewhat with short 310-yard par fours for the 13th and 14th holes. Both have out-of-bounds on the left, and if the alternate green to the left is being used on No. 13, the tree that overhangs the green from the right rear can gather in and ruin what otherwise would be a good approach shot. No. 14 is uphill and calls for a blind shot to a green protected on the left by a long narrow sand trap extending from front to back of this elongated green.

An unusual, different, and fun golf hole best describes the 374-yard par four 15th. The green which is not visible from the tee is nestled at the bottom of a somewhat elongated valley and makes for an interesting approach shot in that it sort of catches your ball, making it fairly easy to get it close. A tee shot ending up in the center of this fairway will have a second shot straight down the valley to the green.

Having gone downhill for the previous hole, we now must go back uphill for the par four 384-yard 16th. Out-of-bounds on the right is one problem here, with the other one being a blind approach shot to the green. Aim for the tall pole at the top of the hill and take an extra club for this uphill shot. No. 17 is a rather ordinary par three at 174 yards to a green guarded by a sand trap on the right. Although this hole doesn't look it, you will find that it plays a little uphill.

The 457-yard par five 18th plays much longer than noted on the score card. It is level off the tee with two bunkers and a cluster of Russian olive trees at the corner where the fairway veers off to the right. A big hit can easily clear these hazards. The fairway rises considerably and narrows sharply to an elevated green protected by a large sand trap to the left and above the green. Any loose approach shot missing the green to the right will kick down into a grove of evergreen trees and could easily prove costly. This is an excellent finishing hole to a most enjoyable round of golf on a fine old golf course.

ADDRESSES OF DENVER GOLF COURSES

18-HOLE COURSES

1.	Applewood Golf Course	14001 W. 32nd Ave., Golden
2.	Arrowhead Golf Club	10850 W. Sundown Trail, Littleton
3.	Aurora Hills	50 S. Peoria, Aurora
4.	City Park Golf Course	2500 York, Denver
5.	Englewood Municipal Golf Course	2101 W. Oxford Ave., Englewood
6.	Foothills Golf Course	3901 So. Carr, Denver
7.	Hyland Hills Golf Course	9650 Sheridan Blvd., Westminster
8.	Indian Tree Golf Club	7555 Wadsworth Blvd., Arvada
9.	J.F. Kennedy Golf Course	10500 E. Hampden Ave., Denver
10.	Lake Arbor Golf Course	8600 Wadsworth Blvd., Arvada
11.	Meadow Hills Golf Course	3609 S. Dawson, Aurora
12.	Overland Park Golf Course	S. Santa Fe Drive and W. Jewell Ave.
13.	Park Hill Golf Club	3500 Colorado Blvd., Denver
14.	Evergreen Golf Course	Evergreen
15.	Raccoon Creek	7301 W. Bowles Ave., Denver
16.	Riverdale Golf Club	1 mile west of US 85 on 124th.
17.	South Suburban	7900 S. Colorado Blvd., Denver
18.	Springhill	17979 E. 6th Ave., Aurora
19.	Wellshire	3333 S. Colorado Blvd., Denver
20.	Willis Casse	W. 50th Ave. and Vrain, Denver
21.	West Meadows	6937 S. Simms St., Littleton
22.	Heather Gardens (9-holes)	2888 S. Heather Gardens Way, Aurora
23.	Harvard Municipal (par 3)	E. Iliff and S. Washington, Denver
24.	Twilight Golf Club (Par 3)	1090 S. Oneida, Denver

Denver Golf Courses

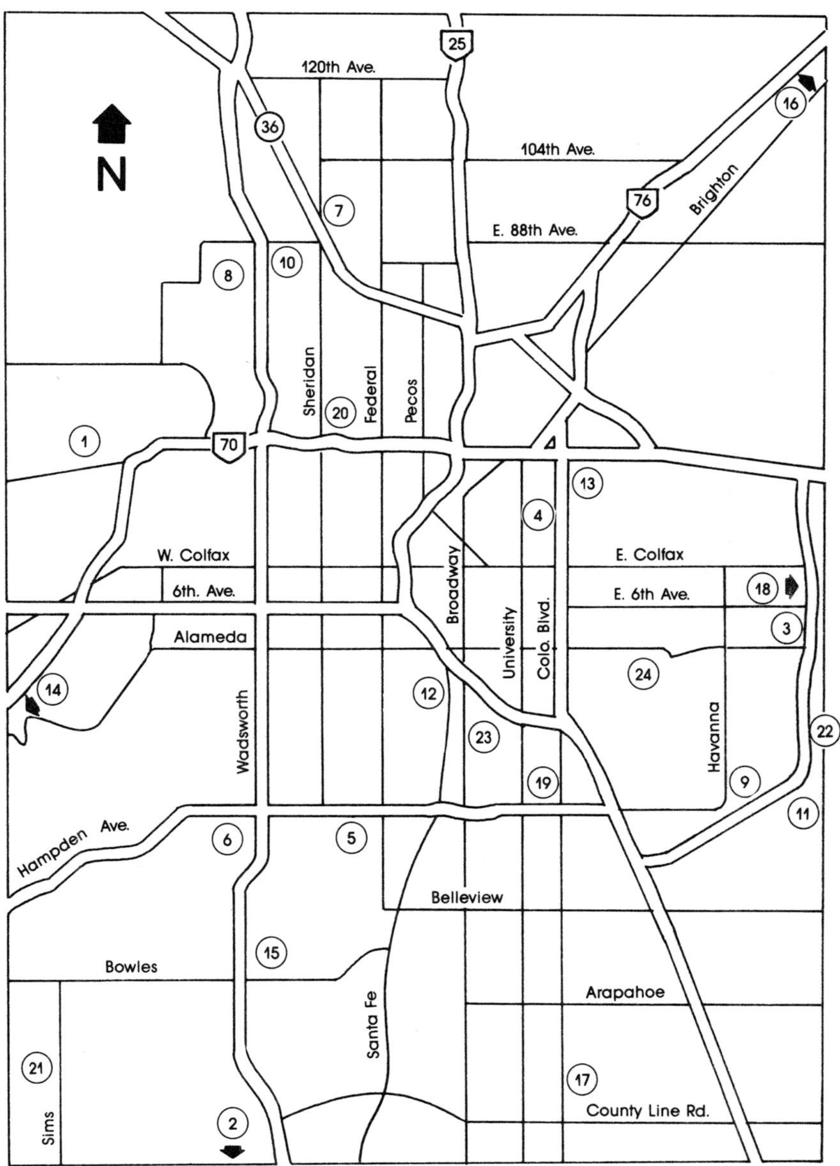

Tamarron's difficult left-hand dogleg starter hole.

Third shot on No. 4 at Copper Mountain.

Looking back from the 14th green at Vail.

The par four 17th at Beaver Creek with ski slopes beyond.

The beautiful 1st hole at Broadmoor East.

No golf course, but Maroon Bells near Aspen offers this fabulous view. Don't miss it.

No room for error on the demanding 6th at Tamarron.

No. 18 at Keystone just before the storm.

The difficult par three 5th at Eagle Vail.

Collegiate Peaks from the nine-hole course at Buena Vista.

Enjoy the peace and quite of the fine Meeker Golf Course.

View from the 13th green at Estes Park with Longs Peak beyond.

Early-fall view of back nine at the Vail Golf Course.

Typical view of Tiara Rado near Grand Junction.

Don't be short on this par three at Rifle Creek.

The sweeping dogleg left par four 4th at Hillcrest in Durango.

SECTION 3

WESTERN SLOPE AND MOUNTAINS

ASPEN GOLF COURSE

LOCATION:	Aspen, Colorado. West edge of Aspen on Highway 82. You will see the course on your right.
TELEPHONE:	925-2145
COURSE FACILITIES:	Fully equipped pro shop, riding golf carts, pull carts, club rental, driving range, chipping and putting greens.
CLUBHOUSE FACILITIES:	Breakfast, lunch, sandwiches, dinner, beer, mixed and soft drinks, swimming pool, and tennis courts.
LODGING:	The Red Roof Inn is located at the golf course. Plenty of other fine accommodations in the Aspen area.
RESTAURANTS:	Colucci's Restaurant is at the Red Roof Inn, and, of course, is quite convenient. If you like Chinese food, Arthur's in Aspen is a must. Aspen's cup runs over with fine places to eat.

GOLF COURSE:

	Par	Course Rating	Yardage
Championship	71	72.6	7165
Regular	71	69.1	6469
Ladies	71	71.1	5518

I have never played on a public golf course with such thick, lush fairways and impeccably manicured greens. Obviously someone should be complimented for a job well done. This course is flat, and the fairways yield excellent lies. Water, in the form of small irrigation ditches and lakes, seems to be everywhere. Study the signs on the tee boxes and the layout of the course as shown on the back of the score card before playing each hole. You have the feeling that this golf course seems to be "in control" on more holes than most other courses. Obviously this is because of the irrigation ditches that cross the fairway so many times. The location of these ditches, as well as the lakes, forces the golfer to either layup short or assume the risk of carrying the hazard. Strategically placed fairway bunkers and grassy berms add further difficulty to this fine golf course. The greens are large, and you will find very few level spots on them, but they are among the best you will ever putt. Small cherry trees indicate the 150-yard marker, even on the par threes, so if there appears to be a yardage discrepancy just double check for the cherry trees.

Almost every hole at the Aspen Golf Course has plenty of trouble in one form or another, and No. 1 is no exception. This 395-yard hole plays straight off the tee, then bends a little left after your drive. A fairway bunker sits at the left corner and another trap lies close to the left front of the green. A small irrigation ditch full of fast running water cuts across the fairway from right to left away from the golfer a short distance out from the green. This ditch is the biggest problem here, as it is on most succeeding holes, and the weak hitter might want to lay up short. The good golfer can go for the green with his second shot and should find par easily within reach.

The 2nd hole, although not as long as the 1st, is more difficult because water comes into play, and the landing area for this 383-yard par four is quite narrow. This fairway doglegs right, and a good size lake sits at the inside corner and extends into the fairway, leaving very little room for error off the tee. The green is trapped left and right, and about 40 yards in front cutting across the fairway is this pesky little irrigation ditch. Going for the green in two will depend on the length of your drive.

No. 3 should be an easy one at 169 yards and par three, but the trap in front of the green and the lake to the right front make this hole quite respectable. No. 4 is a short par four at 360 yards that doglegs right around a lake entrenched at the inside corner. An irrigation ditch crosses the fairway shortly before the dogleg and will be troublesome to the short hitter. A bunker on each side of the fairway just after it bends right will bother the long hitter. A good target off the tee is the right edge of the far sand trap. This green is guarded to the left front by a bunker and to the right by another small irrigation ditch.

Aspen Golf Course No. 7
512 yards par five

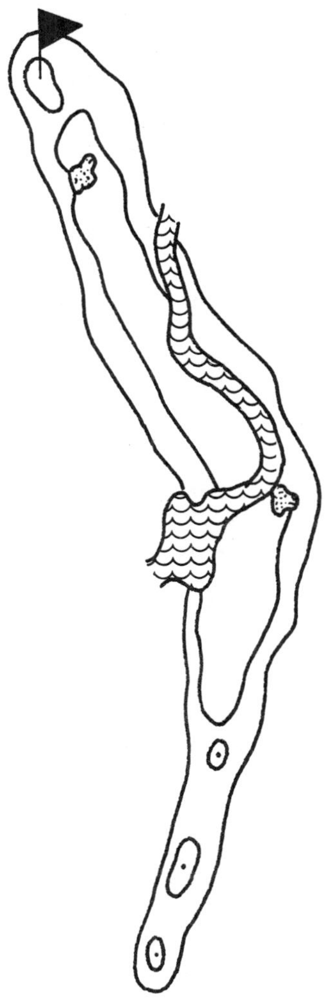

The 399-yard par four 5th hole plays straight off the tee, then bends gently right. Again the landing area off the tee is quite small with a lake to the left and a fairway bunker to the right. The entire left side of this fairway is harassed by the presence of the troublesome irrigation ditch which also curls around behind the green. Aim just a little left of the fairway trap with your drive. Protecting this undulating and irregularly shaped green is a left front sand trap.

For a change, water is not a problem on the 388-yard par four 6th. Although the ditch does cross this fairway early, it will not bother many golfers. This fairway is quite roomy, but a bunker to the right and a grassy mound to the left both guard the landing area. The green is protected by a left front trap, but this hole should yield its share of pars.

No. 7 is both interesting and difficult. This number 3 handicap hole is 512 yards in length, doglegs left, and has a lake at the outside corner and a fairway bunker short of the outside corner of the dogleg. A tee shot of 210 yards will leave you short of the ditch. A big hit may clear it, but it is quite risky, and the lake to the right extends down the fairway's right side about halfway to the green. The green itself is not trapped, but a fairway bunker awaits about 40 yards out to the left front of the green. This is an excellent golf hole. (see sketch pg. 139)

The 173-yard par three 8th should be routine for most golfers. It plays level and straightaway, with no trouble except for the left side trap at the green.

No. 9, which is the number 1 handicap, is just a great golf hole. It is level off the tee for a short distance, then uphill at the landing area, which is guarded rather tightly by two fairway bunkers. The irrigation ditch crosses the fairway early and is not much of a problem, but another one crosses a little beyond the fairway bunkers, and it can prove troublesome. The fairway doglegs right at the bunkers, and any way you play this hole it will demand a long approach shot to the green, which is trapped to the right front. Getting on this green in regulation is a real challenge.

The back nine begins with an interesting 347-yard par four that calls for a lofted wood or long iron to the corner of a left-hand dogleg, then a short iron approach through an opening in the trees to a green a little below the golfer. A long fairway trap sits short of the dogleg in the left rough, and the green is guarded by left and right front bunkers. Accuracy from tee to green is essential for par.

No. 11 is another good one at 417 yards and par four. Your drive is a picturesque shot from an elevated tee through a small opening of aspen and cottonwood trees, down a fairway that doglegs right. Lakes to the left and right come into play shortly past the dogleg, and the irrigation ditch crosses between them. The fairway, however, is roomy at the landing area which is well short of the ditch and lakes. A sand trap crowds the green's left side. This is a very respectable long par four, but the strong hitter should have little trouble.

The 12th hole is another long par four at 420 yards. The irrigation ditch crosses the fairway early, then runs along the right for a short distance, but should not be a lot of trouble. A sand trap in the right rough and a grassy mound to the left narrow the landing area. The green is protected by a large trap to the left front and another to the right front.

The number 2 handicap hole is No. 13. This 517-yard par five plays straightaway, and is another tough one. Only about 20 yards separate the two fairway traps that guard the landing area off the tee, and another irrigation ditch crosses the fairway at just the wrong place. This ditch lies about 150 yards out from the green, and depending on the length of your drive, it may or may not be a problem. A sand trap and grassy mound sit about 60 yards out from the green, which is closely protected by another trap to the left front.

No. 14 at 122 yards and par three should be an easy one, but it requires an all-carry shot over a lake to a green bunkered to the right front. Don't leave it short.

Continuing the string of interesting holes on the back nine is the 450-yard 15th. It plays straightaway with a grassy mound to the left and a fairway trap to the right guarding the landing area. Favor the fairway's left side a little off the tee. The irrigation ditch crosses the fairway about 40 yards in front of the green, raising the question of going for the green in two or laying up short. Two traps watch over and protect the narrow entry to this green. Not a difficult par five, but the ditch in in front of the green has a tendency to lengthen the hole somewhat.

The trouble is all left on the 402-yard par four 16th. This fairway bends slightly left, has a lake at the corner, and the irrigation ditch extends along the left from tee to green. The ditch further complicates this hole by crossing the fairway about 15 yards in front of the green, making it necessary for an accurate, all-carry approach shot. Guarding the green is a trap to the right front and a small pond 40 yards out to the right.

No. 17 is a tough little par three at 176 yards. Except for the left front greenside trap, the trouble is all right here in the form of the irrigation ditch from tee to green and the lake adjoining the green's right side.

No. 18 is anything but an easy finishing hole at 402 yards and par four. It doglegs right, and the irrigation ditch crosses the fairway twice, once early on and again immediately in front of the green. Two fairway traps sit at both sides of the dogleg, and two small lakes occupy the right rough, making it next to impossible to cut the corner. The green is trapped to the front and right front, and the ditch is only 30 yards out from the green. The location of this ditch again puts a lot of pressure on the golfer's approach shot.

Aspen is one of Colorado's most scenic areas, so take time to enjoy it while you're there. Visit Maroon Bells, but do it at a leisurely pace and drink in the splendor of this beautiful setting. Camping, fishing, hiking, and horseback riding are also popular sports in the area. The Aspen Music Festival in July and August is a recognized and popular event. A trip over Independence Pass is a thrilling and exciting experience, so in addition to golf allow enough time for some of these other interesting activities.

BEAVER CREEK GOLF CLUB

LOCATION: Avon, Colorado. Take the Beaver Creek Exit #167 off Interstate 70 west of Vail. Head south and follow the signs.

TELEPHONE: 949-5750 ext. 4715

COURSE FACILITIES: Fully equipped pro shop, driving range, putting and chipping greens, club rental and riding golf carts.

CLUBHOUSE FACILITIES: Breakfast, lunch and dinner are available at The Charter, while sandwiches, beer and soft drinks can be obtained at the oncourse snack bar. Other facilities include a swimming pool, showers, and excellent accommodations for group meetings from 25 to 900 people.

LODGING: The Charter at Beaver Creek is at the golf course. You will find an abundance of places to stay up and down the Eagle/Vail Valley.

RESTAURANTS: The Vail area has many fine restaurants, and it's hard to go wrong on any of them. Best to ask around.

GOLF COURSE:

	Par	Course Rating	Yardage
Championship	70	69.2	6217
Regular	70	67.0	5747
Ladies	70	70.3	5268

Of the four championship golf courses in the Eagle/Vail Valley, Beaver Creek is one. Although 1983 marks only the second year of play, the course is in excellent condition, and time will only improve this challenging and exciting facility. The course architect, Robert Trent Jones II, did an outstanding job of complementing this already beautiful and secluded valley. While not as long as some tournament links, this course offers excellent play because of the rolling hills, twisting creek, lakes, and narrow fairways. Sand traps are large, irregular, and numerous, while the greens are of good size and endowed with all the character and speed needed to challenge the best putters. For a vacation or a single round, you'll have a memorable experience at Beaver Creek Golf Club.

Although not rated as a difficult hole, No. 1 offers a certain amount of concern as you survey this two-level fairway from the highly elevated 1st tee. The upper 1st portion of this fairway drops off to a much lower level about 240 yards off the tee. At this point a deep ravine and Beaver Creek cut across the fairway making the division between the two levels. The distance from tee to ravine only plays about 200 yards, so it's best to use a long iron or fairway wood off this 1st tee. The second half of this 472-yard par five two-level fairway narrows considerably, and Beaver Creek runs along its right side. Play your second shot left of center for best angle of approach to the green. This green is well protected with a sand trap to the left, one to the right front, and another in the left front rough. Be grateful if you can start out with a par on this beginning hole.

The number 3 handicap hole is the 177-yard par three 2nd, and it's a good one. There's little room for error, and club selection is important because we have a highly elevated tee and a heavily trapped long narrow green well below the tee box. Beaver Creek extends along the entire length of the hole's right side, and a ball hit short of the green will bounce sharply right into the creek or sand trap. Play this hole like it was 150 yards and shoot for the left center of the green.

The 3rd at Beaver Creek is just a magnificent golf hole! It is par five, doglegs left, and is the most difficult hole on the course. The creek crosses this 512-yard fairway twice, and continues to haunt the golfer along the right side all the way to the green. It's best to play a fairway wood or long iron off this tee, do the same thing for your second shot, then hit a short iron to this rather sizeable well-trapped green. (see sketch pg. 145)

At 140 yards and par three, the 4th hole should not be difficult, but the creek runs down the right center of this fairway and angles off to the right immediately in front of the green. Add the two greenside sand traps, and it makes you work to get a par.

Beaver Creek No. 3
512 yards par five

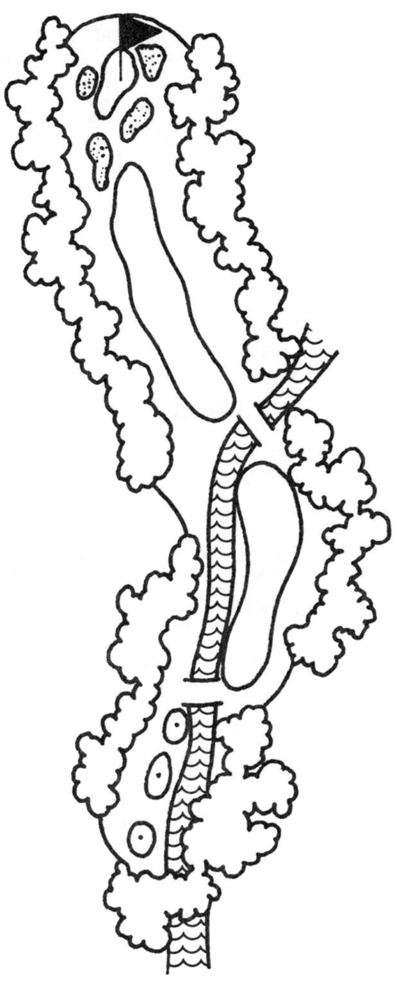

Beginning with the par four 386-yard 5th hole, the golf course opens up somewhat as the valley widens. The trees here are small and recently planted, but the creek continues to be a menace as it winds along the right side of this fairway, which means it can come into play on either your first or second shots. Out-of-bounds is to the right, and the green is protected by two left-side and two right-side bunkers. No room for a careless shot anyplace on this hole.

The short 334-yard straightaway par four 6th is a good-looking golf hole. It has water along the left side in the form of a creek which runs into a good size lake, then a creek coming out the far end of the lake and curling in front of the green. Two sand traps inhabit the right rough, and a well-hit tee shot can easily catch the second trap. The lake is more of a mental hazard then anything else, but because it lurks off to the left, one must not get careless off the tee. This green is also well trapped left and right.

No. 7 is another short par four at 348 yards. The green is not noticeable from the tee, and the fairway doglegs left. A large sand trap guards this inside corner at 125 yards from the green. The big hitter can draw it over the right edge of the trap and have a short chip shot to the green, but most golfers will do best to play for the center of the fairway. The two bunkers at this green are huge, and the green is quite small, all adding to the challenge of the hole.

The 8th is another short one at 312 yards, par four and straightaway. Two large sand traps are situated in the right rough starting 175 yards from the tee, and from that point to the green the fairway's left side offers heavy rough and trees. The small creek crosses the fairway about 40 yards in front of the green, which is guarded by left and right front bunkers. As with all the previous holes, accuracy on every shot is a must for par.

No. 9 is straightaway and gradually uphill. Two sand traps guard the landing area 180 to 225 yards off the tee. This is the place to hit the heavy timber and leave yourself a short iron shot to this well-trapped green.

The back nine begins with a fine par three at 164 yards to an elongated green guarded by two huge left and right sand traps. This fairway slopes severely left, so make sure you hit the green on this one.

Continuing uphill, the 315-yard par four 11th has a slight left-hand bend, a fairway trap in the right rough 225 yards from the tee and out-of-bounds all along the left from tee to green. This rather small green is protected by three ominous and well-placed sand traps, two in front and one at the right rear.

No. 12 is a superb par three at 163 yards, with the green guarded on the right by a lake and on the left by a yawning sand trap. A wayward tee shot can be quite expensive on this number 4 handicap hole.

From the tee on the 479-yard par five No. 13 it seems that all you can see is sand traps! Two guard the landing area off the tee, but are widely separated and make for a friendly and inviting fairway. Three more dominate the hillside in the right rough starting 115 yards out from the green, and another three are sandwiched around this wide, thin green making it possible for some attention-getting pin placements. Be careful of the out-of-bounds along the fairway's right side.

We come back to the wooded area of the golf course with the 382-yard par four 14th. It's open off the tee, but a small creek in the left rough parallels, then cuts diagonally across the fairway about 130 yards from the green. Plenty of trouble remains on this hole after you cross the creek, so be careful and look before you hit. This irregularly shaped green is well trapped to the left front with an exceptionally large bunker and a smaller one to the rear.

Accuracy is essential on the 307-yard par four 15th. Beautiful aspen trees line both sides of this narrow fairway and the ever present creek runs along the right rough. This fairway kicks right to left and bends slightly right, so a nice little fade would be a great shot off the tee. The green is well bunkered with right front, left front, and rear sand traps. On the far side of the green are the remains of some original homesteads in Beaver Creek Valley, including the Holden barn, smoke house, and bunk house.

The green on the 173-yard par three 16th hole nestles back in among a grove of aspen trees, and in the fall of the year has to be one of the most beautiful holes on the golf course. The green is slightly elevated with a large sand trap at the left front and a smaller one at the left rear. Should you lose a ball to the left on this hole it's gone forever! Keep it straight — there's no room for error.

The 331-yard par four 17th is a relatively straight-playing hole. The creek starts off to the left of the tee and runs along the fairway until it crosses over to the right side about 40 yards in front of the green. A lake lies behind and a little to the right of the green, but it's not noticeable from the fairway, so don't be long with your approach shot. This green is also well bunkered left and right, and the fairway narrows considerably as we get back to the upper part of the valley.

At 373 yards and par four, the 18th hole takes you home in style! It's a slight dogleg to the left, but watch out for the lake in the left rough and aim for the narrow opening through the trees. This fairway slopes to the left, and a bunker in the right rough beckons at 215 yards off the tee. The green on the other side of Beaver Creek snuggles up to the side of a hill and is trapped to the left and rear. This is a splendid finishing hole and a great way to end up the day, playing one of Colorado's outstanding mountain golf courses. Come back to Beaver Creek. The golf will get better and better year after year.

BRECKENRIDGE GOLF CLUB

LOCATION: Breckenridge, Colorado. Take Interstate 70 west of Denver to the Frisco Exit. Go approximately 5 miles south on Colorado Highway 9, then ½ mile east on Tiger Road.

TELEPHONE: 453-2251 453-9104

GOLF COURSE:

	Par	Course Rating	Yardage
Championship	72		7150
Regular	72		6895
Ladies	72		6300

The Breckenridge golf course has been under construction during 1982 and 1983. Both the course and the clubhouse are scheduled for completion sometime in 1984. This Jack Nicklaus designed course appears to have all the earmarks of another outstanding golf course in Colorado's mountains. The challenges it will offer are the best creation of both man and mother nature. Be sure to check this course out beginning in 1984. Breckenridge is one of the very popular ski areas in Colorado, so you will find plenty of good restaurants and motels in the immediate area.

COPPER MOUNTAIN GOLF CLUB

LOCATION: Copper Mountain, Colorado. Interstate 70 about 75 miles west of Denver. Exit the Copper Mountain interchange, go back under the highway, and you will see the golf course in front of you.

TELEPHONE: 968-2339

COURSE FACILITIES: Fully equipped pro shop, riding golf carts, pull carts, club rental, driving range, chipping and putting greens.

CLUBHOUSE FACILITIES: Restaurant serving breakfast, lunch, sandwiches, dinner, beer, mixed and soft drinks. Tennis courts and locker room facilities are also available.

LODGING: Located nearby in Copper Mountain Village is the mountain conference center, which houses hotel-style and condominium lodging units, hot tub, sauna, retail shops, and excellent conference meeting facilities. Other motel facilities are available in nearby Dillon, Frisco, and Vail.

RESTAURANTS: In addition to the restaurant in the clubhouse, several other very good eating establishments are located adjacent to the golf course, as well as at the Plaza Hotel in the conference center.

GOLF COURSE:

	Par	Course Rating	Yardage
Championship	65	64.2	5270
Regular	65	62.7	4934
Ladies	65	63.2	4344

The first nine at Copper Mountain was built in 1978, and for such a new golf course is in excellent condition. Par is only 33, but the many water hazards and sand traps make it play much more difficult than you would expect. Accuracy and well-placed tee shots are a must if you plan to score well on this well-maintained front nine. The back nine was opened for limited play in late summer of 1983. The greens are great and in good condition, but the fairways are thin, and the grass will need a couple of years before it reaches a condition comparable to the front nine. In the meantime, even though you play winter rules, this back nine will fight you all the way before yielding to par. Copper Mountain offers a good assortment of challenging golf holes that will give any golfer a real workout. Don't miss an opportunity to play this course.

The golf course begins with a short 301-yard par four that doglegs left and uphill about 200 yards off the tee. A small brook crosses the fairway at this point, so a lofted wood or long iron should leave you short of this hazard. Trees closely line the left side of the fairway off the tee. Your approach shot is uphill, over the brook, to a green that slopes severely toward the golfer. This is not a difficult hole, but don't attempt to cut the corner.

No. 2 is a 150-yard par three from an elevated tee to a well-trapped green that is considerably below the golfer. Take at least one and maybe two less clubs than normally used for this distance. This is an easy hole if you can stay out of the bunkers.

The 386-yard right-hand dogleg par four 3rd is in control all the way. This hole plays downhill off the tee, and a fairway wood or long iron is the most you can hit. Two sand traps guard the inside corner, out-of-bounds is right, and a stream crosses the fairway about 235 yards from the tee. Your second shot is a mid-iron over a large pond to a green that is trapped to the right front and right side. No room for an errant shot on this hole.

Stay away from the right side on the 545-yard par five 4th hole. Water is everywhere on that side. Again, it's best to play a lofted wood or long iron off the tee. This should leave you short of the stream that crosses the fairway about 250 yards from the tee. The fairway's left side on this hole provides no room because of the stream and heavy thick bushes. Two large bunkers occupy the right rough short of the stream. The fair-

Copper Mountain No. 4
545 yards par five

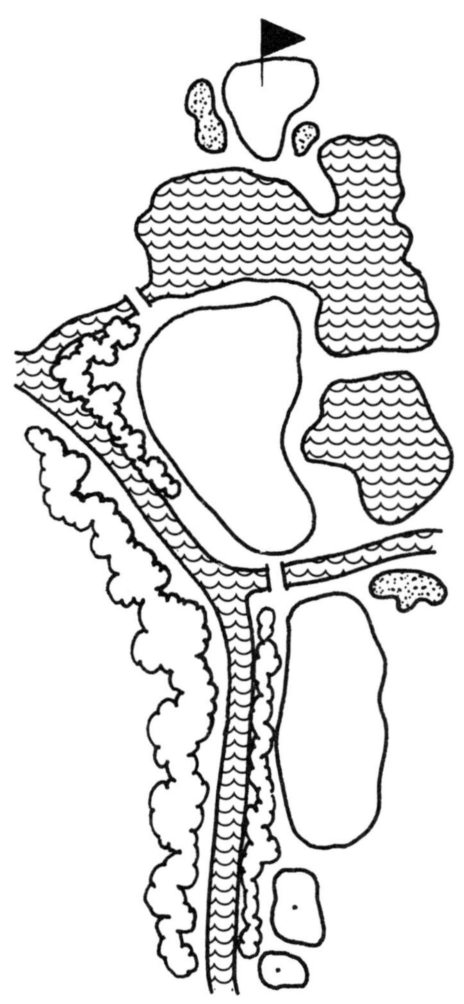

way bends a little left after it crosses the stream, then bends back right slightly as you approach the green. After your drive, another 5 wood or medium-long iron should leave you short of a lake immediately in front of the green. The green is trapped right front, left side, and to the rear. If you haven't already found the water, a short iron approach should get you on this green in regulation. This is another hole that forces the golfer to play its game and not his. (see sketch pg. 152)

This golf course may be short, but it has plenty of tough golf holes. No. 4 was a good example, and the 391-yard par four 5th is another one. This hole plays level and straight, but water crowds the entire right side, and out-of-bounds is very close to the fairway's left side. There's not a lot of room here. A menacing sand trap lurks in the right rough near the landing area, and another one sits in the left front rough about 30 yards out from the green. Two more traps crowd the green's right front and rear. This is another good golf hole with trouble from tee to green.

No. 6 is a short 129-yard par three, but it is a good one. It plays over a stream and deep grassy rough to a green that is heavily trapped on the left and guarded on the right by the stream. All of this makes for a small target and a fine par three.

You can take a breather on the 96-yard par three 7th. The green is deep and is trapped left front, right front, and right rear, but is an easy hole. No. 8 is not so easy and again calls for a well-placed tee shot. This 343-yard par four hole doglegs left, with bunkers guarding both corners of the dogleg, leaving no more than 20 yards between them in the landing area. Out-of-bounds is right, although the fairway is quite roomy short of the bunkers. The big hitter can cut the corner, but it is very risky. Your second shot is uphill over a small brook to a green that is trapped left front and right front. Make every effort to stay below the hole for your putt.

The front nine finishes with an interesting 126-yard par three that plays downhill and over an exceptionally large sand trap in front of the green. Another trap dominates the sloping terrain to the green's right. Avoid the sand and you can easily have a par.

No. 10 is another short one at 139 yards and par three. It plays over a portion of a small lake in front of the tee to a large green trapped right front, right rear, and left side. Again, stay out of the sand.

The next hole, No. 11, is probably the most difficult hole on the golf course. It is a par five that plays 477 yards long and has two doglegs, one 200-plus yards off the tee and another just short of the green. Both of these doglegs are left. At the inside corner of the first dogleg is a large flat hill or plateau, and the really big hitter can hit over it. However, most golfers will want to play it honest and go straight down the fairway to the corner and hit a fairway wood from there to a point short of and to the right of the green. This second shot is uphill over a bumpy and quite rolling fairway. From there it is a short iron to the green, which is heavily trapped left and right.

The 147-yard par three 12th plays level off the tee and is no problem if you can stay out of the sand traps to the green's left, front, rear, and right front.

No. 13 is one of the longer par fours on the course at 395 yards and plays even longer because it's gradually uphill all the way. A well-hit drive will still leave a medium-to-long iron to a green that is surrounded by trees and is further complicated by a three-tiered bunker to the green's right front.

No. 14 is an excellent par three at 192 yards. It plays downhill to a green heavily trapped to the right front and right side. Everything kicks left to right here, so aim for the green's left side.

One of the most picturesque holes on the course is the 152-yard par three 15th. It plays uphill through a small opening in the pine trees to a large green that slopes up and away from the golfer. This green is surrounded by trees and is further complicated by a three-tiered bunker to the green's right front.

The 315-yard par four 16th plays straightaway with the fairway sloping left to right and many pine trees crowding the left side. The green is surrounded by pine trees and sits below the golfer as he approaches it from out in the fairway. No sand traps, but a thick grove of evergreen trees reigns to the right front of the green and can prove a much larger problem than any sand trap.

All 3-par holes on this golf course have been interesting, and No. 17 is no exception. It is 139 yards in length, and plays through an opening lined with huge pine trees. The green is shallow and trapped to the front, as well as to the left front. This is a pretty hole with the sage brush growing on the slope behind the green and the mountains looming up in the far distance.

Plans are to remove the trees at the end of the dogleg on the 385-yard par four 18th. This hole plays sharply downhill, and most tee shots find the trees and thick grass either to the right or at the end of the fairway. Even with the trees removed, I think it might be best to hit a medium iron off the tee, which will still leave another medium iron to an elevated green severely trapped to the right front and right side. This is probably the most difficult approach shot you will have to make on the golf course because of the bunkers and railroad tie abutments. If you miss the green and find the sand, your only shot may very well be back out the same way you came in.

Except for the 18th hole, I thoroughly enjoyed playing Copper Mountain. I'm sure you will, too. Don't let the courses's par 65 fool you, because it's more than most golfers can handle.

CORTEZ MUNICIPAL GOLF COURSE

LOCATION: Cortez, Colorado, northeast of town on Highway 145.

TELEPHONE: 565-9208

COURSE FACILITIES: Fully equipped pro shop, club rental, pull carts, riding golf carts, driving range, and putting and chipping greens.

CLUBHOUSE FACILITIES: Snack bar serving hot sandwiches, lunch, beer, and soft drinks.

LODGING: Several good motels in the area, located along Highways 160 and 550.

RESTAURANTS: Best to ask at the pro shop or your golfing partner.

GOLF COURSE:

	Par	Course Rating	Yardage
Championship	72	70.4	6818
Regular	72	68.3	6347
Ladies	72	70.0	5529

The Cortez municipal golf course was expanded into an 18 hole layout only two years ago, so you will find the 12-year-old front nine somewhat more mature than the back nine. Although the greens on the back side are very good, those on the front side are outstanding and make putting a real pleasure. The course is relatively flat, has many doglegs, quite a few sizeable trees, and several small, but hidden water hazards near the greens. The rough is not the well-watered grass found on many golf courses and is quite sandy, so it will be to your advantage to stay in the fairway. One serious hazard on this golf course is the sign attached to a property fence behind the par three 12th green. This sign reads *"Trespassers Will Be Shot - Those I Miss Will Be Prosecuted"*. Don't be long off the tee on this hole! You will enjoy playing this 6500 ft.

elevation Press Maxwell designed golf course, and it will do nothing but get better as the back nine improves with age.

The 1st hole at Cortez is a 480-yard straightaway par five, down a roomy fairway to a rather deep green, which is guarded by a small pond to the left front and a long narrow sand trap to the right. No. 2 is a good par four at 405 yards that is straightaway over the crest of a small hill. It's slightly downhill for your second shot to a green that is quite deep and juts out at the end of the fairway. Although out-of-bounds extends along the fairway's left side, it is too far away to bother many golfers.

The 3rd hole is a very interesting par three at 164 yards. It calls for a well-hit iron over a lake to a wide, medium depth green. The right side of this green is elevated, and the result can be some touchy, breaking putts.

The number 1 handicap hole is the 510-yard par five 4th. This fairway has an early left-hand dogleg which can be troublesome. The strong hitter can cut the corner over the cottonwood tree, but most golfers will do best to hit past the corner with a fairway wood off the tee. The fairway has a right-hand bend in it about 150 yards from the green, a small irrigation ditch running along the left side, and no trouble around the green.

No. 5 is a medium length par four at 385 yards with a left-hand dogleg that is guarded at the inside corner by a heavy group of cottonwood trees. It's possible to cut the corner with a big hit, but most of us will do better hitting for the center of the fairway. This medium width, but quite deep green is protected by a left side sand trap. Missing this green to the right will result in a touchy downhill chip that will be very difficult to stop.

The 400-yard par four 6th plays a bit downhill and has a right-hand dogleg beginning about 150 yards from the green. Best not to cut this corner because of the sandy soil and grassy clumps in the right rough. No. 7 is a routine 155-yard par three that plays a little uphill to a large, deep green.

The 365-yard short par four 8th hole is straightaway over the crest of a hill to a green that is not visible from the tee. Two long, narrow sand traps guard the left side of this green. No. 9 is a good driving hole. It is level off the tee, then downhill over a valley and up to the green. There's a right rear sand trap to catch any approach shot hit too strong.

The back nine begins with a 480-yard par five that is quite similar to No. 1. The only difference is the presence of more humps and valleys in the fairway and the small water hazard to the right front of the green. No. 11 is a very interesting golf hole at 350 yards and par four. It's not long, but your tee shot must carry over a sizeable lake that is quite intimidating. Most golfers will do best by hitting over the middle of the lake. However, the strong hitter can cut off most of this lake and leave himself with a short wedge to the green. Be careful of the left side sand trap.

The 135-yard par three 12th presents no problems other than being shot at and out-of-bounds behind the green. No. 13 is a 374-yard par four that doglegs right with out-of-bounds on the right. Along with a fairway trap just short of the outside corner of the dogleg, you will find another of those small water hazards at the green's left front. The green is round, medium size, and the back half is higher than the front.

No. 14 is another 374-yard par four. It is level off the tee, down and over a valley, then gradually uphill to the green. When the wind is blowing out of the west, be sure to take an extra club or two for your approach shot.

The par five 496-yard 15th is the number 2 handicap. It's another hole with an early left-hand dogleg. Again, the big hitter can cut the corner, but most of us will be better off hitting to the corner and playing in from there. The left rough is extremely difficult; so avoid it at all cost.

No. 16 at 155 yards and par three is similar to No. 12. Out-of-bounds lurks behind the green, and another small pond sits halfway to the green. The 369-yard par four 17th is straightaway to an irregularly shaped green with the right side of the green being higher than the left. A right front sand trap guards this green.

Although only 375 yards in length and par four, the 18th is a respectable finishing hole. Out-of-bounds watches over the fairway's right side with plenty of tree trouble in the left rough. This hole plays gradually uphill and seems much longer than indicated. No hazards at greenside, it's still a touchy one to putt.

The Cortez area has been popular with tourists for years. The country here is beautiful and you will want to be sure to visit the cliff dwellings at Mesa Verde National Park. The combination of scrub oak and aspen trees makes the fall colors in this area spectacular! All of these attractions merely add to the enjoyment of playing a challenging and interesting golf course.

DOS RIOS GOLF AND COUNTRY CLUB

LOCATION: Gunnison, Colorado. One and one-half miles west of Gunnison on Highway 50. Turn south at the sign indicating the golf course.

TELEPHONE: 641-1482

COURSE FACILITIES: Fully equipped pro shop, riding golf carts, pull carts, club rental, driving range, chipping green and putting green.

CLUBHOUSE FACILITIES: Restaurant serving breakfast, lunch, sandwiches, dinner, beer, mixed and soft drinks.

LODGING: There are several very good motels both east and west of Gunnison on Highway 50.

RESTAURANT: In addition to the restaurant in the clubhouse, there are a good number of other fine places to eat in town. Ask at the pro shop.

GOLF COURSE:

	Par	Course Rating	Yardage
Championship	71		6690
Regular	71		6219
Ladies			5782
Gold			4850

The Gunnison area is an outdoor sportsman's paradise, and the completion of an additional nine holes at the Dos Rios golf course is the frosting on the cake. Long known as a short, rather easy, and tight-playing golf course, it has now become a super test of the golfer's ability to play this challenging, but sometimes frustrating game. The course crosses the Gunnison River and Tomichi Creek several times, and water comes into play on 17 holes! The new construction, which is now the front nine, could just as well be nine holes of golf in Scotland. The resemblance is almost beyond belief! Although this new front nine is wide open, the rolling natural terrain, thick deep rough,

Dos Rios No. 4
535 yards par five

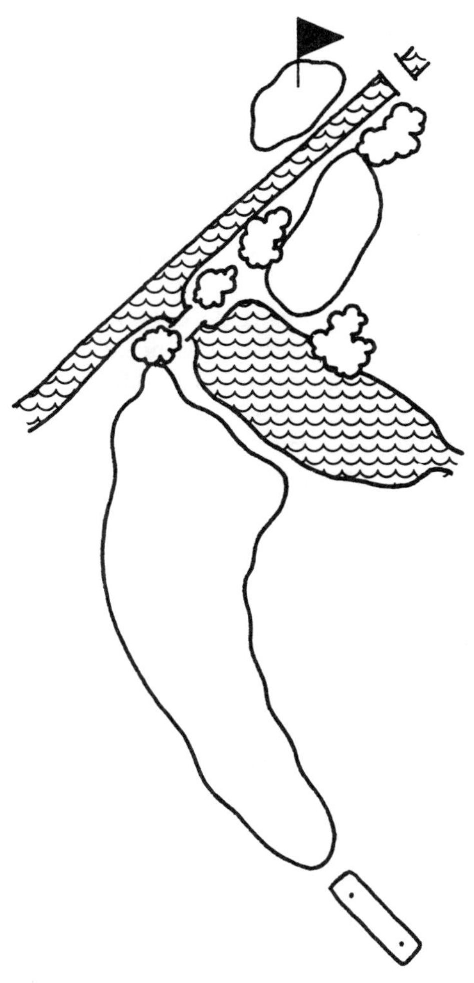

and many water hazards will give the best golfers a real workout. The back nine, with its many large trees, ponds, and streams, continues to demand accurate tee shots, and the course now finishes with 4 varied and challenging par fours. It will take a few years before the new front nine reaches top quality condition, and several sand traps are yet to be added, but when all this happens, Dos Rios will be one of the most exciting golf courses in Colorado.

The golf course introduces you to water early, because the 395-yard par four 1st hole has you tee it up on Dos Rios Island and hit over the Gunnison River through a narrow opening in the cottonwood trees to a fairly tight fairway on the other side. This is a placement shot that must be left short of the irrigation ditch that crosses the fairway about 220 yards off the tee. The proper tee shot should leave the golfer with a medium iron approach to a large undulating green with many grassy humps around it.

No. 2 is a 405-yard par four that doglegs right. There are lots of humps and mounds in the fairway including two larger ones at each corner of the dogleg. An irrigation ditch runs along the fairway's left side, then crosses over just short of the green, runs along the green's right side, and curls around in back. This makes for a tiny target as you approach the green.

With no room to be short, the 190-yard par three 3rd calls for an all-carry shot over a lake. From the front of the tee box this hole will play about 170 yards.

No. 4 has to be one of the more spectacular holes on the course. It is 535 yards in length, par five, doglegs right, and plays over a large lake as well as the Tomichi River. The hole is designed for the golfer's second shot to be hit over the lake to a landing area short of the river. From that point it is a deceptive short iron approach to the green on the other side of the river and at the foot of a 900-ft. rocky cliff. (see sketch pg. 161)

If you tee the ball up on the south side of Tomichi Creek, the par four 5th hole plays to 420 yards. From the north side it is a 395-yard hole. This fairway, like most, is dominated by an abundance of humps and hollows.

Another good par three is the 195-yard 6th hole. Water is the problem on this hole, as lakes crowd the fairway's left side and the green's left and rear. Grassy mounds also surround this green.

If you thought No. 4 was spectacular, then No. 7 is not far behind. This 495-yard hole is a double-dogleg par five. It plays over a lake off the tee to a narrow landing area that is guarded on the left by a second lake. From that point the fairway bends left, and the second shot is over a portion of another lake. Depending on the accuracy of the player's first two shots, his approach to the green may or may not be over water. It's best to play this hole honest and not try to reach the green in two. A sand trap is scheduled to be placed between the green and the lake in front to discourage players from trying to do this. As if there wasn't already enough trouble on this hole!

No. 8 is another good one at 390 yards and par four. The shot is straightforward off the tee, then it doglegs left. Target the water tower in the distance for your drive. Lots of mounds, berms, hollows, etc. abound on this fairway and at both corners of the dogleg.

The number 1 handicap hole is the 395-yard par four 9th. It plays straightaway, but requires an accurate, well-placed drive. The second shot is over the Gunnison River, with a medium iron for the good golfer, to a green that is guarded by the river in front and trees and bushes on the other three sides. Most players will probably want to lay up short of the river and approach the green from there. Few golf holes are better than this one anywhere in Colorado.

We are back to the old original golf course now with the 138-yard par three 10th. I think this is one of the best looking golf holes I have ever played. The shot is through an opening of cottonwoods and over a pond that snuggles right up close to the front of the green. Trees line the opening all the way to the green. From the back tees, this is a super challenge at 188 yards.

No. 11 is short at 300 yards and par four, but the pond and irrigation ditch to the fairway's right and the ditch crossing in front of the green keep most golfers honest. The green is also trapped to the right front. Favor the left side of this fairway because it widens considerably in that direction.

The 494-yard par five 12th plays level and straight, but a menacing pond occupies the right rough near the landing area. At the 150-yard marker this fairway bends a little right, and huge cottonwoods line both sides of the fairway to within a short distance of the green. Play this fairway left center off the tee.

No. 13, which used to be the old No. 1, is a 317-yard par four that plays straight off the tee, then bends left slightly at the 150-yard marker. No particular problems here except for the large cottonwoods at the inside corner.

The 14th hole is a rather routine 167-yard par three that plays level with no problems other than the sand trap to the left of the green.

I like the next three holes, because they place such a premium on accuracy both on and off the tee. The 15th is 322 yards in length and par four. The fairway doglegs left, then crosses an irrigation ditch, leaving an approach shot through an opening in the cottonwoods. Cottonwoods also line the fairway's left side and guard the inside corner. The tee shot here is a lofted wood or long iron. A pothole bunker is scheduled for placement in front of this green in the near future.

No. 16 is another fine golf hole at 362 yards and par four. A straight well-placed tee shot is necessary here in order to avoid the irrigation ditch and long narrow sand trap in the right rough. Target the bush at the outside corner of this left-hand dogleg. A drive of 220 yards in the middle of the fairway will leave a short iron approach to the green, which is guarded on the right by a small pond. This number 2 handicap hole also offers water on the left shortly off the tee and large cottonwoods guard the inside corner.

The 17th is another tight-driving hole. This one is 348 yards, par four, and doglegs right after a well-placed drive. An irrigation ditch crowds the fairway's right side, then crosses over shortly in front of the green. Several large cottonwoods add further protection to a green which is always a touchy one to putt.

Nothing fancy about the 18th hole, but it never seems to be an easy one to par. It is 376 yards long, par four, and plays level and straight from tee to green. An irrigation ditch does crowd the left side of the fairway, and the green is trapped to the right with another bunker scheduled for the left in the near future. A large cottonwood growing to the green's left is of further concern as you approach this final green. These last four holes are good ones, and are a real test of your ability as you complete play on this stimulating and deceptive golf course.

The country around Gunnison is one of my favorite places in Colorado. The trout fishing in this area is the best in the state, it's a great place to hunt in the fall, and skiing at Crested Butte to the north is considered to be some of the best. Now with this outstanding 18-hole golf course, plus another 18 holes soon to open at Crested Butte, what else is there? This is great outdoor country. Come and enjoy it.

THE EAGLE VAIL GOLF CLUB

LOCATION: Avon, Colorado. Go west of Vail and take Exit No. 171 off Interstate 70. Follow the access road to Avon for about 2 miles then turn left at the Eagle Vail Golf Club sign and follow the signs.

TELEPHONE: 949-5267

COURSE FACILITIES: Fully equipped pro shop, club rental, riding golf carts, driving range, and putting green.

CLUBHOUSE FACILITIES: Restaurant serving breakfast, lunch, sandwiches, dinner, beer, mixed and soft drinks. A swimming pool, tennis courts, and showers are also available.

LODGING: There are plenty of fine places to stay in the Vail area.

RESTAURANTS: In addition to the restaurant in the clubhouse, you will find excellent restaurants in Vail Village.

GOLF COURSE:

	Par	Course Rating	Yardage
Championship	72	70.9	6819
Regular	72	68.7	6289
Ladies	72	71.0	

Eagle Vail is a "must play" golf course. It is a marvelous layout and strikingly beautiful. The course architects, Bruce Devlin and Bob Von Hagge, have done an excellent job of building a championship 18 holes of golf while maintaing the natural beauty of the Colorado Rocky Mountain terrain. Add 11 water holes and 60 sand bunkers to all the existing natural hazards provided by mother nature, you have a great golf course. This course was built in 1974 and always is in superb condition. Bordered by the Eagle River to the north and White

River National Forest to the south, Eagle Vail tests the skills of the expert and provides all golfers with a truly unique golfing experience.

No. 1 starts from an elevated tee, 125 feet above the fairway. This 517-yard par five is a good starter hole because the fairway below is wide and inviting. A sand trap dwells in the right rough about 200 yards off the tee. Three more bunkers beckon a wayward shot short of the green and to the right. Be careful of the shot to the green because it is firm and well trapped.

The 2nd hole plays level from tee to green and doglegs right at about 220 yards. Bunkers guard both the inside and outside corners of this fairway. The green is well trapped to the right front and rear. If laying up on your second shot, it's best to approach the green from the fairway's left side.

For the next four holes we cross under the highway and must contend with the Eagle River. No. 3 is a straightforward 158-yard par three to a well-trapped irregularly shaped green. The Eagle River parallels this fairway, and a loose shot to the right will find the water. Favor the left side of this picturesque double green. Putts on this green run toward the river, while balls hit in the river run toward Grand Junction.

No. 4 is a short 349-yard straightaway par four, but there's big trouble if you push either a long drive or your approach shot to the right. A fairway trap lies in the left rough 227 yards off the tee, narrowing the landing area considerably. The three bunkers crowding this green must not be overlooked. Play this hole down the middle all the way.

The 5th hole is a short one at 128 yards, but is one of the many interesting holes at Eagle Vail. The shot is from an elevated tee over the Eagle River to a long, narrow, well-trapped green that slopes from back to front. No. 6 is another short par four at 273 yards, but it is anything but easy. One must contend not only with the Eagle River in front of the elevated tee box, but also along the left side of the fairway and green. The safe shot here is a 200-yard drive aimed left of the fairway bunker in the distance. From that point you can pitch onto this severely sloping, narrow double green.

For No. 7 we go back under the highway to a straightaway 295-yard par four that offers a good assortment of obstacles. Out-of-bounds is to the right, as well as a fairway bunker 241 yards from the tee. Stone Creek and two sizeable water ponds come into play on the left. This green is closely protected by water and three bunkers. Not an easy hole by any means.

No. 8 is called Nicklaus' Nemesis, because he took a 9 here in the 1978 Gerald Ford Invitational. Stone Creek haunts the fairway's right side, and it can be sure trouble trying to reach this 493-yard par five in two shots. The fairway doglegs left 124 yards from the green, so play to that point and hit a short iron to the small, firm, and elevated green. Two bunkers guard the green's front side, and two more occupy the outside corner of the dogleg.

The number 1 handicap hole is the 434-yard par four 9th. Accuracy is more important than distance on this spectacular and scenic hole, which plays downhill all the way. A fairway wood or long iron off the tee will leave you with a long approach to the green, but the green is large and makes for a good target. You are up in the trees now, so don't stray off the fairway.

One of the most talked about holes at Eagle Vail is the short 138-yard par three 10th. The green is about 200 yards below the tee, and will play 25 to 30 yards shorter than the card reads. Three sand traps surrounding the green and a heavy thicket of tall shrubbery to the green's right front are always a constant threat here at No. 10.

A big drive off No. 11 tee will leave you short of Stone Creek, which crosses the fairway about 310 yards from the tee box. Stone Creek continues to haunt this hole because it crowds the fairway's right side all the way to the green. With a wind at your back, it is possible for the strong hitter to reach this green in two, but most golfers should play their second shot safely in the fairway, well left of the big rock. Add the two bunkers guarding the green to the problems already mentioned, and this hole becomes an outstanding test of length and accuracy.

The par four 349-yard 12th hole is not long, but you must keep your drive in the fairway. Traps and out-of-bounds are left and water and out-of-bounds are right, so there is no room for a careless tee shot here. The pond, short of the green, will catch a long pushed drive or a short second shot. Hit your approach to the middle of the green regardless of pin placement. Two bunkers guard the front and left rear of this green.

Eagle Vail No. 16
312 yards par four

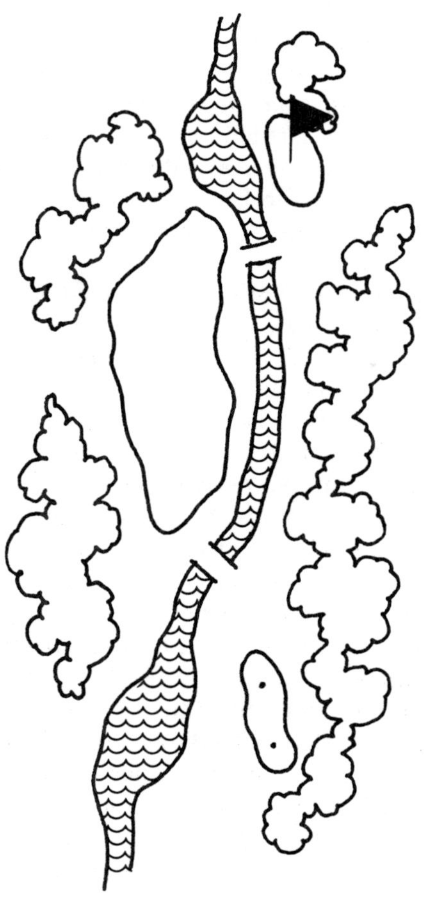

There is no water to contend with on the 177-yard par three 13th, but it's no time to relax. Play for the right side of this long narrow green, but avoid hitting to the right of the sand trap or you will be out in the woods.

The long straightforward 517-yard par five 14th might offer a birdie opportunity if you can avoid the traps and out-of-bounds on the right and Stone Creek on the left. Three traps surround this green which slopes from back to front.

I like the 338-yard par four 15th. It is the number 2 handicap and an extremely exciting golf hole. The smart golfer will use a lofted wood or long iron off the tee to avoid the trap and water on the fairway's left side and forest on the right. Your approach shot is up and over a waterfall to an elevated green guarded by a bunker to the front and Stone Creek to the left. When approaching this green, use a little more club than you think might be necessary.

The 312-yard par four 16th, as described in the Eagle Vail yardage book, is "one tough little bugger." Stone Creek must be negotiated twice, once off the tee and again approaching the green. This hole doglegs right after a 190-yard tee shot favoring the fairway's left side. Don't hit it right, or your ball will find Stone Creek. No sand traps at this green, but it is shallow, elevated, and quite sloping. (see sketch pg. 169)

Another picturesque hole is the 123-yard downhill par three 17th that plays somewhat shorter than indicated. The hole is lined on both sides by evergreen and aspen trees, with Stone Creek on the left adding further concern. This green slopes a little front to back and is guarded by right front and left rear bunkers. Although a short one, it is anything but a sure par.

No. 18 is a challenging and dramatic finishing hole. It is a combination of all that typifies Eagle Vail — an elevated tee box, woods, water, and a well-trapped, sloping green. This hole plays downhill all the way, but you must keep your ball in play or a good round of golf can get away from you in a hurry. Be grateful if you can walk away from this 518-yard hole with a par five.

GRAND LAKE GOLF COURSE

LOCATION: Grand Lake, Colorado. One-half mile north of town on Highway 34, turn left and follow signs.

TELEPHONE: 627-8226

COURSE FACILITIES: Fully equipped pro shop, driving range, putting green, club rental, pull carts, and riding golf carts.

CLUBHOUSE FACILITIES: Bar and lounge serving ready made sandwiches, beer, mixed and soft drinks.

LODGING: Suggest you contact the visitor center located near the west entrance to Rocky Mountain National Park. Most places in Grand Lake are older and somewhat rustic, but still very comfortable. You will also find a number of motels along Highway 34 going to Granby.

RESTAURANTS: There are some interesting and very good restaurants in the area. You will do best to make local inquiry about them.

GOLF COURSE:

	Par	Course Rating	Yardage
Championship	72	70.1	6473
Regular	72	70.1	6310
Ladies	74	73.3	5929

The Grand Lake Golf Course, a real sleeper among Colorado's mountain courses, is carved out of the aspen and pine forests of the Rocky Mountains. In 1966 the front nine was constructed and 8 years later work was started on the back nine. All the fairways are tight, treelined curves, and an errant tee shot leaves the golfer with a lost ball, an unplayable lie, or little chance of chipping the ball back into play. Only the boldest golfers will consider taking the driver out of the bag. Don't expect to putt these mountain greens well the first time out, for they are much grainier than normal, and the amount of break is always confusing. Be sure to bring a sweater, umbrella, and rain gear, as seasonal storms will pop up with little warning.

The par five 1st is a sweeping dogleg right 490 yards, with the tree lined fairway narrowing to a very tight area on both sides and behind the green. The 2nd, though only 350 yards in length, asks for an accurate blind first and a very difficult approach to an elevated green. An unseen marsh on the right side of this fairway can catch any drive hit out to the right. The 175-yard par three 3rd is a well-bunkered downhill one-shotter with trees behind and to the left of the green. No room for a wayward shot here.

Nos. 4, 5, and 6 are tight 400-yard parallel par fours, all demanding accuracy off the tee. The 7th is another short par three, again well bunkered short of the green.

The 490-yard par five 8th hole curls sharply left through the forest, leaving a blind uphill 2nd and 3rd shot to a wide, thin green. Lots of room around the green, but getting there can be a the problem. Number nine is a 360-yard sharp dogleg left, with the trees on both sides threatening to grab either your first or second shot. A 4 wood off the tee and a short iron to the green should be the clubs here. The green is deceiving, elongated and almost impossible to get down in two putts.

No. 10 is a sharp dogleg left, calling for a 200-yard downhill tee shot and an accurate middle-to-short iron shot to a difficult, undulating green. The 11th is a picturesque 175-yard all-carry par three over a lake to an elevated green that will rarely yield a two-putt. Big hitters can relax and hit the driver off the 12th tee to a wide-open fairway. The problem here is your approach to the green because of a severe dogleg left about 125 yards from the green and the thick tall trees at the bend, making it difficult to cut the corner. Roller-coaster mounds on the back of this green make putting a real challenge.

The 350-yard 13th is the tightest hole on the course, with water guarding the left and trees on the right. Your landing area is only about 40 yards wide, and the deceiving second to an elevated green is my own personal plague. No. 14 and No. 15 are parallel 400-yard par fours, quite wide open off the tee, but once again narrowing at the green. No. 16 is a short 160-

Grand Lake No. 18
530 yards par five

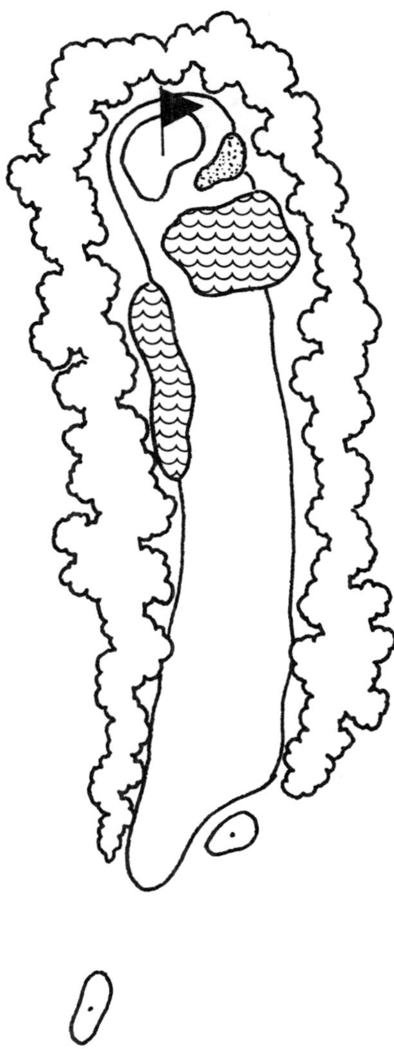

yard par three from an elevated tee. An accurate first shot guarantees par, otherwise bogey can be a blessing.

No. 17 doglegs right, and a well-placed tee ball leaves a middle-to-short iron to a level green. The par five 18th is a 530-yard nightmare, requiring two accurate wood shots and a precise approach over a lake guarding an elevated green. One of the best finishing holes in the state, 18 yields very few birdies. (see sketch pg. 173)

While in Grand Lake be sure to see the town and the surrounding area. Take a boat ride on Grand Lake, and if you have time, do some fishing on Lake Granby and Shadow Mountain reservoir.

HILLCREST GOLF CLUB

LOCATION: Durango, Colorado. From the center of town take 6th Street up the hill to 8th Avenue. Turn left on 8th Avenue and follow the signs to Ft. Lewis College. You will soon see the golf course when you get to the top of the mesa.

TELEPHONE: 247-1499

COURSE FACILITIES: Riding golf carts, pull carts, club rental, driving range, putting and chipping greens, and a fully equipped pro shop.

CLUBHOUSE FACILITIES: Snack bar serving lunch, sandwiches, beer, and soft drinks.

LODGING: There are lots of good motels in Durango. Most of them are located either downtown or north on the main street going through town.

RESTAURANTS: There is no shortage of good and interesting places to eat in Durango. Check the downtown area, or ask your golfing partner.

GOLF COURSE:

	Par	Course Rating	Yardage
Championship	71	69.0	6567
Regular	71	67.3	6236
Ladies	72	70.9	5545

If you like fast greens, you will love Hillcrest. Other than being located in a beautiful setting on top of the mesa above Durango, these fast and slippery greens are the most distinguishing feature of the golf course. The green on hole number 3 is about as slick as any I have ever putted. You will also find the fairways well maintained and in excellent condition. Hillcrest offers a good variety of interesting golf holes, with the last three being especially challenging. No way to coast in on this golf course, because the number 1 handicap hole is 18. This is a good course to walk. It gives you a better chance to enjoy the spectacular mountain peaks and scenery in the distance.

The first nine starts out with two 384-yard par fours. No. 1 doglegs right, and numerous spruce trees guard the inside corner and right side of the fairway. This hole plays level from tee to green and should not offer the golfer a lot of trouble. Cutting the corner can be a little risky because you can easily have a thin sandy lie in the rough or end up behind a spruce tree. No. 2 doglegs sharply left at the 120-yard marker. Target the spruce tree in the fairway at the inside corner when lining up your drive. This hole also plays level with a sand trap at the left front of the green.

No. 3 is an excellent par three at 177 yards. It plays level from tee to green, but a nasty sand trap sits into the side of a small mound located immediately in front of the green. One must carry this bunker to reach the green, and at that point your troubles are just starting. This green is so fast that three putts are more the rule than the exception.

The 4th hole plays from an elevated tee down a fairway that sweeps left along the edge of a sizeable lake that follows the fairway to within 10 yards of the left side of the green. Out-of-bounds is right off the tee, and the green is trapped to the right front. For some reason this is a difficult green to hold, so play a little short when hitting into it. Take a look in the lake to your left as you walk toward this green. You are sure to see a number of nice size trout swimming around.

Lots of room characterizes the fairway of the 401-yard par four 5th. This hole plays downhill off the tee, then a little uphill as you approach the green. The green is elevated and guarded by a right front trap.

I like the 468-yard par five 6th. It plays uphill to a green surrounded by water on three sides. Target your second shot to the left of the spruce tree seen at the top of the hill behind the green. This water is not noticeable from the fairway.

No. 7 is a dandy. It's a par four, 409 yards long, and plays gradually downhill all the way. Target the inside edge of this left-hand dogleg and try for a little fade. This will leave you in the best position to approach the green.

No. 8 is a par three at 156 yards with a trap immediately in front of the green. Not a hard hole, but stay out of the sand. The 9th hole is a short but interesting par four at 291 yards. Out-of-bounds is right, and the rough to the fairway's left drops off severely at the landing area. This hole plays sharply uphill, and the green is not noticeable from the tee. A solid drive will get you to the top of the hill, leaving a short iron approach to the green, which is trapped left and right front.

The 10th hole is a par five at 532 yards. It plays straight and level, with numerous small pine and spruce trees loosely spaced along both sides of the fairway. A right front trap crowds the green. No. 11 is a short par four at 304 yards. Out-of-bounds is right, and about 60 yards short of the green in the fairway is an evergreen tree that can spell trouble for a long drive. Also several pine trees cluster quite close to the green's left side. Best to use a fairway wood or long iron off this tee.

All the par threes on this course are good ones, the 168-yard 12th a good example. It plays from an elevated tee, over a good size lake that comes to within 10 yards of the front of the green, and calls for an accurate tee shot to a wide but shallow green.

No. 13 is a fine golf hole. It's 402 yards long, par four, with the fairway sweeping gradually left. Small pine and spruce trees line the fairway, which kicks right to left. This will usually leave the golfer in a position where the ball will be above his feet for a second shot. A small stream comes out of the lake from the previous hole and extends along the fairway's left side. The green is trapped to the right front. Pars will not come easy on this hole.

Your target is just right of the apricot tree which sits a short distance out from the tee on the 352-yard par four 14th. Out-of bounds is right and a large lake in the left rough extends around to the rear of the green. This lake is reachable off the tee, so accuracy is a must with your drive.

The 143-yard 15th is another good par three. It plays straightaway over a bumpy fairway to a green that is trapped left front. The real trouble on this hole is the sagebrush rough close to the fairway's right and behind the green. This is anything but an easy par three.

The next three holes are all very demanding, and I'm sure many a match or tournament has been won or lost on these final holes. Although No. 16 is a rather short par four at 354 yards, it seems to play much longer than indicated. It's level off the tee, then uphill, and a good drive will get the golfer near the top of the hill. Your second shot is apt to be blind, but hit it straight up the fairway. The green is trapped left front and right side.

No. 17 is a good par five at 543 yards. It plays level with a big, sweeping right-hand dogleg. Out-of-bounds is right all the way to the green as well as behind it, and a large lake threatens near the outside corner of the dogleg. Don't try to cut the corner on this hole, because it's just too far for all but the exceptionally long hitter.

The 18th hole, at 434 yards and par four, is the number 1 handicap, and is a real challenge to keep a score intact. It plays level, doglegs left after a long drive, and leaves a long-to-medium iron approach shot to a green guarded by a large bunker to the right front. The fairway is treelined, so play it down the middle all the way. This long par four is a great way to wrap up an interesting round of golf on another of Colorado's fine mountain golf courses.

Durango is one of Colorado's most interesting and scenic areas. Great outdoor country abounds here, and don't forget to ride the narrow guage train from Durango to Silverton. The train whistle is a nostalgic sound regularly heard from the golf course. You can't help liking this country, so plan to stay long enough to thoroughly enjoy it.

KEYSTONE RANCH GOLF COURSE

LOCATION: Keystone, Colorado. From Denver go west on Interstate 70 about 70 miles to Dillon Exit No. 205 - then east on U.S. 6 about 4 miles - exit right on Swan Mountain Recreational Road - take Soda Ridge Road (which will be the road straight ahead of you as you exit from Highway 6) and go about 1 mile - then turn right on Summit County Road No. 150 to Keystone Ranch.

TELEPHONE: 468-4250

COURSE FACILITIES: Fully equipped pro shop, riding golf carts, club rental, driving range, chipping and putting greens.

CLUBHOUSE FACILITIES: Restaurant serving lunch, sandwiches, dinner, beer, mixed and soft drinks. These facilities, along with the pro shop, are housed in the 50-year-old ranch house which was the residence of the Smith-Reynolds family whose cattle once grazed this beautiful valley.

LODGING: Keystone Lodge.

RESTAURANTS: A wide variety of excellent places to eat are available at the Lodge and in Keystone Village. The restaurant in the ranch house at the golf course is very good. You do not lack for a choice here at Keystone.

GOLF COURSE:

	Par	Course Rating	Yardage
Championship	72	72.7	7090
Regular	72	70.1	6521
Ladies	72	71.1	5720

The Keystone Ranch Golf Course is located in a valley that was formerly a working ranch. Elevation here is 9300 ft., and the course offers a good assortment of treelined fairways, various types of water hazards, links open-type natural terrain, and large irregularly shaped sand traps. This course designed by Robert Trent Jones, Jr., will be appreciated by experts, enjoyed by intermediates, but beginners will surely find it frustrating. Formerly the hunting ground of Ute and Arapaho Indians and surrounded by the high peaks of Colorado Rockies, this is truly a magnificent setting for a golf course. You will need every shot in the bag to score well at Keystone Ranch.

The golf course begins with a medium length 508-yard par five that plays from a highly elevated tee down a heavily treelined fairway. These trees are quite intimidating, as is the bunker sitting in the right rough near the landing area. Another bunker lies in the left rough short of the green and can easily catch a second shot. This large, undulating, deep green is trapped left front and left rear, and a large spruce tree is growing in the center of the left front bunker. This is not an easy starter hole, but if you can keep the ball in the fairway, you have a good chance for par.

No. 2 is a straightaway par four that plays longer than its 408 yards. Again the fairway is treelined, parallels No. 1, and is quite narrow. This fairway kicks a little left to right and plays gradually uphill. The green is trapped to the left rear. Again, it's important to keep the ball in the fairway for par.

The course begins to open up a little with the 406-yard right-hand dogleg par four 3rd, but it doesn't get any easier. This hole plays uphill, and the green is not visible from the tee. Two bunkers guard both sides of the landing area at each corner of the dogleg. Try to split these bunkers with your tee shot, or if you are a strong hitter, it's possible to clear the right bunker. A 3 wood will get the good golfer to the corner. This green requires an accurate approach shot, because it plays uphill, and is trapped to the left, right, and right front. Another large evergreen tree is growing in the right front trap. Out-of-bounds to the right guards this fairway from tee to green.

One must play short of the small stream crossing the fairway on the 391-yard par four 4th hole. A lofted wood or medium-to-long iron is the club to use off this elevated tee. It's almost impossible, even for the big hitter, to clear this stream and certainly not worth the risk. The green is guarded on the left by the stream and the right and right front by sand traps. This all makes for a small target and a demanding approach shot.

The course relaxes a little with the 169-yard par three 5th, which plays over a small creek and thick heavy rough to a green that is trapped to the right, left front, and rear. This green is quite wide, but not very deep, and is a little tough to hold.

The number 1 handicap hole at Keystone is the 527-yard par five 6th. It plays straightaway over a grassy meadow to a fairway guarded by a large lake on the left and a huge bunker on the right at the landing area. For your second shot it will usually be best to lay up short of the small stream cutting across the fairway diagonally from right to left away from the golfer. If you do this, the landing area is quite small, but it is less risky than trying to hit over the stream. Across the stream you will find a sand trap about 40 yards out to the green's right front, another adjacent to the green at the right front, and another one to the right rear. Also guarding this interesting, hilly, and two-level green is the stream which runs along the green's right side. Lots of opportunities to lose a stroke on this demanding hole.

Another interesting par three is the 174-yard 7th. Water crowds the fairway on the left from tee to green, and a sand trap beckons at the green's right side. The course is remindful of many of the Scottish links at this point, with sage brush in the rough in place of heather and gorse.

Sand traps dominate the scene as you view the 391-yard par four 8th fairway. Three of them lurk at the inside corner of this left-hand dogleg, and another tightens up the landing area at the outside corner. The second shot is to a highly elevated green that is severely trapped by two yawning, wide, thin bunkers, one above the other at the green's left front. The green is quite wide, not very deep, and a difficult one to hold.

No. 9 is a different and interesting golf hole. From an elevated tee on top of the nob of a small hill, the shot is over a portion of the large lake that is in the center of the golf course. A good drive off the tee should leave a short iron to the green, which is well trapped to the left front, left side, and rear. The lake makes additional demands on an accurate approach shot by crowding perilously close to the green's front and right side. This 318-yard par four hole is a good one and a fitting climax to an exciting front nine.

No. 10 is a long par four at 421 yards. It plays straightforward off the tee, then bends slightly right around a fairway trap in the right rough. Another trap sits out to the left front of the green, while a much larger one nestles up to the green's right side. Nothing fancy about this hole, but it will yield few pars.

Another hole with sand traps galore is the 313-yard par four 11th. Four of them are in the right rough guarding that side of the fairway, while three more watch over the entrance to this elevated green. This fairway kicks left to right towards the bunkers, and trees line its right side. It's a short par four made longer by the sloping fairway and numerous sand traps.

No. 12 is a short par three at 143 yards, playing downhill to a well-trapped green. The ground drops off sharply to the left of this two-level green. It's not a hard hole, but stay out of the traps.

The number 2 handicap hole at Keystone is a good one. It is a par five at 529 yards, and again, sand traps are the dominant feature. One sits in the right rough near the landing area of this left-to-right sloping fairway, and two others are encountered in the right rough on the way to the green. The green is surrounded by bunkers, and all you can see as you approach this wide, shallow, two-level green, is the flag waving up there among all those sand traps! Lots of breaking putts are the rule on this No. 13 green.

The par threes are the least difficult holes on this golf course, and the 138-yard 14th is no exception. The tee is elevated, and the large green is trapped to the left front and right side. Stay out of the sand, this hole should yield a par.

No. 15 is a 375-yard par four that plays downhill and doglegs left. Three huge bunkers dominate the inside corner, and another guards the outside corner. The big hitter can cut the corner here and have a short chip shot to the green. The target for most golfers is just left of the right fairway bunker. Entry to this green is guarded by three well-placed, hungry sand traps.

The 16th should not be a hard hole if you can stay out of the sand traps. It is 392 yards long, par four, and plays slightly uphill. The fairway is bunkered left and right at the landing area off the tee, so make every effort to split these traps with your drive. Left and right front greenside bunkers provide a narrow entry to this rather deep green.

The next two holes are great finishing holes. No. 17, at 402 yards and par four, limits the length of your tee shot to no more than 220 yards. Any more than this and you will find your ball in deep, thick, grassy rough. This will leave a mid-iron approach that must clear a wide expanse of heavy rough, which grows to within 10 yards of the green's left side and front. Further complicating this hole is a small left front sand trap and a larger one to the green's right side. This is an excellent golf hole forcing both accuracy off the tee and for the golfer's approach shot.

No. 18 tops off a challenging round of golf with a demanding 516-yard par five that plays over a large lake off the tee, then doglegs left with the lake crowding the fairway's left side all the way to the green. Most golfers will do best to target a little left of the first bunker on the far side of the fairway. This should leave a long fairway wood to short of a green that is tightly bunkered left and right. The long hitter can bite off a little more over the lake and might be able to reach this green in 2, but it's quite risky, and I would recommend playing it relatively safe.

In addition to golf, Keystone offers a wide assortment of outdoor activities such as tennis, fishing, historical sightseeing tours, horseback riding, jeep tours, raft trips, sailing on Lake Dillon, swimming, western barbecues, backpacking, and bicycling. Luxury accommodations are offered in the 152 room Keystone Lodge, and excellent meeting facilities are available for groups up to 700. Keystone is a complete resort, and you will enjoy everything about it.

PAGOSA PINES GOLF CLUB

LOCATION: Pagosa Springs, Colorado. From the west side of town at Fairfield Pagosa Resort turn north off Highway 160 and go north one-half mile. The clubhouse and golf course are just over the hill.

TELEPHONE: 731-4141 ext. 4155

COURSE FACILITIES: Fully equipped pro shop, riding golf carts, pull carts, club rental, driving range, chipping and putting greens.

CLUBHOUSE FACILITIES: Available at the course are lunch, sandwiches, beer, mixed and soft drinks. An exceptionally fine selection of golf clothing, accessories, etc., is available at the pro shop.

LODGING: In addition to the excellent accommodations at the Fairfield Pagosa Lodge, the town of Pagosa Springs has several good motels.

RESTAURANTS: The Southface and Great Divide at the Fairfield Pagosa Lodge are close, convenient, and both offer outstanding food and service. Other local restaurants are located in town.

GOLF COURSE:

	Par	Course Rating	Yardage
Championship	71	70.2	6744
Regular	71	68.7	6124
Ladies	71	68.5	5202

Pagosa Pines offers an abundant assortment of exciting and challenging golf holes. Thrown in for good measure is the impressive view of the San Juan Mountains seen in the distance. Most of the fairways are treelined, and the course is quite hilly, so practically everyone rides a golf cart rather than walk. The greens are large, very fast, and all possess more than their fair share of break. This superb golf course is situated in another of Colorado's fine outdoor sports areas. Fishing, hiking, horseback riding, hunting, river rafting, tennis, and skiing are just a few of the year-round activities available to all who love the great outdoors.

In addition, the Fairfield Pagosa Lodge offers the best in excellent room accommodations and fine food. Don't miss Pagosa Pines. It plays on a par with all the other great Colorado mountain golf courses.

No. 1 is a good starter hole of only medium difficulty, par four and 384 yards in length. It plays downhill a little, and the green is trapped left and right with sizeable and rather deep bunkers. The fairway is quite roomy and slopes a little right to left. The small lake 30 yards to the right rear of the green should not come into play.

The 409-yard par four 2nd is considerably more difficult than the 1st. It plays level, then uphill off the tee, with out-of-bounds and plenty of tree trouble left, but a firm drive will get the golfer most of the way up the hill. The fairway doglegs left at the top of the hill to a very undulating green. The green is guarded by a large pine tree growing 50 yards to the left front, another 30 yards out to the right front, and two more to the left of the green. Also heavy, deep, grassy rough carries 10 yards behind the green.

Although the par three 3rd is only 115 yards, it's a little tricky because it plays over a rather deep gully that comes to within 30 yards of the green, which is surrounded on three sides by tall pines. Don't leave it short.

No. 4 is a fine golf hole at 505 yards and par five. It plays level and straightaway, then doglegs right well short of the green. There is a deep ravine in front of the tee box, and the fairway is heavily treelined on both sides. About 10 yards in front of the green is a 10 to 12 foot deep grassy gully 30 feet across that protects the entire entrance to the green. Most players will want to hit short of this depression and pitch on from there. Stay in the fairway on this number 1 handicap hole, and you will have a good chance for par.

The course eases off a bit with the 335-yard par four 5th. It plays from a highly elevated tee, downhill, with a fairway that sweeps broadly to the right. Out-of-bounds is left, a bunker challenges at the outside corner, and lots of tall pine trees crowd the fairway's right side. One of the largest of these trees sits by itself at the inside corner and presents a real problem for those who try to cut the corner. Another huge pine tree lies to the green's right front. A fairway wood or long iron is the club to use off this tee.

I would rate the 559-yard par five 6th as one of the most difficult holes on the course. Out-of-bounds is left, and the fairway is open off the tee for about 200 yards, but the rest of the way it is very narrow and heavily treelined. The chances of most golfers getting into these trees are pretty good. To further complicate matters the fairway kicks left to right and is quite bumpy with numerous humps and hollows. Keeping all your shots in the fairway is a must on this hole. Guarding the green is a huge pine tree growing only 6 yards to the left.

The 417-yard par four 7th is another good one. It is treelined on the right, and two tall pines guard the left-hand dogleg a little short of the corner. A lake and thick grassy rough are a menace to the fairway's left side. Most golfers can hit all they want off the tee, so play it straightaway. From the dogleg on in, it is open all the way to the green, which is trapped left front.

No. 8 is just a great par three at 177 yards. The big problem here is the lake which comes up to the front side of the green and the sand trap to the green's left side. Don't be short here or you will surely find the water.

The front nine finishes with a 384-yard par four that plays moderately uphill over a rolling fairway that is quite roomy and for a change without any tree problems. Out-of-bounds is left in the thick grassy rough. An oblong trap situates in the side of the nob of a small hill to the left front of the green and another trap sits opposite to the right. This is anything but an easy hole.

The problem on the 302-yard par four 10th is the nasty fairway bunker located in the right rough at the foot of a sizeable and thick grassy mound. The green is trapped left front, and a large pine tree grows to the green's right side. The long hitter should use a fairway wood or long iron off this tee in order to avoid the fairway bunker.

Except for the sand trap immediately in front of the green, the 117-par three 11th should cause little trouble. However,

Pagosa Pines No. 7
417 yards par four

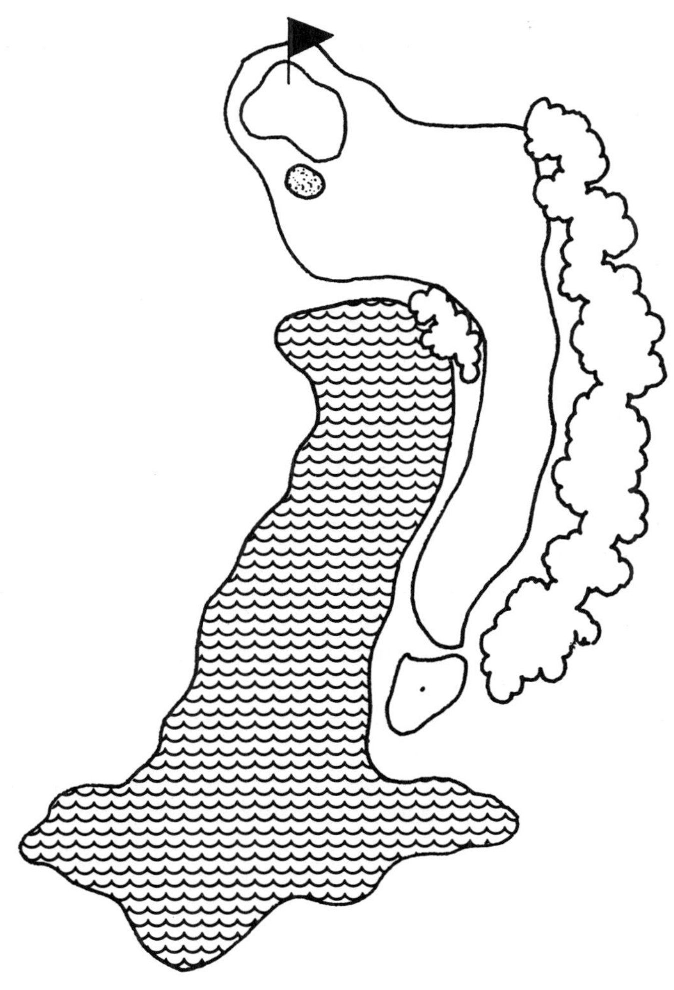

the 311-yard par four 12th quickly makes up for things. It's not a long hole, plays straightaway, but is very narrow, being only 35 to 40 yards wide. A deep grassy upward sloping bank extends along the fairway's left side, and the ground drops off sharply on the right into thick grassy rough and tall pine trees. No room for a loose drive or an errant approach shot on this hole.

No. 13 is a long par four at 422 yards. It's a straightforward playing hole, although it does seem to bend a little to the right. Out-of-bounds is right, and the green is severely trapped left, rear, and right front. No tree trouble occurs on this number 2 handicap hole.

You will find plenty of tree trouble on the 361-yard par four 14th hole. Scrub oak and pine trees line both sides of this fairway, which plays downhill from an elevated tee, then uphill to a green trapped to the right. This bunker is not noticeable from the fairway below. A large pine tree crowds the green's left front, so it's best to approach this green from the fairway's right side.

Another interesting hole is the 338-yard par four 15th. It plays straightaway over a small valley and down a treelined, but roomy fairway. Several shallow valleys and humps break up the fairway, which bends left about 100 yards from the green. A sand trap intimidates the green's left side.

The par four 16th plays sharply uphill, sweeps around to the left, and is heavily treelined. If you can do it, a nice little draw would be the shot on this 311-yard hole. If not, then favor the fairway's left side off the tee. This green is a two-level one, with the lower one to the left. A large pine tree guards the green's right front, and two more guard the left side. Closely behind the green is deep grassy rough.

Tucked away among the large pine trees is the 147-yard par three 17th. The small trap cut into the front of a grassy mound to the right front of the green presents a small problem, but this should not be a difficult hole for most golfers.

No. 18 is a good finishing hole at 550 yards and par five. The tee shot is downhill from an elevated tee, and the fairway bends wide around to the right. Out-of-bounds is right, and two gigantic pines at the inside corner force the golfer to hit it straight down the fairway. After the dogleg, it's straight, level, and open to the green. However, at greenside are two large sand traps, one to the left front and another to the right. The trap to the left front is below the green, and the one to the right is above the green.

Pagosa Pines is such a beautiful place that even if you don't score well, you will enjoy your day on the course. This is a "must play" golf course, so put it on your list of important things to do.

POLE CREEK GOLF CLUB

LOCATION: Winter Park, Colorado. Eleven miles north of Winter Park off U.S. Highway 40. Follow the signs.

TELEPHONE: 726-9225

COURSE FACILITIES: Fully equipped pro shop, riding golf carts, pull carts, club rental, driving range, chipping and putting green.

CLUBHOUSE FACILITIES: None as of this date (August 1983), although sandwiches, beer and soft drinks are available at the pro shop.

LODGING: The Winter Park and Granby areas offer a wide choice of motels and condominiums.

RESTAURANTS: Same as above.

GOLF COURSE:

	Par	Course Rating	Yardage
Championship	72	70.9	6882
Regular	72	67.3	6230
Ladies	72	66.6	4956

Pole Creek offers one of the finest sites for a golf course in Colorado. The varied and natural terrain of this two-year-old course is magnificent. Some of the holes are typical of mountain courses, with tall pines lining the fairways and inspiring views. Others are reminiscent of the links of Scotland, with natural features and open fairways. Several offer an assortment of water and sand to create a completely different character. No look-alike holes exist at Pole Creek. Each one is unique and exciting.

This course needs a couple years to mature before it reaches the quality condition of older mountain golf courses. However, when that time arrives, you will be treated to one of the most challenging courses in the state. In the meantime, enjoy the well-cared-for, interesting greens and play winter rules in the narrow, challenging fairways. This golf course is destined to be known and talked about far beyond the boundaries of Colorado.

Pole Creek begins with a rather friendly 1st hole at 323 yards and par four. It plays straight off the tee, over Pole Creek, to a wide and inviting fairway. Your approach shot is uphill to a green that is trapped right front and left rear. The putting surface is not visible from the fairway, so judge your distance from the 150-yard marker.

I like the 474-yard par five 2nd. It is long and straight with a narrow treelined fairway extending before the golfer, and the high jagged peaks of the Continental Divide can be seen in the distance. Also seen is a fairway trap in the left rough at the landing area and another bunker in the right rough about 100 yards short of the green. Left front and right side sand traps add further concern when approaching this green. Where the 1st fairway was roomy, this one is very tight, and keeping the ball in play is a must for par.

The next hole is a short 303-yard par four that should cause little trouble, although two fairway bunkers and a right front greenside trap are there to reach up and grab any mis-hit shots. No. 4 is a deceiving 161-yard par three over a lake that crowds the front of the green. If you are short, you're in the water. If you're long, you're in Pole Creek. This hole, however, seems to play a little shorter than the indicated yardage.

The 336-yard par four 5th is quite interesting in that Pole Creek crosses the fairway diagonally from left to right away from the golfer, then continues along the fairway's right side all the way to the green. This situation actually divides the fairway, creating one to the right and one to the left. The safe shot is to the right, while the more risky shot is over Pole Creek and to the left. The green is not trapped, but Pole Creek creates all the trouble necessary on this hole.

No. 6 is a 159-yard par three that plays a little longer than indicated. Most of the trouble here is to the green's right in the form of large bunkers, but another trap to the left front can also be a problem.

The 552-yard par five 7th is a very interesting and different golf hole. It doglegs sharply left, a large bunker and tall pine trees guard the inside corner, and the fairway is heavily treelined off the tee. It's your second shot that becomes a real challenge. This shot must clear a lake at the bottom of a valley, as well as Pole Creek and the heavy growth along its banks. The green is drastically elevated and heavily trapped to the front, left front, and left side. Only the best golfers will reach this green in two, and most will reach it in four or more.

No. 8 is 395 yards in length and par four. It is the number 1 handicap hole and plays much longer than the indicated yardage. Favor the right side of this straightforward fairway because your ball will kick right to left. Trees line the right side of the fairway, and two bunkers guard the landing area off the tee. The green is well trapped to the left front and left side, and its contour is much higher in the back than in the front. This is a tough green to chip and putt because of the two tiers.

The 359-yard par four 9th calls for a straight tee shot favoring the fairway's right side. Stay well right of the round hump in the left rough just short of the 150-yard marker. If you don't, you will probably lose your ball down in the sage brush well below the left side of the fairway. This tightly bunkered green makes for a small target, and No. 9 is anything but an easy hole.

One of the best and toughest holes on the course is the 551-yard par five 10th. The tee shot is over Pole Creek, uphill to a right-hand dogleg, which is guarded at the inside corner by a large fairway bunker. Trees line the fairway from this point all the way to the green. The second shot is also uphill, and another bunker sits at the outside corner of a second right-hand dogleg. Tall pine trees come into play at the inside corner, and the green is trapped left and right front. Getting on this green in regulation will be an accomplishment for any golfer, and pars will be hard to come by for most players.

No. 11 is a beautiful par three. It is 166 yards in length and plays downhill to a large green that is surrounded by six sand traps. The fairway is treelined on both sides and behind the green. Sand is the big problem here.

Lots of tough holes come into play on this back nine, and the 387-yard par four 12th is one of them. This hole doglegs sharp-

Pole Creek No. 13
391 yards par four

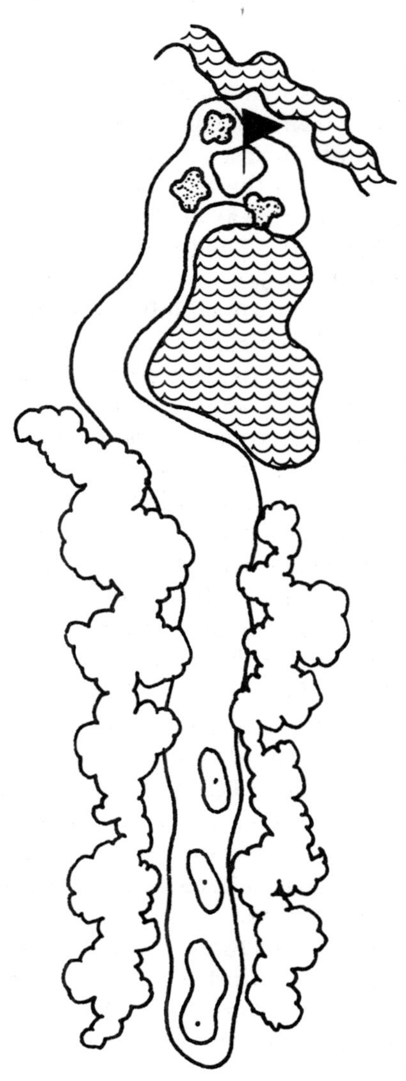

ly left after your drive and plays uphill from the corner to the green. The strong hitter can cut the corner, but if left short, you will be looking for your ball in the thick grassy rough. Most golfers should play straight down the fairway to the corner, then uphill to short of the green, pitch on from there and hope to get it close enough for a par putt. Trees line both sides of the fairway after it doglegs, and the green is well trapped right front, left front, and left side.

The 391-yard 13th is a demanding par four. Trees line this slightly downhill fairway early off the tee, and a large lake threatens immediately in front of the green. Most golfers will be safe to hit a driver off the tee, but the long hitter ought to use a lofted wood. The fairway curls around the left side of the lake, but if you have hit a good drive, a medium iron second shot should reach the green by going straight over the lake. This two-tiered green is trapped left and right front as well as to the rear, and Pole Creek runs along the green's back side. It will take four fine shots to par this hole. (see sketch pg. 193)

The next two holes are short par fours, and anything but easy. No. 14 is 345 yards and plays straightaway over Pole Creek to a landing area no more than 30 yards wide. One of the largest bunkers in Colorado guards the left front of this wide but narrow kidney-shaped green. A pin placement behind this huge trap will require the perfect approach shot to get it close to the pin. No. 15 also plays straightforward, but the lake extending into the fairway forces an iron or lofted wood off the tee. Pole Creek runs along the fairway's left side, then crosses immediately in front of the green and crowds the green's right side. This all makes for a tiny target for your approach shot. Breaking putts will be the rule on this green.

The 178-yard par three 16th plays level from tee to green over Pole Creek which serves as a protector of the green's front, right, and back sides. Four sand traps guard the green's left side. This hole presents another small target and seems to play a little shorter than indicated.

Although not long, the 326-yard par four dogleg right 17th, requires the golfer's best effort for par. This hole plays uphill all the way, and three bunkers guard the outside corner of the dogleg. It's possible to cut the corner here, but only with a strong hit. A short-to-medium iron should be the club for your uphill approach to this green, which is severely trapped to the front. Plenty of room extends behind the green, so don't be short and find yourself in the sand.

No. 18 is a challenging finishing hole at 489 yards and par five. It's short as par fives go, but seven sand traps have a way of making it much longer. Your drive is from an elevated tee, down a fairway that bends slightly left and slopes left to right towards a large bunker in the right rough at the outside corner. The left rough offers pine trees early on and sage brush the rest of the way to the green. Two bunkers inhabit each side of the fairway about 60 yards short of the green, and the green is heavily trapped to the front. The safe approach to this elevated green is to lay up short and pitch on with a short iron. Going for this green in two is quite risky. Be satisifed to get a par on No. 18.

It's only a matter of time before Pole Creek becomes one of Colorado's most popular mountain golf courses. The greens are already great, and the layout of the course is exciting and challenging. Allow a few years for the grass in the fairways and rough to thicken a little more and you will be playing one of the finest golf courses in the state. Put Pole Creek on your "must play" list.

QUAIL RIDGE GOLF COURSE

LOCATION: Fruita, Colorado, 1450 16 Road.

TELEPHONE:

GOLF COURSE: Three of the holes are yet to be completed, so final statistics are not available at this time.

Quail Ridge is a new golf course presently under construction that is scheduled for limited play in the fall of 1984. It is an 18-hole, privately owned course that will be open for play by the public. The course architect, Dick Phelps, has made good use of the natural terrain and adobe hills that are peculiar to this part of Western Colorado.

Although there are no sand traps, the 200 foot elevation change, several canals, and huge water reservoir will offer more than enough challenge. Water comes into play on thirteen of the eighteen holes.

Facilities here will include a clubhouse, restaurant, tennis courts, fully equipped pro shop, driving range, chipping and putting greens. Riding golf carts, pull carts and club rental will also be available.

SINGLETREE GOLF CLUB

LOCATION: Edwards, Colorado. Fifteen miles west of Vail on Interstate 70. Take the Edwards Exit No. 163, head north, and follow the signs.

TELEPHONE: 926-3533

COURSE FACILITIES: Fully equipped pro shop, driving range, putting green, pull carts, riding golf carts, and club rental.

CLUBHOUSE FACILITIES: Restaurant serving breakfast, lunch, sandwiches, dinner, beer, mixed and soft drinks. Other facilities include showers, swimming pool, and tennis courts.

LODGING: No facilities available at the course. Vail Village offers a good choice of accommodations.

RESTAURANTS: In addition to the restaurant at the clubhouse, you have a wide choice of excellent places to eat throughout the Vail area. Ask around.

GOLF COURSE:

	Par	Course Rating	Yardage
Championship	71	71.5	7024
Regular (blue)	71	69.7	6435
Ladies	71	67.5	5293

Singletree is another of Colorado's terrific mountain golf courses. Designed by Bob Cupp and Jay Morrish of Golforce, Inc., it was first open for play in July of 1981. The course is similar to many Scottish links in that it is quite open, and good use has been made of natural hazards and undulating terrain. Many of the traps are deep pothole-type bunkers resembling those of the Old Course at St. Andrews. The front nine is hilly, calling for well-placed shots from tee to green. Although the back nine is flatter, it is also longer with par at 36. You might think the lack of trees would make this an easy golf course, but nothing could be further from the truth. The many traps, creeks, ponds, deep rough, and other natural hazards give the golfer more than enough obstacles to overcome in one day. Singletree is superb! Don't miss an opportunity to play this course. The challenge it presents is genuine.

The course begins with four demanding par fours, all calling for a best effort from the golfer if he expects to end up with a respectable score for the day. The 1st is an uphill 373-yard straightforward hole to a fairway that is roomy, but quite undulating. A deep left front trap extends along the entire left side of this two-level green. The hole plays longer than indicated, and the green is lightning fast! No. 2 is 382 yards downhill and sort of curls around a hill on the right. Out-of-bounds is on the right, but the landing area off the tee is quite spacious, and most golfers should have little trouble finding the fairway. Although this two-level green is large, it is tightly bunkered right front and right rear.

Next comes the number 1 handicap hole and rightly so! From an elevated tee it's downhill to a 40 ft. wide gully 266 yards off the tee and 118 yards from the center of an elevated green. This hole is further complicated by a grove of large cottonwood trees in the fairway's right edge just short of the gully. Three well-placed traps crowd the right, right rear, and the left rear of this rather wide, but thin green. Favor the fairway's left side off the tee, avoid the gully, and stay out of the two rear bunkers, and you might have a chance for a par on this 386-yard hole.

The 311-yard par four 4th is rather short, but still quite demanding. A small gully runs along the fairway's right side and cuts diagonally across in front of the green. The fairway kicks left to right, but does open up pretty well in the landing area. Most of the trouble here is right except around the green where a huge trap extends along the green's left side. Another pothole-type trap sits between the green and the larger bunker.

No. 5 is a 167-yard par three over a rather treacherous little valley to a green that is about the same elevation as the tee. Two left front traps, both of different elevations, beckon below the green. A larger bunker abuts the green to the right rear. Accuracy is a must for par.

No. 6 is a beautiful par four at 365 yards. The hole plays downhill through a valley to a wide-open fairway. A small stream bubbles out of the hillside on the left about halfway to the green, then curls toward the green, and empties into three small ponds. These ponds guard the green's left front and left side. Bunkers to the right and rear add further challenge to this very interesting hole.

The 7th hole is of medium difficulty at 424 yards. This rather lengthy par four is straightaway from an elevated tee to a roomy and inviting fairway. However, out-of-bounds is on the left, and about 280 yards off the tee are three pothole-type bunkers haunting the left side of the fairway. Another tiny pothole bunker that can't be seen from the fairway is a real nuisance immediately in front of the green.

The 179-yard par three 8th hole can best be described as having wall-to-wall sand traps! There are four in front of the green and another long, narrow one behind. Railroad tie terraces back up the front traps as well as the rear bunker. Pinpoint accuracy is required here unless you wish to play out of the sand.

We finally come to a par five on the 568-yard 9th, and it is the number 3 handicap hole. The tee is slightly elevated, and the fairway bends a little left, with two bunkers lurking at the inside corner about 270 yards off the tee. Adding further challenge to this hole are two groups of large trees guarding both sides of the fairway about 200 yards out from the green. The green is guarded by a left rear trap. It will require five properly executed shots to par this hole.

We start off the back nine with another par five at 560 yards. Out-of-bounds is on the left and a nasty fairway bunker lurks 245 yards out from the tee on the right. A large lake lies perilously close to the left front and left side of this green. Most golfers will not be able to reach the lake in two, but it might be wise to come up and take a look before hitting your second shot. Missing this green to the left guarantees a water penalty, so be careful.

The 142-yard par three 11th is supposed to be the number 18 handicap hole, but it offers its share of challenges in the form of a yawning canyon-type gully that is out-of-bounds on the left and two greenside traps that closely protect this wide

Singletree No. 15
499 yards par five

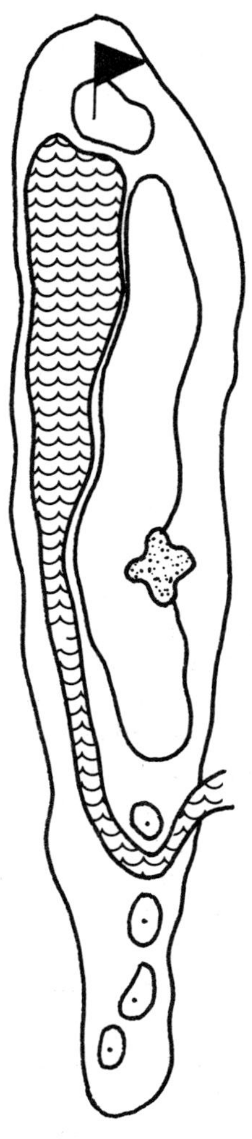

shallow green. We jump from a rather easy hole to a considerably more difficult one at the 409-yard par four 12th. This number 2 handicap hole plays level, but does bend gently right about 200 yards off the tee. A 30-yard-long fairway bunker lies adjacent to the corner, and out-of-bounds is left and right.

Although not a long hole, the 343-yard par four 13th presents some interesting obstacles. With out-of-bounds left and right, a sand trap at the inside corner where the fairway doglegs a bit to the right, and a green that is well protected by water on the left and by three bunkers on the right, this hole should yield its share of pars. Another opportunity for par is the 170-yard 14th hole. The green is tucked away behind a fairly good size pond, so don't miss to the left or be short.

No. 15 is a rather short par five at 499 yards, but it offers plenty of trouble. Out-of-bounds is to the right, and a very large sand trap lies 215 yards out from the tee in the right rough. A small stream crosses the fairway in front of the tee, then flows down the left side into a large lake that extends all the way to the green. A big hit pulled left could find the front edge of this lake, which is a constant threat all the way to the green. Accuracy off the tee is essential to score well on this hole. (see sketch pg. 200)

If you fade the ball, the 404-yard par four 16th should be to your liking. This fairway is level, roomy, and sweeps around to the right with a sizeable grove of small pine trees at the inside corner. A large right front trap and a smaller one in the back watch over this green.

A profusion of sand traps greets the eye from the tee box at the 358-yard par four 17th. Three of them are situated 231 yards off the tee in the left rough, and two more occupy the right rough starting about 100 yards from the green. A good target off the tee is the second trap on the right. Three pothole-type bunkers surround the green, adding further complication to this already heavily trapped hole. Your approach to the green is slightly uphill. Stay out of the sand if you hope to par this hole.

No. 18 is a great finishing hole! The fairway bends gently left and a fairway bunker lies at the inside corner 174 yards from the tee. From this point to the green the fairway slopes sharply left to right. Don't be short with your approach, because there is a very attractive two-level water hazard immediately in front of the green. Two rear sand traps make pinpoint accuracy essential for anyone attempting to reach this green in regulation. Most golfers will do best to lay up short of the water and pitch on from there. This 395-yard par four hole is a fitting climax to an exciting round of golf on one of Colorado's most impressive and challenging golf courses.

THE SNOWMASS CLUB GOLF LINKS

LOCATION: Aspen, Colorado. From downtown Aspen go west on Highway 82 for 6 miles, turn left at the sign indicating direction to Snowmass Village and go 3 miles. At that point take Highline Road, which is the one going straight ahead, and go about one-half mile, then turn right, and this road will lead you to the Snowmass Club.

TELEPHONE: 923-5600

COURSE FACILITIES: Fully equipped pro shop, riding golf carts, club rental, driving range, and putting green.

CLUBHOUSE FACILITIES: Breakfast, lunch, sandwiches, dinner, beer, mixed and soft drinks, showers, swimming pool, tennis courts, sauna, steam bath, jacuzzi, handball and squash courts, complete Nautilus training center, and excellent locker room facilities.

LODGING: Snowmass Club.

RESTAURANTS: The Snowmass Club. Other restaurants are located just a few miles away in the village.

GOLF COURSE:

	Par	Course Rating	Yardage
Championship	71	71.2	6817
Regular	71	68.7	6065
Ladies	71	62.3	5008

Further proof of the excellent quality of golf found in Colorado's mountains is The Snowmass Club Golf Links. Although not an old golf course, Snowmass is in top condition. The course is quite open, and good use has been made of the natural rolling terrain as provided by mother nature. The course architect, Ed Seay, has supplemented this beautiful setting with an abundance of sand traps and lakes that come into play all too often. The greens are large, irregularly shaped, and all quite undulating. This is a rather short golf course from the regular tees, but the championship tees will give the best golfers a real workout. Snowmass is the complete resort, offering a wide choice of sports activities for the entire family. Non-guests of the Snowmass Club may play the golf course, but at a slightly increased fee.

The golf course starts out with two par fours of medium difficulty, playing gradually uphill and bending a little to the right with fairway traps at the inside corner and greens that are heavily bunkered, especially No. 2. Keep the ball in the fairway and out of the sand and these first two holes should get your round started off with a couple of pars.

The 490-yard par five 3rd is the number 1 handicap hole, and although not a long one, has its share of problems. It continues gradually uphill, and a bunker sits at the outside corner of this right-hand dogleg. Mt. Daly looms impressively in the distance, and the Snowmass ski area watches from high on the mountain to the left as you proceed up this fairway. A small sign just off the fairway in the right rough at about the point of the dogleg indicates 200 yards to the water, which is a small creek crossing the fairway 120 yards in front of the green. A long drive will let you hit over this creek with your second shot, but most golfers will have to lay up short. The green is another one that is well trapped, with bunkers to the front, right, and left rear.

I like the 400-yard par four 4th. A small stream cuts across the fairway shortly in front of the tee, continues down the left side, and crosses the fairway again about 130 yards out from the green. This fairway doglegs sharply left after your drive. A good target off the tee is the trap at the far end of the fairway where it bends left. Another large sand trap with arms going in several directions lies to the right front of the green, and a second one sits to the left. Most any well-hit tee shot will leave a medium-to-long iron to this rather narrow, but deep green.

The 150-yard par three 5th is not difficult, but the stream crosses the fairway left to right going away from the tee box, then runs along next to the green's right side. Two sand traps guard this green, one to the left front and a larger one to the left rear. Between the creek to the right and the bunkers to the left, it all makes for a small target.

No. 6 is a 370-yard par four from an elevated tee box over a small creek and down a fairway that bends gently to the right. Several traps guard the inside corner, so favor the fairway's left side a little. A good target off the tee is the small evergreen tree in the left rough indicating 150 yards from the green. This quite small green is surrounded by bunkers, one to the right front, one to the right, one to the left, and another to the left rear.

At only 350 yards, the par four 7th should be an easy hole, but plenty of trouble awaits to the right in the form of a lake guarding the inside corner of this right-hand dogleg. The tee on No. 7 is highly elevated, and the fairway is quite roomy, so a good drive and a short iron should get most golfers on in regulation. Left side and left rear traps guard the green.

The 8th hole is a 150-yard par three that is an all-carry shot over a lake. A huge sand trap protects the green's right front. This green looks farther away than it is, so play it as indicated on the score card or even a little less.

The front nine finishes with a very good golf hole. It is 390 yards in length, par four, and plays straightaway from an elevated tee. About the distance of a good drive you will find a bunker in the left rough and two more in the right rough. The real challenge comes when approaching this green. It is guarded on the left and left front by a lake and on the right by a large sand trap. No room available to roll a ball onto this green.

The 10th hole plays more uphill than any of the previous ones. Consequently, its 310 yards plays more like 350. The fairway kicks left to right, and the fairway traps to the right are the correct distance to catch a lot of drives. Large left front and left rear traps dig in at the green, which is shaped like a boomerang and is very touchy to putt. Not an easy par four.

The 170-yard par three 11th plays a little shorter than indicated, but the green is heavily trapped to the left, right front, and right rear, so accuracy off the tee is a must for par. No. 12 is quite a golf hole! It is not long at 335 yards and par four, but seven sand traps come into play, which make it tough. This hole plays downhill and doglegs right, but it won't pay to try to

Snowmass No. 14
510 yards par five

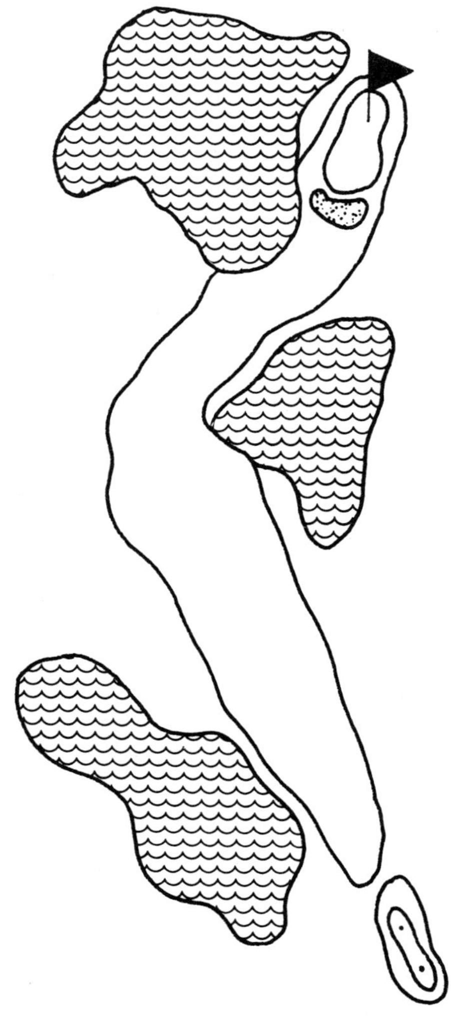

cut the corner. Enough sand traps occupy the right rough to discourage even the reckless golfer. Also two bunkers appear at the outside corner of the dogleg, two more in front and to the right front of the green, as well as another two that cozy up to the green's backside. Play this hole honest by hitting to the corner, then take a short iron to the green.

No. 13 is another medium length par three that shouldn't cause any difficulty. This 160-yard hole plays downhill to a large well-trapped green with bunkers to the left front, right front, and to the rear. It plays a little shorter than indicated.

I think No. 14 at 510 yards and par five is an outstanding golf hole. It demands accuracy with every shot, or you can find a lake with a drive that strays right or another lake with your second shot if you pull it left. This fairway doglegs right and is quite narrow all the way to the green. A wide thin bunker intimidates immediately in front of the green, and the lake to the left snuggles up close, making a small target for shot number three. Don't try to get home in two — you'll never make it!

The next two holes are quite similar, both being about 360 yards in length and with fairways bending around lakes, one to the left and one to the right. No. 16 is the tougher of the two because the lake comes close to the front and right side of the green, making for a delicate approach shot.

No. 17 is a 325-yard par four that is straightaway and plays a little downhill. A drive and a short iron should get most golfers on the green, which is well trapped to the right front, left front, and left rear.

The 540-yard par five 18th is a good finishing hole because of the demand it places on your approach shot to the green. This hole plays straight off the tee, doglegs a little left, then bends again to the right. A bunker awaits in the left rough and three more in the right rough, but plenty of room stretches between them. Two more traps are in the left rough as you approach the green. The lake immediately in front and to the green's right forces an all-carry and accurate approach. Don't be long though, because plenty of trouble hides behind and below the green in the form of water, thick heavy grass, and rocks. Make every effort to come into this green from the fairway's left side, and don't try to reach it in two.

The Snowmass Club Golf Links, like Beaver Creek and Singletree at Vail, will only get better as time goes by. Next time out try it from the Championship tees. But for now, a dip in the pool, and a sauna or steam bath will top off a great day of golf at Snowmass.

SHERATON AT STEAMBOAT GOLF RESORT

LOCATION:	Steamboat Springs, Colorado. From Highway 40 exit on Mt. Werner Rd., turn left on Steamboat Blvd., turn right on Clubhouse Rd., then turn left on Golf Course Road.
TELEPHONE:	879-2220 Ext. 1071
COURSE FACILITIES:	Fully equipped pro shop, riding golf carts, pull carts, club rental, driving range, chipping and putting greens.
CLUBHOUSE FACILITIES:	Complete snack bar serving breakfast, lunch, sandwiches, beer, mixed and soft drinks.
LODGING:	Sheraton at Steamboat.
RESTAURANTS:	In addition to the Sheraton, numerous fine restaurants dot the town of Steamboat Springs as well as the village. Ask around.

GOLF COURSE:

	Par	Course Rating	Yardage
Championship	72	71.0	6906
Regular	72	69.0	6276
Ladies	72	72.7	5647

The Sheraton at Steamboat Golf Course ranks among the finest in the State. This Robert Trent Jones Jr. designed course was built in 1974 and possesses a full complement of all that makes a golf course great. The usual policy is that "guests only" of the Sheraton may play this golf course, but occasionally it is open for play by the public. Call the pro shop for this information.

Although most of the fairways are of good width and quite inviting, little room for an errant shot exists anyplace on the golf course. Yawning bunkers surround most of the greens, and strategically placed fairway traps along with interesting natural hazards add all the excitement the golfer needs for any one day. You can't help enjoying your day playing golf in this strikingly beautiful setting.

The 1st hole is a rather short par four at 354 yards. It plays down a straightaway, rather narrow fairway lined with aspen and shrubbery early on, but opening up somewhat as you approach the green. A sizeable bunker sits in the right rough shortly past the 150-yard marker, and the large undulating green is tightly trapped to the front, left, and rear. This elevated green calls for an all-carry, pinpoint approach shot to the putting surface.

No. 2 is a slightly longer par four at 365 yards, playing downhill off the tee, then uphill to the green. The fairway is well trapped to the left and right in the landing area, at which point it bends right a little. The deep rough to the left spells trouble, and the green is heavily bunkered. All in all, eight sand traps hazard this hole!

The holes keep getting a little longer with the 385-yard par four 3rd. This one also plays from an elevated tee, which is typical of many holes to come, and offers severe rough to the left and a well-placed fairway trap to the right at the bottom of the valley. Three bunkers, one to the left front, one to the right front, and another to the left side, closely guard this quite large green.

The first three holes have been building up to the number 1 handicap 4th, which is a 544-yard par five. This fairway is quite roomy, but is trapped on each side at the landing area. It plays downhill off the tee, then gradually uphill from that point to the green. Out-of-bounds is left off the tee, then both left and right after the first two fairway bunkers. Another fairway trap sits in the left rough about 130 yards from the green. Because of the elevated green, the putting surface is not visible for your approach shot and is well trapped to the front, left, and right front.

The 201-yard par three 5th is a beautiful golf hole. Proper club selection is a must from this highly elevated tee to the green well below the golfer. You should be able to back off one or two clubs because of the difference in elevation. Aspen and pine trees watch over the green from the rear, while a large left front trap creates further concern by crowding the green at that point.

We encounter our first water hazard in the form of Fish Creek at the 342-yard par four 6th. This hole doglegs left around a bend in Fish Creek and calls for a lofted wood or long iron off the tee. Target the 150-yard marker at the far end of the dogleg. The approach is uphill from that point to a green that is trapped left front, right front, and to the rear. It's best not to try to cut the corner here because you will probably end up in either severe rough or water.

In my opinion, No. 7 at 534 yards and par five is one of the most difficult holes on the course. It is straight off the tee to the top of a hill, then left to the green, which seems miles away. A fairway trap guards the outside corner of this left-hand dogleg, and a grouping of thick bushes and rocks protect the inside corner. Another fairway bunker occupies the right rough about 90 yards out from the green. Very few golfers will ever reach this heavily trapped green in two.

No. 8 is another beautiful par three from an elevated tee to a green 161 yards away. This green presents a miniature target because it is surrounded by a lake on three sides, and a long narrow bunker crowds the green to the left. No room for error on this hole.

I like the 322-yard par four 9th. The temptation here is to cut the corner of this right-hand dogleg, but the tall aspen trees and shallow landing area make it very risky. It's best to hit a lofted wood or long iron over the edge of the lake to the corner, then approach the green from there with a short iron. Too long a shot off the tee will put you through the fairway and in deep rough. Don't get cute on this hole — play it safe.

The back nine starts off with a challenging and troublesome par five. This 497-yard hole is roomy off the tee and plays straightaway with no fairway sand traps. Sounds easy, doesn't it? Well, it isn't. The fairway narrows sharply for your second shot, and Fish Creek crosses the fairway about 80 yards in front of the green. This forces the golfer to either lay up short of the creek or "go for it." Most golfers will do best to lay up short, then hit a short iron to the green, which is quite shallow and well trapped to the front and left rear. Many a golf ball has found its final resting place in Fish Creek in front of this 10th green. (see sketch pg. 212)

A profusion of sand traps greets the golfer from the tee at the 172-yard par three 11th. Don't be short here or you will surely

Sheraton Steamboat No. 10
497 yards par five!

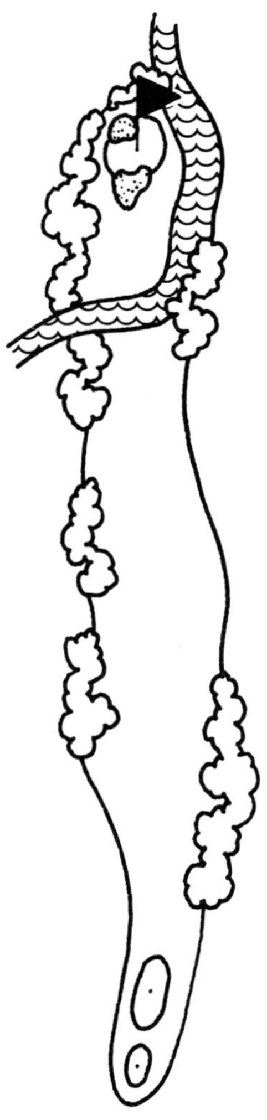

find sand. No. 12 is another respectable golf hole at 373 yards and par four. It plays fairly level and straightaway, but two fairway bunkers guard the landing area, and two greenside bunkers protect the putting surface.

For the number 2 handicap hole we have the 572-yard par five 13th. It's a tough hole, requiring two strong woods and an accurate approach to get on this green in regulation. Trouble lies to the fairway's right side in the form of out-of-bounds and deep grassy rough. This fairway bends a little right, and a fairway bunker sits to the left in the rough short of the outside corner. Two more bunkers lie to the left about 60 yards short of the green, and another two extend out from the green's lower right corner. This is another wide but shallow green.

All of the par threes on this golf course possess unmatched scenic qualities, and the 145-yard par three 14th is no exception. The tee shot here is over Fish Creek to a long and rather narrow green that is guarded by Fish Creek on the left and two bunkers above and to the green's right. This hole will usually play somewhat shorter than indicated, and accuracy off the tee is essential for par.

The next two holes both dogleg right, and neither of them can be taken for granted. No. 15 is 313 yards, par four, over Fish Creek off the tee and over Fish Creek again in front of the green. To further complicate matters, Fish Creek also crowds the fairway's right side at the inside corner of the dogleg. Don't cut the corner here. Play a lofted wood or long iron off the tee to the corner and a short-to-medium iron approach from there. The green is elevated, well trapped left front, right side and rear, and presents an extremely small target.

No water bothers the 330-yard par four 16th, but the fairway traps at the outside corner of this right-hand dogleg and the heavily bunkered elevated green make this hole play much longer than indicated.

No. 17 is another beautiful par three at 177 yards. The green is well below the golfer as he stands on this elevated tee, and it will play at least one and maybe two clubs less than normally hit for this distance. Two bunkers, one left and one right, guard each side of the green.

The golf course finishes with a par five of medium difficulty at 489 yards. It plays straightforward, and most of the trouble is to the right in the form of deep, thick rough. Fish Creek crosses the fairway early on, and a bothersome sand trap dwells in the right rough near the landing area. Another fairway bunker is well short of the green to the left front and can catch a second shot if you are short off the tee. The green is heavily trapped to the front, left and right.

Steamboat Springs is a year-round sportsman's paradise. In addition to this fabulous golf course, it offers excellent fishing and hunting, as well as some of the finest skiing in Colorado. River rafting, horseback riding, hiking, and rodeo are other popular activities in the area. The charm and appeal of Steamboat is anything but seasonal, so come back often and enjoy the good life in this beautiful country.

SKYLAND RESORT

LOCATION: Crested Butte, Colorado. Base of Crested Butte Mountain.

TELEPHONE: 349-6129

COURSE FACILITIES: Fully equipped pro shop, riding golf carts, club rental, driving range, chipping and putting greens.

CLUBHOUSE FACILITIES: Restaurant serving breakfast, lunch, sandwiches, dinner, beer, mixed and soft drinks. Other facilities include indoor tennis, racquet ball courts, and a health club.

LODGING: Crested Butte has long been known for its excellent skiing, so plenty of good accommodations inhabit the area.

RESTAURANTS: Some excellent restaurants grace Crested Butte. Best to make local inquiry, but it's hard to go wrong.

GOLF COURSE:

	Par	Course Rating	Yardage
Championship	72		7300
Regular	72		7250
Ladies	72		6150

This golf course is scheduled to open for the 1984 golfing season. It's a Robert Trent Jones designed golf course, so you can expect plenty of sand traps. The front nine is more like the typical American golf course, while the back nine is more like the Scottish courses. This is another beautiful and scenic part of Colorado, and many things to do abound here other than playing golf. Bring your fishing pole, because this is great trout fishing country. You will enjoy the town of Crested Butte. It is an old mining town and has preserved the architecture of its time. I'm anxiously looking forward to playing this golf course, which I'm sure will be one of the outstanding courses in Colorado.

TAMARRON

LOCATION: Durango, Colorado. Eighteen miles north of Durango on Highway 550.

TELEPHONE: 247-8801

COURSE FACILITIES: Fully equipped pro shop, club rental, riding golf carts, driving range for irons only, chipping and putting greens.

CLUBHOUSE FACILITIES: Restaurant, snack bar, and lounge serving breakfast, lunch, sandwiches, and dinner, as well as beer, mixed and soft drinks. Also available to guests are indoor-outdoor swimming pool, jacuzzi whirlpool, steam baths, sauna, exercise room, and tennis courts, both indoors and outdoors. Tamarron has excellent meeting facilities for groups up to 600 people, and a good number of interesting and distinctive shops should draw the attention of the non-golfer.

RESTAURANTS: Eat at Tamarron. The food is outstanding.

LODGING: Tamarron. Great accommodations.

GOLF COURSE:

	Par	Course Rating	Yardage
Championship	72	72.5	6900
Regular	72	69.9	6400
Ladies	72	72	5400

Situated in the foothills of Colorado's San Juan mountains, Tamarron's 18-hole championship golf course has been carefully designed to provide the golfer with the highest challenge to his golfing skills. The beauty in this part of Colorado is incomparable, and the golf course offers a little of everything: age-old oak and aspen, ponderosa pine, broad rolling grassy meadows, lakes, streams, and sand traps galore.

Colorado's blue sky and fresh mountain air are thrown in for good measure. Very little has been changed from what mother nature created. Tamarron is more than golf, it is a complete year-round resort offering a wide variety of activities for everyone. One must be a guest at Tamarron in order to play this fine golf course. Don't miss an opportunity to do so.

No easy holes at Tamarron, and the 405-yard par four 1st hole is a good example. A large pine tree dominates the fairway at the corner of this left-hand dogleg and comes into play for your second shot. Hit your tee shot and hope that you are either short or a little past the tree. This green is long and narrow, so take plenty of club when approaching it. Be careful of the small creek at the green's right and the trap in front.

The 530-yard par five 2nd hole doesn't back off any because it is the number 1 handicap. It is a beautiful, treelined, right-hand dogleg that plays downhill, across a valley, then uphill to the green. Many humps and valleys dominate the terrain along the way. A large fairway bunker sits to the left about 140 yards out from the green, while another large trap is located below and to the green's right front. Three other smaller bunkers crowd the edges of this rather long thin green. Par on this hole will be difficult for the best golfers.

The 345-yard par four 3rd calls for a 220-yard downhill tee shot. The fairway doglegs left at that point, and from there it is a short iron over the small creek in front of the green. Two small traps guard the green's right side, and a smaller one sits to the left rear. This hole requires more finesse than strength.

No. 4 is a 190-yard par three from an elevated tee to a large green that is protected by a yawning bunker to the green's left front and two smaller ones to the right. Trees are everywhere, except on the playing area.

The 5th hole is a short one at 335 yards and par four. You can't see the green from the highly elevated tee, and the fairway doglegs severely right. Aim over the tall pine tree at the corner, and a 220-yard drive should find your ball well positioned in the fairway. This green is heavily trapped with one to the right front and two others to the left front.

The course levels out with the 350-yard par four 6th, but water in the form of a lake lines the fairway's right side, and the landing area at 220 yards off the tee is only about 20 yards wide. Accuracy is a must on this hole.

The 150-yard par three 7th might be considered an easy hole except for the all-carry shot over water in front and to the right of the green. The trap to the green's left, along with all the water, makes for a small target.

I think No. 8 is a real challenge. This hole continues level, but your drive is an all-carry shot of about 180 yards over a lake immediately in front and to the left of another lake that cannot be seen from the tee. This fairway narrows sharply at the green which is guarded by two large traps, one to the front and another to the right front. This steeply terraced green calls for some touchy putts.

Although No. 9 at 380 yards and par four is only moderately long, it is anything but a sure par. As one stands on this elevated tee surveying the scene below, he has the feeling that he can clear the lake that juts into the fairway's right side. Don't try it. Stay to the left and you will have a nice open second shot to the green that is trapped to the right front and left.

No. 10 is one of the more interesting holes at Tamarron. Play for about 210 yards off the tee. Any more and your ball will find the rough of a steep embankment that drops down to a much lower level of the fairway. Favor the right side a little off the tee. As you stand at the edge of the fairway's upper level, the scene below presents an awesome picture. Although the green is large, it is almost completely surrounded by monstrous sand traps, as well as plenty of water to the left and to the left rear. A fairway wood or medium iron should reach this green from the edge of the fairway's top level.

From another elevated tee, it's downhill then gradually uphill for the 480-yard par five 11th. A small pond hides in the left rough a little short of the fairway's landing area, and a small stream extends along the right side. This green is well trapped with a large fairway bunker about 40 yards to the front, a long narrow trap guarding the green's right side, and a smaller one to the left front.

No. 12 is a hole of medium difficulty that plays uphill to a par four at 380 yards. This fairway slopes rather sharply right to left, and the quite narrow, but deep green is protected on the left front by a sizeable trap. The picturesque 13th at 160 yards and par three is the easiest hole at Tamarron. The green is well below the tee and is guarded by left and right front bunkers. Take two less clubs off this tee.

The number 2 handicap hole is the 530-yard par five 14th. It plays a little uphill, is straight off the tee, doglegs left for your second shot, then right again shortly before the green. A monstrous bunker lies in waiting in the left rough, so favor the right side of the fairway off the tee. Two other huge sand traps just short of the green add excitement and force an accurate approach to this green that is further protected by a wide, thin bunker to the rear. It will take five perfect golf shots to par this hole.

Although not rated as one of the more difficult holes at Tamarron, the 130-yard par three 15th is nevertheless quite demanding. The wide thin green is bunkered in front by a sand trap the same width as the green. Another smaller sand trap sits behind and a little above the putting surface, which slopes to the middle and is quite difficult to putt.

No. 16 at 415 yards and par four has a two-level fairway, and neither the second level nor the green can be seen from the tee. Play for the center of the upper level fairway, then aim for the target on the tree showing the center line of the green. A large lake guards the left side of the green and the second part of the fairway, which are both well below and to the left of your drive off the tee. Right front and right side sand traps make this green a small target from the plateau above.

The 355-yard par four 17th is not long, but is a tight little golf hole. Water lines the fairway's right side from tee to green, so stay left off the tee. The approach to the green is over a stream, and for a change no traps reach up to grab your ball.

It's all uphill for the short 330-yard par four 18th. A lofted wood or long iron should work best off the tee. Favor the left side of the fairway a little. Don't leave it out to the right or you can be in the bushes, trees, and long grass of the difficult sidehill rough. Four traps surround the green, making for another small target. Keep it in play and this hole should yield to par rather easily.

The more you play Tamarron, the better you'll like it. No question about it being one of Colorado's most challenging and difficult golf courses. In addition to the many activities available at Tamarron itself, be sure to drive through the San

Juan mountains to Silverton and Ouray. These two historic Colorado towns will prove quite interesting. A jeep trip to the higher country in July and August can be a memorable experience. In fact, there's so much to do and enjoy in the great outdoors of this part of Colorado that I'm sure you will want to come back for more at another time.

SMILE
YOU'RE PLAYING GOLF
IN COLORADO

TIARA RADO

LOCATION: Grand Junction, Colorado. From the center of town take Grand Avenue west for about 5 miles or until you come to South Broadway. At this point turn left and go about 2 miles, and you will be at the golf course.

TELEPHONE: 242-9979

COURSE FACILITIES: Fully equipped pro shop, riding golf carts, pull carts, club rental, and putting green.

CLUBHOUSE FACILITIES: Snack bar serving hot sandwiches, lunch, beer, and soft drinks.

LODGING: Plenty of excellent motels in Grand Junction, most of them located off I-70 on Horizon Drive.

RESTAURANTS: Several good restaurants located around the Lincoln Park and downtown areas. The Horizon Drive part of town also offers a wide choice of good places to eat. Best to ask around.

GOLF COURSE:

	Par	Course Rating	Yardage
Regular	71		6145
Ladies	71		5030

Tiara Rado is an excellent golf course situated in a beautiful setting at the foot of the Colorado National Monument in the Redlands area. Twelve years is not a long time for a golf course to mature in this part of the world, but Tiara Rado offers lush fairways and well-manicured greens. The front nine is the older of the two nines and plays skintight, while the back nine is newer and quite open. You will need most of the shots in your bag to score well on this golf course, and the subtle break in the greens is apt to leave you talking to yourself. Don't miss Tiara Rado — it's a fine golf course and also a part of some magnificent Colorado scenery.

The course starts out with a rather easy par four that plays straightaway and offers very little in the way of trouble. A good way to start. Out-of-bounds is on the right, and two large cottonwoods guard entrance to a small green with several mounds around the edges. This 365 yard hole should yield a lot of pars or better.

No. 2 is a tough one, calling for well-placed shots from tee to green. This 470-yard par five plays straight off the tee through an opening of tamarac and cottonwood trees to a rather tight landing area. Most golfers will do best to hit a long iron or fairway wood off the tee and play short of this narrow area between the trees. The fairway opens up considerably for your second shot to short of the green. A small irrigation ditch guards the green's right side. The trees on both sides of the fairway are the big problem on this hole, which I think is one of the best on the golf course.

The next hole, No. 3, is a rather routine 170-yard par three playing straight and level, although a little uphill. Out-of-bounds is to the right and behind the green.

Most golfers will have to play short of the small irrigation ditch that crosses the 4th fairway about where you would expect a good drive to end up. This will leave a long iron or fairway wood for a second shot, and par will not come easily on this 390-yard par four hole. Of further concern here is out-of-bounds, which is quite close to the fairway's right side.

Out-of-bounds is both left and right on the 340-yard par four 5th. This hole plays gradually uphill toward the mountains. The fairway bends gently left, and another small irrigation ditch crosses the fairway shortly in front of the green.

No. 6 is a lengthy par five at 545 yards that doglegs left and has out-of-bounds on the right. The drive is over a small gully in front of the tee. This gully follows the fairway along the left side all the way to the green. A large cottonwood sits just a little short of the inside corner. Your target off the tee is the right bush in the fairway. Out-of-bounds is both sides of the fairway from the dogleg to the green. This hole plays all of its 545 yards and then some.

The 320-yard par four 7th is an interesting golf hole. It plays somewhat downhill with a lake on the right and an irrigation ditch crossing the fairway diagonally right to left going away from the golfer. The tee shot is left of the lake, over the irrigation ditch to a quite small landing area. Use a long iron or lofted wood, and this should leave a short iron to the green, which is surrounded by an orchard of apricot trees. Accuracy off the tee is essential for par here.

No. 8 is a 165-yard one-shotter through a narrow opening among the apricot trees. This is not a difficult par three hole unless you dub one off the tee into the orchard. An irrigation ditch that you can't see from the tee runs quite close to the left side of the green. You might want to take one less club on this hole, because it plays a little shorter than indicated.

The number 1 handicap hole is the 440-yard par four 9th. The fairway doglegs right around a sizeable lake, and it is almost impossible to cut any distance off by trying to carry a portion of this lake. Play it safe, down the middle, through the opening in the orchard. This will leave a long iron or fairway wood to the green. Be grateful for a par here.

You can survey the entire back nine from the vantage point of the No. 10 tee. The fairway, which is well below the golfer, is 340-yards long, par four, doglegs left at a point where a cement irrigation ditch crosses the fairway, and has out-of-bounds along the left side. Not a hard hole, but an interesting one.

No. 11 is a rather normal 160-yard par three that plays level from tee to green, but for a change does offer a couple of sand traps. One sits in the left rough short of the green, and another curves around the green's right side.

Target your drive to the right of the elm tree seen in the distance as you tee it up on the lengthy 435-yard par four 12th. The fairway bends left around this tree which is about 190 yards out from the green. A small pond, not visible from the fairway, sits to the left front of the green about 40 yards out in the rough. Although a lot of trouble does not plague this hole, it's a tough one to par because of its length.

Pinpoint accuracy is a must on the 130-yard par three 13th. This hole plays over a large pond that comes to within 10 yards of the green, which sits at the foot of a craggy hill. The green is wide, but shallow, so don't misjudge your distance here.

Play left of the lone cottonwood tree growing in the right edge of the fairway on the 510-yard par five 14th. This should be a routine par five for most golfers and will yield a lot of birdies to the long hitters.

No. 15 is a short 300-yard par four that plays level and straight, but does bend a little as you approach the green. Your target off the tee is a little right of the flattop rocky hill at the end of the fairway. A sand trap sits at the green's front, and the rough behind the green is quite severe. Best to approach this green from the right.

Play right of the lone cottonwood tree in the distance for the 360-yard par four 16th. Two sand traps, level with the fairway and not easily seen, sit to the right front of this green in the right rough. This hole is quite similar in character to the previous two holes.

One of the best holes on the course is the 400-yard par four 17th. It plays straight and level off the tee, out-of-bounds is very close to the fairway's left edge, and a pond guards the golfer's approach to the green. The placement of this green is interesting in that it lies to the left of the craggy hill that has been so prominent on this back nine. It also crowds the side of steep sloping terrain to its left. As a result of all these natural obstacles, the green is tightly protected and forces an accurate, rather long approach shot to get on in regulation.

No. 18 is a short 305-yard par four from an elevated tee down to a valley below, then up a U-shaped valley to an elevated green. A long iron or lofted wood is the shot off the tee, and it must be well placed or you can easily find the rough on either side of the fairway. This should leave a short iron approach to a wide shallow green whose putting surface cannot be seen from the fairway. This is not a difficult finishing hole unless you find the rough. If you do you are in real trouble.

Grand Junction is the hub of many activities in this part of Colorado. Ranching, farming, mining, and oil are all flourishing industries in the area. The Colorado National Monument and Grand Mesa are scenic attractions that one should see while visiting here. The mild weather in this part of the state makes all outdoor activities popular and, of course, makes it possible to play golf most of the year. Tiara Rado is already a fine golf course, and it will get even better as time goes by. Don't miss it.

VAIL GOLF CLUB

LOCATION: Vail, Colorado. Follow South Frontage Road 1½ miles east of town - turn right and follow the road to the clubhouse.

TELEPHONE: 1-800-332-3666 Colorado only
303-476-1330 Outside Colorado

COURSE FACILITIES: Fully equipped pro shop, riding golf carts, pull carts, club rental, chipping and putting greens.

CLUBHOUSE FACILITIES: Restaurant serving lunch, sandwiches, dinner, beer, mixed and soft drinks.

LODGING: Plenty of accommodations in Vail Village.

RESTAURANTS: In addition to the restaurant at the course, you have a good variety of fine places to eat in the Vail area. Best to ask around.

GOLF COURSE:

	Par	Course Rating	Yardage
Championship	71	70.5	7008
Regular	71	68.0	6282
Ladies	73	73.1	5899

This fine mountain golf course was built in 1967 and is one of the top quality courses in Colorado. It extends up and down both sides of Gore Creek, which comes into play on at least half of the holes. Numerous other water hazards, plenty of sand traps, and an abundance of natural vegetation provide the golfer a real workout for all 18 holes. If you can arrange it, play this golf course in the fall when the aspen are turning. It's one of the most beautiful sights you will ever see! Most of the holes at Vail are relatively flat, so even at an elevation of 8250 feet it's not a difficult one to walk. You can't help enjoying this great golf course.

Vail begins with two friendly par fours, the 394-yard 1st and the 325-yard 2nd. They both play straightaway, are level, and offer little difficulty. They are good warm-up holes, as is the 132-yard par three 3rd, which plays over a small grassy valley to a green whose putting surface cannot be seen from the tee.

Beginning with the 354-yard par four 4th hole, the golf course toughens considerably. This hole plays slightly uphill off the tee, and the green is not visible as you line up your drive. A sand trap sits in the right rough at the inside corner where the fairway bends gently to the right. Out-of-bounds is quite close to the fairway's right side, and the green is trapped left and right front. A drive that stays in the fairway should leave a short iron to the green and a possible par.

No. 5, at 357-yards playing downhill with a right-hand dogleg and heavily treelined, is an interesting hole. A lofted wood or long iron is the best tee shot here, because you don't want to hit through the dogleg into the rough. Stay in the fairway, play for a left-to-right bounce, and you should have a short downhill approach to a friendly green without any sand traps. Accuracy is essential off the tee in order to par this hole.

The number 1 handicap hole is the 423-yard par four 6th, and rightly so. Target your tee shot a little right of the tall evergreen tree in the left rough shortly off the tee. This fairway kicks right to left and doglegs left rather sharply about 170 yards from the green. A large rock appears in the left rough at this point. The terrain on this hole is quite rolling, and you are almost certain to have an uneven lie as you approach the green, which is closely trapped left and right front. This is a fine golf hole with a lot more contour than most of the holes here at Vail.

One of Vail's most breathtaking views of the Gore Range in the distance can be enjoyed from the highly elevated tee of the 177-yard par three 7th hole. The green is well below the golfer, and he must negotiate a left front bunker as well as Gore Creek a little farther to the left. Take about two clubs less for this shot.

Usually 479 yards is not long for a par five, but the 8th hole plays considerably longer because of the trout pond that beckons short of the green by about 125 yards. The driving area is guarded on the left by Gore Creek and on the right by two bothersome sand bunkers. The good golfer can clear this pond easily with his second shot, but most golfers will probably want to lay up and hit a short iron over the pond to the green.

This two-level green is tightly trapped to the right front, left front, left and left rear. Not an easy hole, and lots of golf balls find their final resting place in the trout pond.

The 407-yard par four 9th, with Gore Creek continuing along the fairway's left side, is another good hole. It plays straightaway and level, but the green is demanding in that it is protected on the right by a sand trap and on the left by Gore Creek. Not a lot of room for error when approaching this green. This is a very respectable par four, with Gore Creek the main trouble maker.

No. 10, at 377 yards, is quite similar to the previous hole, only a little shorter. Gore Creek continues along the left, and the green is trapped to the left front. A potential source of trouble is a grouping of trees crowding the fairway from the right. Stay in the fairway off the tee, and No. 10 should be an easy par.

One of the more interesting holes at Vail is the 366-yard par four 11th. The tee shot is over Gore Creek, which now changes to the fairway's right side. A right-hand dogleg in this fairway greets you after your drive, and the green which is trapped on the right is one of the most treacherous on the golf course. Be grateful for a par on this hole.

For a change Gore Creek does not come into play on the 546-yard par five 12th hole, but a bunker in the right rough can catch a short tee shot, and a large cottonwood tree grows in the left portion of the fairway about 116 yards short of the green. However, once past this tree, a short pitch and a putt should yield a par.

The 387-yard par four 13th plays straightaway, but offers a difficult driving area with out-of-bounds left and hidden water on the right. This long narrow pond in the right rough is not noticeable from the tee. The green is trapped left and possesses a rather touchy putting surface.

With the 360-yard par four 14th we head back toward the clubhouse, and I think one of the best holes on the golf course. It usually plays into the prevailing wind, and as a result will play much longer than the indicated yardage. Gore Creek crowds the fairway's left side, then crosses diagonally short of the green, forcing a lofted wood or long iron for a tee shot. Once safely in the fairway, the golfer faces an elevated green

Vail Golf Club No. 14
360 yards par four

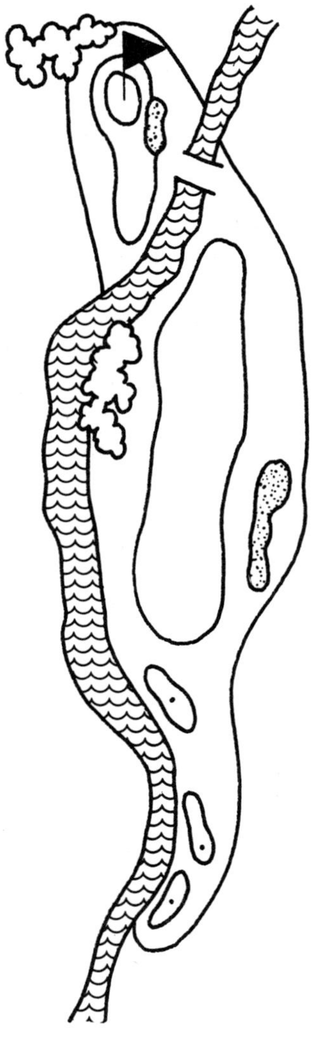

that is set in against the mountains. The second shot must cross the river, and the green is a two-level one where a three-putt is not uncommon. (see sketch pg. 228)

No. 15 is quite a hole! It's only 100 yards, par three, and is supposed to be the easiest one on the course, but it seems to cause more problems than many of the others. The tee shot is from a highly elevated tee, over Gore Creek which crowds the green's front side, to a green that is rather shallow and heavily trapped to the rear. Too short and you're in the water. Too long and you're in the sand. A sand or pitching wedge is the club for most golfers. A memorable hole!

It will take a strong drive to reach the corner of the left-hand dogleg on the 405-yard par four 16th. Favor the fairway's right side, or the trees at the inside corner will block your shot to the green. Two traps at the outside corner of the fairway narrow the landing area considerably, so accuracy is a must from the tee. This hole should yield a good number of pars, but watch out for the right front greenside bunker.

The language in the Vail Golf Club yardage book best describes the difficult 194-yard par three 17th: "Tough is often not adequate to describe this hole. Its length requires a long iron or fairway wood to a green surrounded by water. Jack Nicklaus says, 'it's the best hole on the course'."

Trout ponds surround the teeing area at the 499-yard par five 18th. Two fairway traps guard both sides of this left-hand dogleg at the corner, but the larger problem is the grove of trees, bushes, and thick grass at the inside bend. Cutting the corner here can be very risky, so best to play down the fairway. Two more bunkers come into play guarding the left front of the green as you approach it from the fairway. This is a fine finishing hole that demands the golfers best for par.

It's great to play Vail during the spring and summer, but in the autumn the beauty and color is beyond description by all but mother nature. Colorado is privileged to have many scenic and colorful areas, and Vail, without a doubt, is one of them.

SECTION 4

SOUTHEAST PLAINS AND FOOTHILLS

THE BROADMOOR

The world famous Broadmoor Hotel means many things to different people, but to the golfer it signifies three superb and challenging championship golf courses. Golf was first played at the Broadmoor in 1918. Master golf course architect Donald Ross designed the original tract, which was known at the time as "The Broadmoor Nine." Five years later the course was expanded to 18 holes. In 1954 Robert Trent Jones designed an additional nine holes, and for 10 years the Broadmoor offered 27 holes of golf to its guests. In 1964 Robert Trent Jones completed the design for another nine holes, and since that time guests of the hotel have had the privilege of playing on two of the finest golf courses in the world. Actually the final layout has resulted in a combination of Donald Ross and Robert Trent Jones designs on each course.

In 1976 the Broadmoor South Golf Course was opened for play. This course is an Arnold Palmer Enterprise design, and the architect was Ed Seay. The same high standards of Broadmoor East and West were met and expanded at Broadmoor South. To play any of these three outstanding golf courses is a true golfing experience.

The setting for these courses is absolutely beautiful, and the natural terrain at the foot of Cheyenne Mountain is ideal. One characteristic of all three courses is the large, undulating greens. They are very fast, and if you don't lag it close, you can almost count on a three-putt. The rough can be either friendly or unfriendly, depending on how they cut the grass, and the trees, sand traps, water hazards, and other natural obstacles all combine to make each Broadmoor course challenging to play.

The Broadmoor Hotel is another complete story in itself. Let me just say that its convention and meeting facilities, accommodations, dining, service, fine shops, and many other amenities are second to none, and any stay at the Broadmoor is a memorable and exciting experience.

BROADMOOR EAST

LOCATION: Colorado Springs, Colorado. Take Exit 140 B off Interstate 25 near the south end of Colorado Springs. Get on Nevada and go south until you see the sign indicating a right turn to the Broadmoor. Continue on this street, Lake Avenue, until you come to the hotel.

TELEPHONE: 634-7711

COURSE FACILITIES: Fully equipped pro shop, riding golf carts, club rental, driving range, chipping and putting greens.

CLUBHOUSE FACILITIES: Restaurant serving breakfast, lunch, dinner, beer, mixed and soft drinks.

LODGING: Broadmoor Hotel. One must be a guest of the hotel in order to play golf at any of the Broadmoor courses.

RESTAURANTS: Only guests of the hotel will be served at the golf course restaurant.

GOLF COURSE:

	Par	Course Rating	Yardage
Championship	72	71.6	7218
Regular	72	69.2	6555
Ladies	73	73.6	5954

Broadmoor East is a championship golf course in the true sense of the word. It possesses all of the necessary ingredients: great natural terrain, large fast and undulating greens, strategically placed sand traps in the fairways and surrounding the greens, water hazards, deep grassy rough that can be difficult to recover from, and an abundance of trees, shrubbery, and underbrush, all of which adds up to a golf course of exceptional challenge and beauty.

Cheyenne Mountain forms a unique backdrop for the 385-yard par four 1st hole. The tee is elevated, and pine trees line both sides of the fairway at the landing area. The green is also elevated and trapped to the right front and left side. This is a good starter hole and not as easy as it sounds.

No. 2 is straightaway, uphill, par four, and 330 yards in length. Guarding the fairway are two bunkers, one in the left rough 143 yards from the green and another in the right rough 111 yards from the green. The green is also closely trapped, with two at the left front and another at the rear that is not visible from the fairway. Take a little more club than you might think necessary when approaching this green.

The 366-yard par four 3rd plays straight off the tee, then bends gently right. The interesting part of this hole is the approach shot to the elevated green, which is guarded by three yawning bunkers cut into its lower front side. No room to roll the ball on, so an all-carry shot is essential in order to stay out of the sand.

Target the sand trap seen in the distance on the 367-yard par four 4th hole. This fairway has lots of pine trees lining both sides, and it bends a little to the left. Again, the green is elevated and well trapped with one to the left front and another to the right front.

The short 137-yard par three 5th leaves absolutely no room for error. A canyon crosses the fairway, then turns and crowds the green's left side. Sand traps are situated to the green's right front and rear. This all makes for a small target, requiring an accurate and well-placed tee shot.

The first par five on the course is really a good one. Only 468 yards in length, it plays much longer because it is uphill off the tee, doglegs left, and a lake immediately in front of the green will cause most players to lay up short. Thick, heavy scrub oak and underbrush to the fairway's left side make it risky to cut the corner, and the smart golfer will do best to play it down the middle. From the top of the hill it is 175 yards to the front edge of the water and 205 yards to the back edge. Make your own decision about "going for it." Further complicating this No. 6 hole at greenside are three sand traps, one to the left front, one to the right front, and another to the rear. Approaching this green over the water and bunkers is intimidating and just a little scary!

Broadmoor East No. 7
456 yards par four

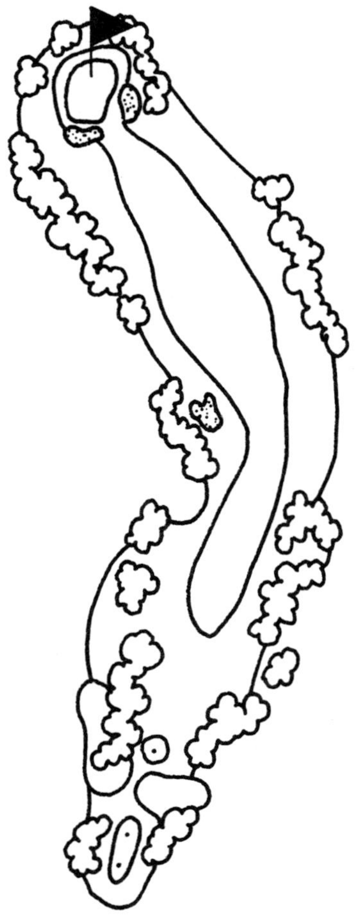

No. 7 is 456 yards and par four. It is the number 1 handicap and an excellent golf hole. The fairway doglegs left 240 yards off the tee, and lots of tree trouble greets you on the same side. Of further concern is the large bunker in the left rough at the inside corner. This hole plays downhill from tee to green, but that doesn't seem to shorten it by any significant amount. Left and right front traps guard entry to the green, which is a tough one to hold with your approach shot. Take time to enjoy the great view of Colorado Springs and the prairie to the east from the dogleg point of this fairway. (see sketch pg. 236)

The 420-yard par four 8th is another fine golf hole. It doglegs left and plays over several sizeable humps and valleys in the fairway. Avoid the area to the right and short of the green, because the shrubbery and underbrush is thick and plentiful over there. Two traps cut into the lower right side of the elevated green are an additional hazard.

No. 9 plays from an elevated tee to a well-trapped green, which presents a large and inviting target. However, at 199 yards it's no cinch par, and the three bunkers make this par three hole a good one.

The back nine begins with three respectable par fours. No. 10 is a long 468 yards, doglegs right, is heavily treelined both sides, and plays to an elevated green that is trapped to the left and right front.

No. 11 has a left-hand bend in it and is 406 yards in length. A wide, tnin fairway bunker extends in from the left rough about 175 yards from the green, so stay to the right of this trap if at all possible. Your approach is over a small valley to a green protected by three sand traps, one to the left front, one to the right front, and another to the rear.

The 404-yard 12th plays from an elevated tee down a fairway that doglegs left at the landing area. Two fairway traps guard both corners of the dogleg. Split these bunkers with your tee shot if possible. Another valley extends in front of the green, and three greenside traps demand an accurate approach shot.

No. 13 is a rather easy 165-yard par three. It plays from an elevated tee to a green well belcw the golfer and is trapped to the left, front, and right sides. This is a good opportunity to pick up a par.

No. 14 is another realistic chance for a par. It's not a long par five at 506 yards because it plays downhill with no fairway bunkers to contend with. However, the fairway is treelined on both sides, and the green is trapped to the left and right sides.

I like No. 15. It is the number 2 handicap at 385 yards and par four. It plays downhill a little and bends slightly to the right. Favor the fairway's left side off the tee. Your approach is over a large pond, and the distance is deceiving, but play it in relation to the 150-yard marker. A right front trap guards the green.

No. 16 is a beautiful par three. This 138-yard one-shotter is all-carry over water to a large green trapped to the left side. Don't be short, but any putt from above the hole is very touchy.

The 401-yard par four 17th plays straightaway and uphill. About 40 yards out from the green in the right rough is a fairway bunker, and for a change we don't have an elevated green. Guarding this green are two sand traps, one to the left front and another not noticeable from the fairway to the right side.

Completing the back nine is an excellent finishing hole at 554 yards and par five. Target your tee shot a little right of the group of tall spruce trees seen in the left rough. Another pond sits immediately in front of the green, and most players will have to lay up short of it with their second shot. Two strong woods and a short iron should get most good golfers on in regulation. The green is trapped left front. Try to favor the fairway's left side from tee to green on this 18th hole.

Don't be discouraged if you don't score well on this golf course. The best players have trouble, so you are always in good company. Try again tomorrow on Broadmoor West. After that, give Broadmoor South a shot. You may not do any better, but you will have played on three great golf courses.

BROADMOOR SOUTH

LOCATION:	Colorado Springs, Colorado. Follow the signs from the main hotel of the clubhouse.
TELEPHONE:	634-7711
COURSE FACILITIES:	Fully equipped pro shop, riding golf carts, club rental, driving range, chipping and putting greens.
CLUBHOUSE FACILITIES:	Restaurant serving lunch, sandwiches, dinner, beer, mixed and soft drinks.
LODGING:	You must be a guest of the Broadmoor Hotel to play the course.
RESTAURANTS:	The Broadmoor.

GOLF COURSE:

	Par	Course Rating	Yardage
Championship	72	71.6	6781
Regular	72	68.5	6108
Ladies	70	72.0	5609

The Arnold Palmer designed South Golf Course is the most recently built of the three courses at the Broadmoor Hotel complex. It places a premium on accuracy off the tee as most holes are bordered on both sides by scrub oak. Hit a ball into the thick scrub oak lining the fairways and you deserve an award if you find it. South has been the site of many amateur tournaments in the last six years, so the championship tees are a real test.

The 1st hole is a 375-yard par four with a sheer drop about 225 yards from the regular tees. The approach is a downhill shot to a thin green protected front and back by large traps.

Use one extra club on the 171-yard 2nd in order to carry the two traps in front of the elevated green. No. 3 is an excellent birdie opportunity, and a big drive could leave you with a mid-iron second on this 449-yard par five. The lay-up area short and left of the green is well trapped as is the green itself.

A rough series of doglegs begin with the 359-yard 4th. Two traps line the left side of the landing areas on this dogleg left par four. Make sure you use enough club to avoid trouble around the green. From the regular tees the 368-yard 5th probably requires a fairway wood to short of the bushes and stream. Nearly everyone comes up short on their approach to this elevated green. Will you?

The 6th hole, a 466-yard par five, demands accuracy on both the drive and position shot short and left of the lake. A big hitter can get home here, but any mistake will prove costly.

A large trap protects entrance to the left-to-right sloping green on the 150-yard par three 7th. No. 8 is an uphill 393-yard par four and presents a very difficult second to a green surrounded by eight traps.

A good drive on the 360-yard par four 9th dogleg right leaves a short iron over two sand traps to an elevated two-tiered green. Check the pin placement and put it close or three putts are almost automatic.

A brief respite from the very tight fairways awaits on the 460-yard par five 10th. This is the widest driving area on the course, and the big hitter will be tempted to carry the traps, avoid the trees, water, and scrub oak, and go for the green in two.

There is another sharp drop-off 250 yards from the tee resulting in a downhill second shot to a difficult two-tiered green on the 369-yard par four 11th.

The big hitter must stay on this side of the gulley 250 yards off the tee on the 405-yard par four 12th. The approach is open to the elevated green which breaks sharply back to front. Only 107 yards long, the par three 13th is well trapped, and the water shouldn't affect most players.

The 14th demands an uphill and lengthy tee shot. At 384 yards the golfer must hit the ball long or be faced with a blind second. Hole No. 15 is another uphill par four, but at only 321 yards it provides a much needed break.

The par three 16th is 147 yards long and guarded front, back, right, and left by traps. Putting is a real challenge on this very difficult green.

Keep your tee ball left in the open spaces on the 362-yard 17th hole. For a change, the fairway widens on this dogleg right par four. The second is to a very thin green with traps in front and behind.

No. 18 is an excellent final hole. It's also a good driving hole with another wide fairway that allows the big hitter to let out the shaft and position himself to reach this 443-yard par five in two. The faint of heart will want to hit a short iron left for his third shot approach to yet another elevated green.

Some of the above distances may vary depending on placement of the tee markers. However, you will find the 150-yard markers to the green in the fairways quite accurate. Enjoy your game here at one of Colorado's finest championship golf courses. For both a thrill and a humbling experience, play South from the championship tees!

BROADMOOR WEST

LOCATION: Colorado Springs, Colorado. Take Exit 140 B off Interstate 25 near the south end of Colorado Springs. Get on Nevada and go south until you see the sign indicating a right turn to the Broadmoor. Continue on this street, Lake Avenue, until you come to the hotel.

TELEPHONE: 634-7711

COURSE FACILITIES: Fully equipped pro shop, riding golf carts, club rental, driving range, chipping and putting greens.

CLUBHOUSE FACILITIES: Restaurant serving breakfast, lunch, dinner, beer, mixed and soft drinks.

LODGING: Broadmoor Hotel. One must be a guest of the hotel in order to play golf at any of the Broadmoor courses.

RESTAURANTS: Only guests of the hotel will be served at the golf course restaurant.

GOLF COURSE:

	Par	Course Rating	Yardage
Championship	72	71.0	6937
Regular	72	67.3	6109
Ladies	73	71.1	5505

Although Broadmoor West is 446-yards shorter than the East course, it offers similar challenges. Actually, the fairways seem to be narrower and more heavily treelined, as well as more sloping and uneven. However, the golfer encounters the same type of large, elevated and slippery greens as on the East course. Huge, troublesome sand traps seem to be everywhere, and water hazards plague most of the par threes.

The course begins with a 359-yard par four that bends gently right at the 150-yard marker. Three bunkers guard the outside corner, and large spruce trees guard the inside corner. A little fade is a good shot off the tee, but be careful of out-of-bounds to the right. This green is level with the fairway, but surrounded by several grassy mounds, as well as sand traps to the front, right front, left rear, and right rear. The left rear trap is not visible from the fairway.

No. 2 is a 460-yard par five that plays straightaway over an uneven fairway with out-of-bounds on the right from tee to green. It is best to favor the fairway's left side here, so aim for the fairway trap in the left rough near the green. Only the strong hitter can reach the fairway traps in the right rough. A small valley lies in front of the well-trapped, elevated green.

There are plenty of small hills and valleys to play over on the 407-yard par four 3rd hole. Three separate but continuous bunkers lurk to the right of the landing area in the rough, and your approach shot is uphill to a green that is protected to the left and right side by two massive bunkers.

Although No. 4 is not long, I think it is an interesting and demanding golf hole. It is 323 yards, par four, and plays over a valley to an elevated green. Shrubbery and tree trouble extend to the right in the area of the small valley about 100 yards short of the green. Two sand traps are a further problem in the right rough as you approach the green from the valley. Favor the fairway's left side off the tee if at all possible. The green, which is trapped right front, left side, and left rear, is cut into the side of a grassy bank.

The 151-yard par three 5th is supposed to be one of the easy holes on the course, but I can't agree. True, it's a short one,but a real premium is placed on accuracy off the tee. The golfer must play over a valley to a green surrounded by water on the right and sand to the left and rear. All of this presents a very small target and plenty of opportunity to lose a stroke or two if you find any of the hazards.

The first significant dogleg is the 407-yard par four 6th. This fairway plays uphill off the tee and bends left about 175 yards from the green. The long ball hitter may cut a little off the corner, but it is quite risky. Two bunkers are cut into a grassy mound to the left of the landing area, and two more grassy mounds watch over the outside corner. This hole plays much longer than indicated, and most players will have a long iron or fairway wood for their second shot. The golfer must also contend with a huge trap to the green's left side. This number 1 handicap hole will not yield to par without a real struggle.

An accurate tee shot is essential on the 306-yard par four 7th hole. Using a lofted wood or medium-long iron will get most golfers uphill and to the corner of this left-hand dogleg. Be careful of the large bunker at the inside corner. It's easy to hit through the fairway and encounter tree trouble if you hit too much club off the tee. Trees are also in evidence to the fairway's left, which discourages most players from attempting to cut the corner. Play it safe to the corner, which will leave a short iron approach shot over a valley to a green trapped left and right front and left and right rear.

Keeping your ball in the fairway is a must on the 439-yard par five 8th. It plays straightforward, is quite narrow, and in addition to being heavily treelined has two fairway bunkers about 175 yards off the tee in the left rough. At the 150-yard marker the rough drops off sharply to the left, while shrubbery, scrub oak, and other underbrush crowd the fairway's right side at this point. This elevated green is tightly trapped on all sides, so an accurate approach shot is important if you expect to par this number 5 handicap hole.

Rounding out the front nine is a typical Broadmoor par three. This 175-yard 9th hole plays from an elevated tee to a picturesque green behind a pond, and the green is closely bunkered to the left front and the lower right front. Use plenty of club on this hole because the water snuggles up close to the green's front edge. Take a moment to enjoy the view of Colorado Springs and the eastern plains from this 9th green.

In my estimation, the 427-yard par five 10th hole is a tough one. In fact, it borders on the point of being unfair. It plays uphill off the tee to a quite narrow, tree and shrubbery-lined fairway that kicks sharply left to right. The two sand traps in the right rough catch a lot of balls hit off this tee. Your second shot is a lofted wood or long iron to a valley that crosses the fairway well below the elevated and heavily trapped green. Trees continue to haunt both sides of the fairway, and two more bunkers in the right rough short of the green also challenge the golfer.

Broadmoor West No. 12
415 yards par four

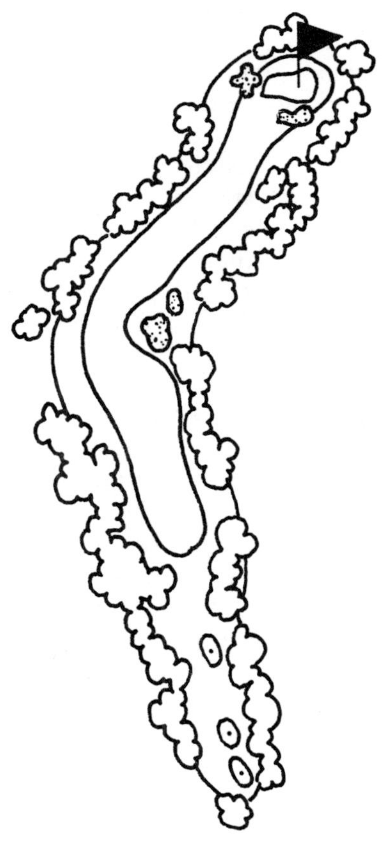

No. 11 is another demanding par three. From an elevated tee it is 163 yards over water and sand to the green well below the golfer. Again, accuracy is a must for par.

No. 12 is a great golf hole. It plays from an elevated tee down a heavily treelined and narrow fairway, then doglegs right about 230 to 240 yards from the tee. The inside corner is bunkered, and huge pine trees make it impossible to go for the green unless your drive is out there 200 to 240 yards. Even then it's a medium-long iron or lofted wood downhill to another well-trapped green. Without a long drive, par is beyond the reach of most players on this 415-yard par four hole. (see sketch pg. 245)

Another fine golf hole is the 353-yard downhill par four 13th. A precise tee shot and an approach of the same high standards will reward the golfer handsomely here, because finesse is more important than strength on this rather delicate golf hole. Two huge bunkers in the left rough are located about 200 yards from the tee, and a well-hit ball can clear them, but it's a little risky for most golfers. You might want to play to the right of these bunkers, although the fairway is quite narrow at that point. This will leave a short iron to the green which is protected by a good size pond to the right front and a sand trap to the left. The front edge of the water is 275 yards from the men's tee.

The number 2 handicap hole, No. 14, plays uphill, bends gradually to the left, is tightly bunkered at both sides of the landing area, and plays much longer than the indicated yardage. Three greenside sand traps give this hole more respect than it really needs. You can be proud of a par on this 357-yard par four.

No. 15 plays downhill, doglegs left, and is 403 yards long, with out-of-bounds left and a bunker in the rough at the inside corner. You will find plenty of room in the fairway to the right of this sand trap. The green is closely bunkered, and an accurate approach is essential in order to stay out of trouble.

For a change no water is encountered on the 182-yard par three 16th. However, it's not a sure par by any means. This hole plays gradually uphill through an opening in the trees to a green protected by four menacing sand traps. In addition, a grove of pine trees to the green's right side cannot be ignored.

It will take a 240-yard all-carry tee shot to cut the corner and clear the trap at the inside corner of the 355-yard, dogleg left, par four 17th. Most golfers will do best to hit a fairway wood to the corner, then a medium iron to the green. Guarding entry to the green are left front, left side, and right side sand traps, as well as a thick grove of scrub oak growing immediately to the left of the left side bunkers.

When playing a golf course of this caliber, the final hole seems to come around all too soon. However, the 459-yard par five 18th measures up to the previous 17, and the golfer continues to have his work cut out for him. This hole plays downhill, and the landing area is well bunkered left and right. At 240 yards off the tee, the fairway bends gently right, so a good drive is essential. Trees line both sides of the fairway from the dogleg to the green. Your approach shot is over a small valley to a green trapped to the right front, right side, and left side.

I'm sure you will agree that Broadmoor West offers a fine complement of interesting and challenging golf holes. If you're normal, I know you will want to come back and play it again. One thing you can count on, the course will still be here and just as difficult and beautiful as ever.

CITY PARK MUNICIPAL GOLF COURSE

LOCATION: Pueblo, Colorado. Take Highway 96 Exit off Interstate 25 and continue west on Highway 96 until you come to the golf course. This will be about four miles.

TELEPHONE: 561-4946

COURSE FACILITIES: Fully equipped pro shop, riding golf carts, pull carts, club rental, driving range, putting and chipping greens.

CLUBHOUSE FACILITIES: Restaurant serving breakfast, lunch, sandwiches, beer, mixed and soft drinks.

LODGING: Most of the motels are located near the intersection of Interstate 25 and Highway 50.

RESTAURANTS: A number of interesting places to eat in Pueblo. Ask at the pro shop or your golfing partner.

GOLF COURSE:

	Par	Course Rating	Yardage
Championship	70	68.8	6498
Regular	70	67.8	6263
Ladies	73	72.5	6028

If you like doglegs you will love City Park, because 10 of the holes bend left or right to some degree. This is a mature and well-maintained golf course with excellent greens and fairways that will always yield good lies. A mixture of medium-to-large trees line most of the fairways. With no water hazards and only a few fairway traps, the curving fairways, greenside bunkers, and slippery greens all add up to a more than adequate challenge to the golfer. This is another golf course that is quite enjoyable to walk.

No. 1 is the first of many doglegs. It is a par four at 365 yards and bends right about 150 yards from the green. A small bunker and several medium-size trees guard the inside corner. A 220-yard drive will get you to the corner and leave an open shot to the green.

The 411-yard par four 2nd is the number 1 handicap, and it also doglegs, but this time to the left. The fairway is treelined from the corner to the green, so favor the right center with your drive. This two-level green is trapped left front and right side. Par will not come easy on this hole.

Out-of-bounds close to the fairway's left is the main concern on the 351-yard par four 3rd. Three large elm trees to the fairway's right at the 150-yard marker narrow the landing area considerably. No sand traps guard the table-top green, and par should not be too difficult on this hole.

No. 4 is another short one at 341 yards and par four. However, out-of-bounds is left, and a large tree that sits in the right rough can be a problem if you leave your tee shot to that side. Most players will not be able to see the green for their second shot because it is over a crest in the fairway and below the golfer.

The par four 410-yard 5th hole doglegs left at the 150-yard marker, and the green is trapped to the left front. This number 3 handicap hole will insist on a medium iron for the good golfer and a long iron or fairway wood for the average golfer to reach the green in regulation.

Tall trees at the inside corner make it impossible for most golfers to cut the corner on the 396-yard par four 6th. It's best to play down the middle to the corner of this right-hand dogleg and approach the green from that point.

The only par three on the front nine is the 132-yard 7th. It plays level from tee to green and is a rather easy hole. The green, however, is quite undulating, and you will find it a difficult one to putt.

The 414-yard par four 8th hole is another dogleg, this time to the left, but only the strongest of hitters should attempt to cut the corner. It will take two well-struck balls to reach this green in regulation. Another problem is a sand trap, not noticeable from the fairway, that crowds the green's left side.

No. 9 is very interesting. It's a 491-yard par five with a double dogleg. Most players can cut a little off the first dogleg, which bends to the left, but the tall elm trees at the inside corner of the right-hand second dogleg force the golfer to play his second shot down the middle. Two traps guard the green, one about 20 yards out to the left front and another to the right front.

No. 10 is a 377-yard par four that doglegs left at the 150-yard marker, and the green is heavily trapped to the left and right front. This green has more character than those on the front nine.

The first of three par threes on the back nine greets the golfer on the 11th tee. This level playing hole is not difficult, but the green is closely trapped to the left and rear.

The number 2 handicap hole is a straightaway, long-playing, 548-yard par five. Out-of-bounds is left, but the fairway is quite roomy. Two traps guard this 12th green, one at the left front and another about 30 yards farther out to the left front.

At 332 yards No. 13 is a short par four. The fairway sweeps around to the right, and a strong drive can easily cut the corner. However, most players will be wise to play for the middle of the fairway, leaving a short iron approach to an unguarded green.

The exceptionally long tee box makes club selection difficult on the 193-yard par three 14th. However, the green is large with no sand traps to be concerned with.

No. 15 is a short but rather difficult 351-yard par four. A fairway trap in the left rough and several Russian olive trees guard the inside corner of this left-hand dogleg. Play this hole down the fairway for best results. Be careful of the left side trap at the green.

No. 16 is the only par four over 400 yards on the back nine. This 425-yard hole doglegs left, and a huge elm tree guards the inside corner. Favor the right side of the fairway, and don't try to cut the corner. No. 17 is a routine par three at 159 yards, and presents an excellent opportunity for par.

I like the 394-yard par four 18th. It's a fine finishing hole. The fairway is a long sweeping right-hand bend, and a large elm tree grows in the center of the fairway about 125 yards from the green. Your approach shot must clear this tree and not catch any of the other large trees guarding entrance to the green.

City Park has a nine-hole course located on the other side of Highway 96. Par is 30, and it has 6 par threes and 3 par fours. If you have time be sure and play it, because it is quite interesting, and it will do wonders for your short game.

PATTY JEWETT GOLF COURSE

LOCATION: Colorado Springs, Colorado. Take the Nevada Exit off Interstate 25 and turn east on Espanola. This road will take you to the golf course.

TELEPHONE: 578-6825 Pro shop
578-6827 Starter

COURSE FACILITIES: Fully equipped pro shop, riding golf carts, pull carts, club rental, chipping and putting greens.

CLUBHOUSE FACILITIES: Restaurant serving breakfast, lunch, sandwiches, beer, and soft drinks.

LODGING: Plenty of good places to stay along I-25.

RESTAURANTS: No shortage of fine restaurants in Colorado Springs. Local inquiry should get you good results.

GOLF COURSE:

	Par	Course Rating	Yardage
Championship	72	71.3	6811
Regular	72	69.7	6463
Ladies	75	73.1	5998

Patty Jewett, originally a private club built in 1896, has the distinction of being Colorado's oldest golf course. Ten years later the interesting old clubhouse was constructed. In about 1916 Mr. Jewett, who was the owner of the property, gave it to the city providing they would name the golf course after his wife and that all monies earned would stay with the golf course for maintenance, expansion, and improvement of the facilities.

The result of all this is a fine old mature golf course, offering an excellent combination of flat, gentle-rolling, treelined fairways, and exceptionally well-cared-for greens. Adding to the difficulty of the course are many sand traps and a large irrigation ditch that comes into play on several holes. The view of Pikes Peak and the mountains to the west is magnificent. Don't miss any opportunity to play this interesting and challenging golf course.

In order to reserve a tee time at Patty Jewett, one must do so in person at the starter house. This will cost $1.00 and may be made as far as seven days in advance.

Now it's time to play golf. A great view of Pikes Peak greets the golfer from the tee box of the 480-yard par five starter hole. Huge cottonwoods line the right side of this level-playing fairway, and an inconvenient bunker sits in the middle of the fairway 200 yards out from the green. All kinds of problems await the slicer on this hole, so do your best to favor the fairway's left side from tee to green.

No. 2 is a routine 147-yard level-playing par three to a medium-size green trapped about 10 yards to the right front. The 3rd hole also plays level and straightforward. It is 365 yards in length and par four, with a troublesome sand trap in the right rough near the 150-yard marker. The green is surrounded by numerous small grassy mounds and depressions and is a tough one to hold because it seems to slope away from the golfer.

No. 4 is a real challenge at 459 yards and par five. Line up a little left of the large cottonwood in the distance guarding the inside corner of this right-hand dogleg. Be satisfied to reach this green in regulation and be careful of the traps behind the large cottonwood and to the green's left front. This is the number 1 handicap hole and rightfully so.

The 382-yard straightforward and level-playing par four 5th is not a difficult hole, but the green is trapped left and right front, and it's a touchy one to putt from above the hole. No. 6 is another rather easy hole at 141 yards and par three. It plays slightly uphill to a green trapped to the left and another one to the right front. Plenty of character and lots of breaking putts on this green.

I like the 395-yard par four 7th. It plays straight off the tee, then bends left later on. The fairway slants a little left to right and the rough drops off moderately to the right. A bunker about 240 yards off the tee awaits in the left rough. Sand traps to the right front and left side guard the green. Avoid the right side of this hole from tee to green because it spells nothing but trouble. After you have putted out, turn around and take a look at the view of Pikes Peak back down the fairway. What a sight!

Another fine golf hole is the 420-yard par four 8th. It plays straight off the tee, then doglegs right. Two reachable bunkers guard the inside corner, but the long-ball hitter can shorten this hole by hitting over these sand traps. Most golfers should play it safe and down the middle. Your approach to this undulating green is slightly uphill, and it is trapped to the right front.

The 341-yard par four 9th is quite interesting. It plays from an elevated tee, downhill, over a large lake, doglegs left, then uphill to the green. To clear this lake off the tee will require a 225-yard all-carry tee shot. Most golfers will do best to hit a 150 to 160-yard mid-iron to short of the lake and another shot of similar length to the green. Watch out for the trap below and to the right front of the green. This is another green with plenty of character, and above the hole is the wrong place to be when it is your turn to putt.

The back nine begins with a 381-yard straightaway par four that is anything but easy. The problem here is the irrigation ditch crossing the fairway. It is reachable with a long drive, but impossible to carry. The strong hitter might want to hit a long iron, but most golfers can hit their driver. An accurate approach shot to this well-trapped green is a must for par.

The 196-yard uphill-playing 11th is a par three of average difficulty. The green is medium size, has good character, and offers plenty of breaking putts.

No. 12 is a 357-yard par four down a fairway that kicks a little right to left and doglegs right. Most golfers should play it in the fairway to the dogleg, but the big hitter can cut the corner here with minimum risk. A thinly spaced gauntlet of evergreens guards the inside corner and is a small problem. The approach to this quite undulating, well-trapped green is slightly uphill.

The 512 yard par five 13th is another interesting and challenging golf hole. It is straightaway off the tee, then after a well-hit drive sweeps to the right around a grouping of evergreens to a green at the top of a small hill. Two sand traps guard the green, one to the front and another to the right. Although lots of room extends in the right rough, it's impossible to get any kind of lie there, so play this hole down the fairway all the way.

The 189-yard par three 14th plays from an elevated tee to a green tightly trapped to the left front, right side, and the left rear. Proper pin placements can make this hole a real challenge.

No. 15 is a 341-yard straightforward-playing par four over a rather uneven fairway that slopes a little right to left to an elevated green trapped left and right front. Favor the fairway's right side off the tee and a par should not be too hard to come by.

The 16th hole is just a good long 506-yard straightaway par five down a rather wide-open fairway to a green that sits over the brow of a small crest in the fairway. A small trap crowds the green's left side, but the only problem here is length.

Patty Jewett offers two long par fours for finishing holes. No. 17 is 430 yards in length and is heavily treelined to the left side. The quite roomy fairway and the green are the same elevation. Several small grassy depressions surround the green, but are not a real problem. Stay out of the trees to the left and you should have a good chance for par.

The 18th hole plays to 421 yards, par four, and is treelined both sides. Crossing the fairway about 30 to 60 yards in front of the green is a large irrigation ditch that comes into play on everyone's second shot. Most golfers will want to lay up short, but the strong hitter can clear it and reach the green in regulation. Of further concern are the two long narrow sand traps guarding each side of the green and extending out to the front for about 20 yards. Par will not come easily for most golfers on this final hole.

Colorado Springs offers many interesting attractions in the area other than this fine golf course. For years this part of Colorado has been vacation land for thousands of people. A few of the many things to do and see here are The United States Air Force Academy, Pikes Peak cog railway, Seven Falls, Cave of the Winds, a visit to Cripple Creek to the west, the Royal Gorge to the south, the Broadmoor Hotel, Cheyenne Mountain zoo, and the Garden of the Gods.

You probably can't get all these things done in one trip, so come back again soon and don't forget to bring your golf clubs.

PUEBLO WEST GOLF CLUB

LOCATION: About 8 miles west of Pueblo on Highway 50.

TELEPHONE: 547-2280

COURSE FACILITIES: Fully equipped pro shop, club rental, pull carts, riding golf carts, driving range, putting and chipping greens.

CLUBHOUSE FACILITIES: Snack bar serving sandwiches, beer, mixed and soft drinks.

LODGING: The Pueblo West Inn is located at the site. Plenty of other good accommodations are available in the city of Pueblo.

RESTAURANTS: The Pueblo West Inn is the only restaurant near the golf course.

GOLF COURSE:

	Par	Course Rating	Yardage
Championship	72	73.5	7400
Regular	72	71.6	6975
Ladies	72	68.9	6385

As you can see from the above yardage, Pueblo West is a long golf course. It is also rated as one of the most difficult in the state. Although the course is quite flat and lacks sizeable trees, plenty of problems must be overcome other than length. Practically every hole is a dogleg, and most fairway traps are level with the ground, making them difficult or impossible to see from the tee box. Greenside bunkers are also hidden and not easily seen on many approach shots. All the greens are somewhat similar in character, with gentle rolling putting surfaces. Water hazards are well placed and add to the challenge of most of the par threes. The rough is prairie grass and sandy, so keep your ball in the fairways, which will most always yield excellent lies. Because of its out of the way location, many golfers are not aware of Pueblo West. If you are in the Pueblo area, take time to play this very challenging course. In fact, it's worth a special trip, which I would recommend doing in the spring when the prairie grass is green, the wild flowers are in bloom, and the birds are all singing their favorite songs.

The front nine begins with a lengthy par four at 475 yards that doglegs left about 200 yards from the tee. A strong hitter can cut this corner, but he can also hit through into the rough if his direction is off line a little to the right. The green is large and guarded by a right front trap. Out-of-bounds is both left and right, as is the case on almost every hole at Pueblo West. This 1st hole is an attention getter and demands the golfer's best right away.

No. 2 is a 503-yard par five, and again the fairway swings left. The landing area off the tee is quite narrow, with two sand traps at the inside corner of the dogleg and a long narrow lake crowding the outside corner. Neither of these hazards are visible from the tee. A huge trap defends the entire front approach to this green, and another smaller one sits to the rear. The 3rd hole is another long one at 467 yards and par four. The fairway bends right, and a big hit can cut the corner, but the landing area is a little tight, so be careful. At the green, you will find right front and left side traps that are much larger than they appear to be from the fairway.

The 413-yard par four 4th is another dogleg, this time to the left. Favor the fairway's left side and be careful of the large traps at the right front and left side of the green. These first four holes are all quite similar, and they play somewhat the same, with length being their main difficulty. Not many courses will start off with holes of such length. The 5th is a 180-yard par three with a small pond that snuggles up to the green's right front. Take plenty of club to this sizeable green.

The first five holes play gradually downhill, so beginning with the 529-yard par five 6th we go back uphill towards the clubhouse. This fairway doglegs left, then straightens out again. A fairway trap at the inside corner is not noticeable from the tee. The green is protected by right and left traps, with the left trap not visible from the fairway. This green dishes in toward the center, so some breaking putts can be expected here.

By comparison to the first four holes the 392-yard par four 7th is a short one. This fairway swings a little right, and small trees dot both sides, as has been the case on most of the previous holes. Although a right front trap offers some concern, this is a good opportunity to pick up a stroke.

No. 8 is a most interesting hole. It is 189 yards, par three, and well trapped right and left front. A water hazard (pond) sits to the front of the right trap, so take plenty of club to this quite deep green. The 398-yard par four 9th doglegs a bit to the right, but the difficulty here is the water reservoir that butts up to the green's left side.

The back nine begins much easier than the front nine, with two 365-yard par four holes that play very much alike. Problems on No. 10 are hidden traps, one at the inside corner of the left-hand dogleg, and another at the green's left side. From the 11th tee, aim for the corner of the white house with the brown roof. The green is not in view from the tee and another hidden trap lies to the left of this green.

No. 12 is a blind tee shot down a 543-yard fairway that bends and slopes right. This is a good place for a big hit with a little fade on it. Favor the right side of this fairway, but watch out for the right front trap that awaits about 30 yards out from the green and another smaller trap to the green's right.

The 393-yard par four 13th continues playing slightly downhill, and two hidden traps greet you 150 yards out from the green. A good drive should leave a short downhill approach to a green that is almost completely surrounded by sand traps. This is not a difficult hole, but these greenside traps cannot be taken lightly.

No. 14 is not only pretty and attractive, but is a testy little golf hole. Because of the water hazard guarding the green's left side and rear, this 167-yard par three places a premium on accuracy. Don't miss the green to the left or you are in trouble.

We start working our way back up towards the clubhouse with the par five 15th. This 575-yard fairway is a long one that is straightaway off the tee, then swings to the left. A big hit off the tee will be helpful here. Another hidden trap lies at the inside corner of the dogleg, and a left front trap stands guard about 20 yards out from this wide, but shallow green. It will take five well-executed shots to par this hole.

The 16th is an average length par four at 408 yards. The fairway bends a little right early off the tee. Take plenty of club for your approach shot, or you can find the small bunker immediately in front of the green. No. 17, at 186 yards, is another interesting par three because of the two-level green. The front half is considerably lower than the back half and can result in some interesting putts.

The number 1 handicap hole at Pueblo West is the 426-yard par four 18th. This fairway plays slightly uphill and bends a little right. The green is well trapped left and right with two huge bunkers, and a sizeable water reservoir challenges about 50 yards in front of the green, giving real concern for the golfer's second shot. It takes a pretty good poke to clear this water, and most golfers will want to lay up short and pitch on from there. This is a tough finishing hole on a golf course that has already given most players a severe test of length and accuracy.

VALLEY HI GOLF COURSE

LOCATION: Colorado Springs, Colorado. This golf course is in the southeast part of town at 610 South Chelton. Take Academy Blvd. to Airport Road to Chelton.

TELEPHONE: 578-6926

COURSE FACILITIES: Fully equipped pro shop, riding golf carts, pull carts, club rental, driving range, chipping and putting greens.

CLUBHOUSE FACILITIES: Restaurant serving breakfast, lunch, sandwiches, dinner, beer, mixed and soft drinks. In addition, a swimming pool for use during the summer months and very good banquet facilities are available.

LODGING: Colorado Springs has long been a favorite place for tourists and visitors, so accommodations are plentiful in the area.

RESTAURANTS: No shortage of good places to eat in Colorado Springs. It's best to make local inquiry.

GOLF COURSE:

	Par	Course Rating	Yardage
Championship	71	69.9	6805
Regular	71	68.5	6392
Ladies	75	70.0	5383

Valley Hi was originally a private golf course. It was purchased by the city in 1977, and the back nine was redesigned to some extent in 1981. Reconstruction work continues on the back nine in an attempt to improve the condition of several of the fairways. In general the course is a good assortment of hills, flatland, sand traps, water hazards, and trees. You will find the greens in excellent condition and a seemingly different challenge awaiting on each hole. Several of the fairways show the result of obvious neglect during past years, but this situation is being taken care of, and it won't be long before they are all up to acceptable standards.

The front nine begins with anything but an easy hole. It plays 563 yards long with a sweeping bend to the left. Avoid the rough to the left of the fairway because it spells real trouble. The long ball hitter can cut a little off the corner, but most golfers will want to play safe and down the fairway. The green of this number 2 handicap hole is trapped to the left front and right side. A par on this 1st hole is a great start.

No. 2 is an interesting par three at 182 yards. The tee shot is over a portion of a lake that extends into the fairway from the right and guards the golfer's approach to the green. The large, undulating green lies below the teeing area a little, and you will find that everything kicks left to right, even on the green.

You cannot see the green from the tee box on the 395-yard par four 3rd hole, because the fairway sweeps around to the right and continues behind large cottonwoods that lay claim to that side of the fairway. However, the green is unguarded, and lots of pars await the golfer on this hole.

No. 4 is a short but difficult par four that requires you to stay in the fairway. This 358-yard fairway is straight and level, but has several real problems. In the left rough, starting about 150 yards from the tee is a hidden pond that extends to the 150-yard marker. In the right rough, near the 150-yard marker, is a small narrow slew that can easily catch any ball hit in that direction. Also another larger pond in the left rough starts about 125 yards from the green and continues to even with the green. To the left and behind the green is a grassy area with numerous mounds and depressions. Any chip shot from this area back to the green will be very delicate indeed.

I think No. 5 is a great par three. It is 169 yards in length, plays level but over the same large pond that came into play on the last hole, and places a premium on proper club selection. You can cut off as much of the water as you feel comfortable with on this hole, and for the timid player a little room stretches to the right of the pond. The green is quite undulating, so getting on in one does not automatically insure a par.

Another good golf hole is the 384-yard par four 6th. The fairway is straight and level, as well as quite roomy. However, out-of-bounds is left and many new trees have been planted in the left and right rough. They are not a factor yet, but will be before long. The green is trapped to the left front and left side. Behind the green is an irrigation ditch, and any ball hit over the green will surely find it.

The 465-yard par five 7th is supposed to be the easiest hole on the course, but it will not be so for many golfers. It plays level and straight, with no traps at the green. However, the narrow slew that was in the right rough on No. 4 is also in the right rough on this hole. It can easily come into play on your 2nd shot if you leave your ball out to the right too much. Again, this slew is not noticeable from the fairway.

Most golfers should par the short 353-yard par four 8th hole. It plays level, bending slightly left, and the only problem is the irrigation ditch that runs about 15 yards behind the green.

The front nine finishes with a very respectable 412-yard par four. This fairway plays gradually uphill and doglegs right at the 150-yard marker. The strong hitter can cut the corner here, but most players should play it up the fairway. A right side sand trap guards entry to the green.

No. 10 is a 412-yard par four that plays from an elevated tee down a fairway that is heavily treelined with sizeable cottonwoods to the left and more sparsely treelined to the right. Your drive will kick left to right, and there is a sizeable cement-lined irrigation ditch crossing the fairway shortly past the 150-yard marker. Most players will not be able to reach this ditch off the tee, which will leave them a rather long second shot to the green. This 10th green is huge and makes for a friendly and inviting target.

The 401-yard par four 11th plays level and bends left near the 150-yard marker. Line up your tee shot a little right of the evergreen and cedar trees growing in the left rough. The really big hitter might be able to cut the inside corner on this hole, but it's a little risky to try it. Sand traps guard the green to the front and right front. This is an interesting hole calling for a well-placed drive and an accurate approach to the green.

Another hole that is supposed to be rather easy is the 328-yard par four 12th. However, because of the narrow landing area and the lake at the inside corner of the right-hand dogleg, this hole can cause lots of problems. You cannot see the lake from the tee box, but believe me it's there. Play a fairway wood or long iron off the tee to short of the lake, then approach the green over the water and hope you get it close. This large elevated green possesses substantial character, and is not an easy one to putt.

The number 1 handicap is the 459-yard par four 13th. It plays level off the tee with a long sweeping bend to the right. Play it down the middle, because there's no way to cut the corner. Many new trees have been planted in the rough lining both sides of the fairway. This hole will only get more difficult as time goes on.

No. 14 should be a rather routine par three for most golfers. It plays straightforward, level and to an exceptionally large green that provides a wide and inviting target.

No. 15 and 16 were under reconstruction at the time I played the golf course, and I was unable to play them. The 15th is a 381-yard par four and the 16th is a 190-yard par three. Distance and par will remain the same on both holes. The work being done on these two holes is expected to improve the quality of the fairways.

The 491-yard par five 17th is an excellent golf hole. It plays over a large drainage ditch in front of the tee, down a fairway lined with hundreds of newly planted trees that are not a factor yet, but will be in a few years. A natural drainage ditch runs in the right rough and develops into a pond shortly in front of the green. This pond will force most players to lay up short and approach the green over the water. Only the very strongest of hitters should elect to go for the green in two. Par on this number 3 handicap hole is an accomplishment.

Although No. 18 is not long at 349 yards, neither is it an easy par four, and plenty of opportunity for trouble exists. The fairway plays straight, uphill, kicks right to left, and is heavily treelined on the left with large cottonwoods. Favor the fairway's right side off the tee. The green is cut into the side of a hill on the right and the fairway drops off sharply to the green's left side. Missing this green to the right leaves a touchy downhill chip shot, and missing it to the left leaves a difficult uphill pitch. Keep the ball in play, and you should par this final hole.

SECTION 5
NINE-HOLE COURSES

COLORADO'S BEST-KEPT SECRET

It's difficult to say enough good things about Colorado's nine-holf golf courses! I was more than impressed with their splendid condition and interesting challenge. You will find some of the most exciting golf holes in the state on these nine-hole courses.

For the most part these golf courses are located in out-of-the-way places and are overlooked by all but local golfers. Their peaceful and secluded settings are a rarity nowadays, and you will be missing a real treat if you don't search them out.

You will love the natural rolling terrain at Wray, the treelined fairways and canyons at Trinidad, the hills and valleys at Lamar, and the peaceful seclusion of the courses at Meeker and Rifle. If you are traveling through or around Colorado, don't overlook these fine golf courses. I know you will be impressed and well rewarded for taking the time to play any of them. Another thing that will please you — the people you meet all know the true meaning of western hospitality.

PAGE	GOLF COURSE	CITY

NORTHEAST PLAINS AND FOOTHILLS

DENVER METRO AND SUBURBS

WESTERN SLOPE AND MOUNTAINS

293	Monte Vista Country Club	Monte Vista
294	Montrose Golf Club	Montrose
295	Mt. Massive Golf Club	Leadville
296	Ranch at Roaring Fork	Carbondale
297	Rifle Creek Golf Club	Rifle
299	Salida Golf Club	Salida
300	Steamboat Golf Club	Steamboat Springs
301	Westbank Ranch Golf and Country Club	Glenwood Springs
302	Yampa Valley Golf Club	Craig

SOUTHEAST PLAINS AND FOOTHILLS

305	Cimarron Hills	Colorado Springs
307	City Park Municipal Golf Course	Pueblo
308	Colorado City Golf Club	Colorado City
310	La Junta Golf Club	La Junta
311	Limon Municipal Golf Course	Limon
312	Meadow Creek	Colorado City
313	Patty Jewett	Colorado Springs
314	Rocky Ford Golf Club	Rocky Ford
315	Spreading Antlers Golf Club	Lamar
316	Trinidad Municipal Golf Club	Trinidad
318	Walsenburg Golf Club	Walsenburg

BUNKER HILL COUNTRY CLUB

LOCATION: Brush, Colorado. Take Exit number 89 off Interstate 76 and go south about ¼ mile to Mill Street. Turn right on Mill and you will see the golf course on the right.

TELEPHONE: 842-5198

Bunker Hill is a well-conditioned golf course with thick, lush fairways and impeccably manicured greens. I'm sure many of you have driven by Bunker Hill on I-76 and said to yourself, "That sure looks like a good golf course. I ought to stop and play it sometime." Well it is, and you should! This course is not long at 6166 yards for the two nines, but every hole is a good one. I particularly like No. 6, 7, and 9. The 6th hole is not difficult at 313 yards and par four, but the approach to the green makes for an attractive shot. A lofted wood off the tee to the corner of this left-hand dogleg will leave a short iron to the green which slopes noticeably toward the golfer. Any putt from above the hole will be extremely fast.

No. 7 is the number 1 handicap hole at 407 yards and par four. It plays straightforward and gradually uphill off the tee, then slightly downhill to the green. It will take a medium-to-long iron or even a fairway wood to get on this green in regulation.

The longest hole on the course is the 518-yard par five 9th. Trouble waits to the left early on in the form of a small pond, but most golfers should be able to avoid this hazard as it's only about 175 yards off the tee. Another long narrow pond crowds the fairway's right side at the 150-yard marker and comes to within about 60 yards of the green. This is a good par five that requires the golfer to stay in the fairway from tee to green.

Course facilities at Bunker HIll include a fully equipped pro shop, riding golf carts, pull carts, club rental, driving range, putting and chipping greens. The clubhouse offers breakfast, lunch, sandwiches, dinner, beer, mixed and soft drinks.

Make it a point to play Bunker Hill. You will find all the holes interesting, and you will love putting on these excellent greens.

CITY PARK NINE

LOCATION: Ft. Collins, Colorado, 411 S. Bryan Street. From downtown Ft. Collins go west on Mulberry to City Park, turn right on Bryan Street, then take the first left which will lead you to the clubhouse.

TELEPHONE: 221-6650

City Park Nine is one of Northern Colorado's oldest golf courses, with play beginning here in 1939. Consequently, the course is covered and the fairways lined with many huge elm, spruce, and pine trees. Nowadays it is customary to think of nine-hole courses as short or even par threes, but this is not the case with City Park Nine. If you play the nine holes twice, the yardage is 6394 yards and par is 72, which makes it a respectable golf course. The fairways, rough, and greens are well groomed, and coupled with the many large trees, the two long par fives, the water hazard in front of No. 6, and the numerous possibilities of being out-of-bounds off the tee make this course interesting and exciting to play. City Park Nine is another course that is quite enjoyable to walk.

Facilities here include a fully equipped pro shop, club rental, pull carts, riding golf carts, driving range, putting green, and chipping green. Soft drinks, beer, candy bars, and other vending machine items are available in the golf shop.

City Park Nine No. 6
355 yards par four

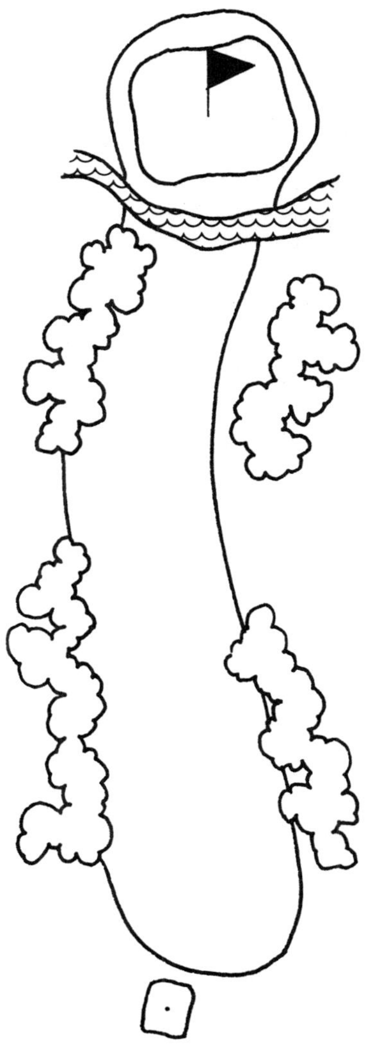

HAYSTACK MOUNTAIN GOLF COURSE

LOCATION: Northeast of Boulder at the base of Haystack Mountain. You can also find this golf course by going half-mile north and a half-mile west of the IBM plant located between Boulder and Longmont.

TELEPHONE: 530-1400

There are only two regulation 18-hole public golf courses in Boulder, so if you can't get on either of these or are short of time, Haystack might be your answer. It is an executive-length 9-hole public course at 1952 yards with par being 32 for men and 33 for ladies. Green fees are reasonable, and no reservations are accepted. It has the only lighted driving range in the area and is open until 11 p.m.

HIGH PLAINS GOLF CLUB

LOCATION: Yuma, Colorado. Go one mile north of Highway 34 on Colorado Highway 59. Turn east and go .3 miles to the golf course.

TELEPHONE: 848-2813

High Plains gets your attention immediately with the first three holes playing to 555 yards and par five, 445 yards and par four, and another par five at 531 yards. They are all straightforward treelined fairways, and if you can get by these three holes in good shape, you have a chance for a respectable score.

In general this course is rather flat, has lots of trees bordering the fairways, and is quite long at 6814 yards for the two nines. The fairways, as well as the large greens, are well maintained and in excellent condition.

In addition to the first three holes, I feel that No. 7 offers a good challenge. The fairway of this 375-yard par four bends a little right beyond the top of the hill, and a good drive should leave a medium iron to the green. The problem is the lake in the right rough and a finger of the lake extending across the fairway only 10 yards in front of the green. A well-placed and accurate approach shot is a must here. No. 9 is also a good hole because of its length. This 444-yard par four plays straight and level off the tee, then uphill to the green.

Practice facilities include a driving range and putting green. Rental clubs are also available at the pro shop. Clubhouse facilities include a restaurant serving breakfast, lunch, sandwiches, dinner, beer, mixed and soft drinks.

Because of its length and treelined fairways, High Plains offers the golfer a definite challenge. Come on out and see if you are up to it.

HOLYOKE GOLF CLUB

LOCATION: Holyoke, Colorado. Go three blocks east of the stoplight at the junction of Highway 6 and Colorado Highway 385, then one block north.

TELEPHONE: 854-3200

Ten years ago this was a sand greens golf course. Today it can boast excellent, well-maintained grass greens and thick, lush fairways. For the two nines this course is a respectable 6410 yards, and the numerous large elm trees lining the fairways further complicate matters. Another problem is the sizeable drainage draw that comes into play on holes No. 2, 3, and 9. The greens here are not large, and they all make for small targets. I especially like holes No. 6 and 9. The 6th is a long, treelined 444-yard par four, and because of its length is a tough hole. No. 9, at 373 yards and par four, is an excellent finishing hole. It plays straightaway, is treelined, and your approach to the green is quite demanding. The green is small, elevated, and the drainage draw crosses the fairway just in front, requiring an accurate all-carry shot to the green. It's easy to leave it short. I'm sure a lot of golf matches have been won or lost on this 9th hole.

Most people look at me in disbelief when I tell them about the fine golf course in Holyoke, Colorado, but it's true! Come on out and see for yourself. You will be glad you made the trip. This is not only the land of tall grain bins and pivot irrigation systems, but also of a mighty fine golf course.

Riding golf carts, pull carts, and golf clubs are available for rent, and practice facilities include chipping and putting greens. Sandwiches, beer, and soft drinks are available at the clubhouse.

LAKE ESTES GOLF COURSE

LOCATION: Estes Park, Colorado. East of town off Highway 34 on your right.

TELEPHONE: 586-9871

Lake Estes is an executive course with par at 31, which is usually beyond the reach of most players. Four of the holes are really good par fours, and the 186-yard par three 9th over the Big Thompson River does not yield to par easily. In fact, all nine holes demand the golfer's best effort if he expects to score well.

The course is flat, easy to walk, and the view of the high mountain peaks to the west is magnificent. Just walking around on this golf course makes you glad to be alive and able to enjoy life in this beautiful setting. Don't miss it.

Facilities here include a partially equipped pro shop, practice putting green, club rental, pull carts, and soft drinks.

SUNSET MUNICIPAL GOLF COURSE

LOCATION: Longmont, Colorado. From downtown Longmont go west on 3rd Avenue to Sunset Street. Turn north on Sunset and go 2 blocks to Longs Peak Avenue and turn left. This road will take you to the parking lot for the golf course.

TELEPHONE: 776-3122

The first round of golf was played at Sunset in 1920, which makes this golf course one of the oldest in the state. The greens are small, and the well-conditioned fairways are lined with many large trees. Although there are few side hill lies, the golfer will be confronted with either an uphill or downhill lie on practically every fairway shot. Sand traps guard all but two of the greens, and out-of-bounds on the right is a problem on three of the holes. No water hazards plague this course, but the many trees make up for this shortcoming. The view of the snowcapped Rocky Mountains and Longs Peak to the west is inspiring, so don't forget to drink in this fabulous Colorado view while enjoying your round of golf at Sunset.

Course facilities include a fully equipped pro shop, club rental, putting green, pull carts, and electric golf carts. Soft drinks, candy bars, and other vending machine items are available at the golf shop.

WASHINGTON COUNTY GOLF CLUB

LOCATION: Akron, Colorado. South of town on highway 63.

This golf course is more for local use, but the public is quite welcome. If you like to play off buffalo grass fairways, that is what you will find at Akron. However, a very pleasant surprise is the superb condition of the interesting grass greens. They are some of the best in this part of the state.

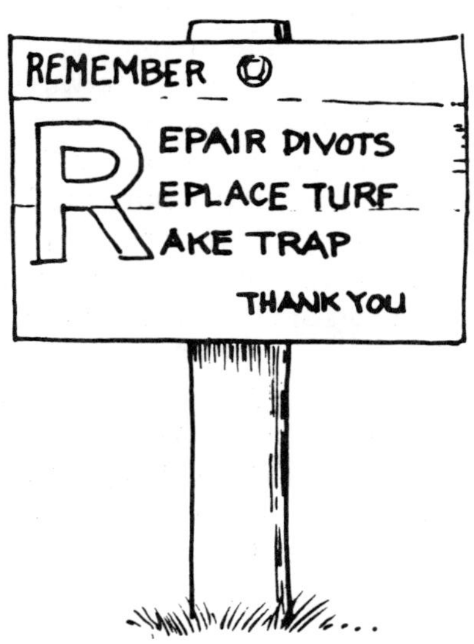

WRAY COUNTRY CLUB

LOCATION: Wray, Colorado. Go 1 mile north of town on Colorado Highway 385. Turn left at the golf course sign.

TELEPHONE: 332-5934

The Wray Country Club golf course is a real jewel! It is laid out among the hills and valleys of this interesting country, and the well-conditioned fairways and greens are some of the best in Colorado. At 5974 yards this is not a long golf course, but it plays much longer because of the elevated greens. Consequently, all-carry approach shots are a must. Every hole at Wray is a challenge, but my favorites are the par three 6th and the par five 7th.

The 175-yard 6th hole plays from a tee at the top of a hill to a green sitting in the bottom of a valley. This green is much higher on the left than the right. If you miss the green, do it to the right front. Club selection here is always a problem and can be anything from a 5 iron to a lofted wood.

Because of all the humps and valleys and the setting of the elevated green at the end of the fairway, No. 7 is really a beautiful golf hole. This 535-yard par five fairway is long, narrow, and will provide few level lies. The sandy, native grass rough on both sides spells real trouble, so do your best to keep the ball in play.

Course facilities include a pro shop, a few riding golf carts, pull carts, driving range, chipping and putting greens. No clubhouse facilities are available to the public.

It's worth making a special trip or going out of your way to play this fine golf course. Do it soon.

HEATHER GARDENS

LOCATION: Aurora, Colorado. Take the Iliff Exit off Highway 225 west of Denver and go east a very short distance to Abilene, turn south on Abilene to Heather Gardens Parkway, then right and the clubhouse is on the left.

TELEPHONE: 751-2390

Heather Gardens is a semi-private golf course, owned by the residents, but open for play by the public. You will find the course in superb condition with thick, lush fairways and immaculate greens. Other interesting features of this par 32 executive golf course are the number and size of the sand traps and the severe undulations possessed by most of the greens.

I especially like holes No. 7 and 9. Not many executive courses offer a par five, but Heather Gardens does with the 7th, and you will find it anything but a cinch par. The hole plays level and straightaway with out-of-bounds left, a fairway bunker in the right rough, and a lake extending into the fairway from the right at the 150-yard marker. Evergreen trees line the near side of the lake, and protecting the entrance to the green is a huge sand trap at the left front and a smaller one at the left side. Three putts will be commonplace on this very undulating green.

The 344-yard par four 9th is not long, but the large lake in front of the tee box and the bunkers guarding each side of the landing area make this hole another good one. A small unseen pond sits to the fairway's left shortly off the tee. Guarding the green and complicating your uphill approach shot are three bunkers, one to the right front, one to the left side, and another to the right rear.

It's a rare treat to play on a golf course as well conditioned as this one. Come out and enjoy the experience. Facilities here include a fully equipped pro shop, riding golf carts, chipping and putting greens. Lunch, sandwiches, dinner, beer, mixed and soft drinks are also available.

DENVER NINE-HOLE COURSES

FOOTHILLS

LOCATION: 3901 So. Carr, Denver, Colorado

TELEPHONE: 989-3901

Par three adjacent to 18-hole course.

HYLAND HILLS

LOCATION: 9650 Sheridan Blvd., Westminster, Colorado

TELEPHONE: 428-6526

Par three adjacent to 18-hole course.

INDIAN TREE

LOCATION: 7555 Wadsworth Blvd., Arvada, Colorado.

TELEPHONE: 423-3450

Par three adjacent to 18-hole course.

KENNEDY

LOCATION: 10500 East Hampden Ave., Denver, Colorado

TELEPHONE: 755-0105

Par three adjacent to 18-hole course.

SOUTH SUBURBAN

LOCATION: 7900 So. Colorado Blvd., Littleton, Colorado.

TELEPHONE: 770-5500

Par three adjacent to 18-hole course.

HARVARD MUNICIPAL

LOCATION: East Iliff and South Clarkson, Denver, Colorado.

TELEPHONE: 744-9448

Recently constructed par three located in Harvard Park.

TWILIGHT GOLF CLUB

LOCATION: 1090 South Oneida at Leetsdale and Monaco, Denver, Colorado.

TELEPHONE: 388-5641

Par three course with pro shop, driving range, restaurant, and lounge.

ALAMOSA PUBLIC GOLF COURSE

LOCATION: Alamosa, Colorado. Approximately ¾ miles north on State Street from downtown Alamosa.

TELEPHONE: 589-2260

This fine golf course is level, flat, and a pleasure to walk. It's no telling how long the many gigantic cottonwood trees that dominate this course have been growing here. Although sand traps are scarce, water hazards come into play on four of the holes, and the heavily treelined left-hand dogleg 2nd is always a tough one. The par three 6th at 218 yards is another difficult hole, mainly due to its length, and is the number 1 handicap. However, I like the 363-yard 7th the best. This hole calls for a straight 220-yard to 230-yard drive, then an accurate approach over water guarding the entire front of the green. The fairway doglegs right after your drive, and large cottonwoods come into play at the inside corner.

This 30-yard-old course has improved considerably over the past several years with the addition of an underground sprinkler system, and the fairways and greens are all in excellent condition. If you are spending any time in the San Luis Valley, be sure to play at Alamosa.

Two other interesting attractions in this area are the Great Sand Dunes, Colorado's biggest sand box, located 32 miles northeast of Alamosa at the foot of the Sangre de Cristo Mountains, and the Cumbres and Toltec scenic railroad which is a narrow-guage train ride from Antonito, Colorado, to Chama, New Mexico. No trip to the San Luis Valley is complete without taking advantage of these activities.

COLLEGIATE PEAKS GOLF CLUB

LOCATION: Buena Vista, Colorado. Go 1.3 miles west of stoplight (at Main Street and Highway 24) on Colorado Highway 306. Turn right when you see the small green and white golf course sign.

TELEPHONE: 395-6622

Collegiate Peaks is a privately owned golf course that is open to the public. The greens are excellent, but some of the fairways need more time and care before reaching top quality condition. The layout of the course is really a good one, with Cottonwood Creek, several small lakes, and many large cottonwood trees all combining to make it anything but an easy golf course. Holes No. 2, 4, 5, and 9 are particularly fine golf holes, and it will be a struggle for most golfers to make par on any of them.

Riding golf carts, pull carts, and rental clubs are available in the clubhouse, as well as sandwiches, mixed drinks, beer, and soft drinks. If you are in the Buena Vista area, take time to play Collegiate Peaks. It is an easy one to walk, the scenery is exciting, and the golf course offers a real challenge.

COTTONWOOD GOLF CLUB

LOCATION: Delta, Colorado. From the north end of the city limits, continue north on Highway 50 for about half a mile. At that point the highway bends left, but continue straight for about one block and turn right on Road 38. Continue on this road until you come to Road 1600 at which point you turn left and go until you come to Road H75. Turn right on Road H75 and you will soon see the golf course. Signs will help you follow these directions.

TELEPHONE: 874-7263

The Cottonwood Golf Course was built in 1965 and has excellent fairways and greens. The course is flat, easy to walk, but lacks many trees and sand traps. The water hazards on Nos. 6 and 8 are good ones, and the dirt rough between all the fairways is really tough to recover from. One of the best things about Cottonwood is that you can play golf here almost all year. Very few days during the winter are lost to weather.

Course facilities include a fully equipped pro shop, riding golf carts, pull carts, rental clubs, driving range, and putting green. Sandwiches, beer, and soft drinks are served at the golf shop.

Because of its out-in-the-country, out-of-the-way location, this golf course may be overlooked by many golfers. If you are in the area or passing through, take the time to play Cottonwood. It's a good test of golf, and the greens are some of the best in Western Colorado.

GLENWOOD GOLF CLUB

LOCATION: Glenwood Springs, Colorado. Exit from Interstate 70 at Glenwood Springs and turn right to the stop light (about 1 block). Turn left and go one mile west, and you will see the golf course sign on your right. Follow these signs to the golf course.

TELEPHONE: 945-7086

The Glenwood Springs golf course has been here since 1955, so it has all the characteristics of a mature and well-cared-for facility. Trees of various types line most of the fairways and very definitely have an influence on the outcome of your score. Practically all of the fairways have either a right or left slope to them, but on the other hand seem to be quite roomy. This is another rather short golf course at 5812 yards for the two nines, but only a few golfers can ever total up their score and have it read par 70.

All the par threes are interesting, but I think the 5th and 7th holes are the most demanding. No. 5 is a 425-yard par four with out-of-bounds right and trees lining the left side of this level and straightforward fairway. It will take two long and well-struck balls to get on the green of this number 1 handicap hole in regulation.

I feel that No. 7 offers the golfer more challenge than any of the other holes at Glenwood. It's a par four that plays 418 yards, but the lake in the left rough is reachable off the tee if you pull or hook a well-hit drive. Trees line the fairway's right side, which will give the slicer some problems. The fairway curls around the far end of the lake, and the green hides about 40 yards behind it. This water cannot be ignored, and the hole will not yield to par without a real battle.

Course facilities here include a fully equipped pro shop, riding golf carts, pull carts, club rental, and putting green. At the clubhouse you can get breakfast, lunch, sandwiches, beer, mixed and soft drinks. This is another course that is fun to walk, although it is more hilly than some.

Glenwood Springs is a good place to spend the night, because it has an abundance of motels and restaurants. Be sure to take a swim in the famous Glenwood Hot Springs pool. After a round of golf it will make those sore muscles feel like new.

LINCOLN PARK GOLF COURSE

LOCATION: Grand Junction, Colorado. 14th and Gunnison Avenue in Lincoln Park.

TELEPHONE: 242-6394

Lincoln Park is an older well-established golf course with wide, friendly fairways and beautiful mature trees. The course is flat, easy to walk, presents no water hazards, and only an average number of sand traps. However, out-of-bounds right on five holes, its length, and the many large trees give this course all the respectability it needs. The 6th and 7th holes are excellent, with No. 6 being a long 570-yard par five that plays straightforward all the way, but with out-of-bounds and lots of huge trees on the right quite close to the edge of the fairway. Favor the fairway's left side all the way to the green, and you will have a good chance for par. Don't plan on reaching this green in anything but regulation, because it's too long.

No. 7 is a tough par three at 212 yards. It plays straight and level from tee to green, but gigantic cottonwood trees line the fairway's right side, and several more extend to the left of the green. This green is also elevated several feet, and the adjacent mounds give it additional character.

A fully equipped pro shop, driving range, putting and chipping greens, riding carts, pull carts, and rental clubs are available. Lunch, sandwiches, beer, and soft drinks are served at the golf shop.

You can't help enjoying your round of golf on this fine, old and well-kept golf course. If you are in Grand Junction, make every effort to play it.

LOS CUMBRES GOLF COURSE

LOCATION: Crestone, Colorado. Shortly south of Moffat, Colorado, on Colorado Highway 17, turn east on Road T towards Crestone. Go 9 miles on Road T and the golf course will be on the left just past the Baca Grande Inn.

TELEPHONE: 256-4856

I was quite surprised to find such a superbly conditioned golf course in this out-of-the-way part of Colorado. The fairways and greens on this par 34 ten-year-old course are outstanding and will give any country club in Colorado a run for their money. Don't miss playing this golf course, because it's a privilege to play golf on fairways and greens of this caliber. At no extra charge you get the freshest air for miles around, and the view of the Sangre de Cristo mountains to the east is breath taking.

This course is quite short at 4848 yards for the two nines, but the 5th, 6th, and 9th holes will play on anyone's golf course. The par four 5th at 418 yards curls right around the edge of a lake and calls for a well-placed drive to a narrow landing area that kicks left to right toward the lake. Approaching this green can be tricky, because one must play over a portion of the lake to a green that is trapped left and right front. Also a grassy bunker sits behind the green. No. 6 is another good one at par four and 376 yards. It plays straightaway with out-of-bounds left and two fairway bunkers guarding the landing area. A small lake protects the green's front side, and it will take a medium-long iron for most golfers to reach this green in regulation. Many players will be wise to layup short of the lake and approach the green from there. The 387-yard par four 9th makes a good finishing hole. It plays straightforward, then doglegs sharply right about 100 yards from the green. Two bunkers guard the landing area, one at the outside corner and one at the inside corner. Another sand trap is located to the green's right as well as to the left. Aim for the American and Colorado flags waving in the distance as you set up for your tee shot on this 9th hole.

Facilities here include riding golf carts, pull carts, club rental, and a driving range. Tennis, swimming, as well as meals, are available at the Inn. Fishing, hiking, and horseback riding are all enjoyable activities available in or near this area, as well as visits to the Great Sand Dunes, Alamosa-Monte Vista National Wildlife Refuge, and a ride on the Cumbres and Toltec narrow-gauge railroad. This San Luis Valley area is an interesting part of Colorado. Take time to enjoy it.

MEEKER GOLF COURSE

LOCATION: Meeker, Colorado. From Colorado Highway 13 at the south end of town turn at the Co-op and cross the bridge. Immediately after crossing the bridge turn right and go about one mile. Turn right again at the golf course sign.

TELEPHONE: 878-5642

You will thoroughly enjoy playing the Meeker Golf Course. It is out in the country, and the sounds you hear are of cattle grazing on the other side of the fence and running water in the numerous irrigation ditches. The fairways are well cared for, and the greens are excellent. If you miss any putts on these greens, you need more practice.

Par at Meeker is only 68, so it's not a long course and possesses only one sand trap, although more are planned. Very few trees spot the course, but if you stray from the fairway, you are apt to end up in a deep gully, irrigation ditch, out-of-bounds, or deep grassy rough.

Lots of good holes at Meeker, but I like No. 6, 8, and 9 the best. No. 6 is an uphill 377-yard par four with plenty of deep rough on both sides. Target the flag seen in the distance on No. 4 green. A mild left-hand dogleg greets you about 135 yards from the green. The 8th hole is a downhill 338-yard par four with a dogleg to the right and out-of-bounds on the same side. Your ball will kick sharply right when it hits the fairway, so allow for this or you are apt to be out-of-bounds and in the irrigation ditch that also extends along the fairway's right side. The 313-yard par four 9th plays straightaway and uphill. Keep it in the middle here, or you may never find your ball in the deep rough. The only sand trap on the course sits to the green's left side and is not noticeable from the fairway.

Course facilities here include riding golf carts, pull carts, club rental, driving range, chipping green, putting green, and a fully equipped pro shop. At the clubhouse you can obtain lunch, sandwiches, dinner, mixed drinks, soft drinks, and beer. Meeker is a little out of the way for most travelers, but if you

Meeker Golf Course No. 8
338 yards par four

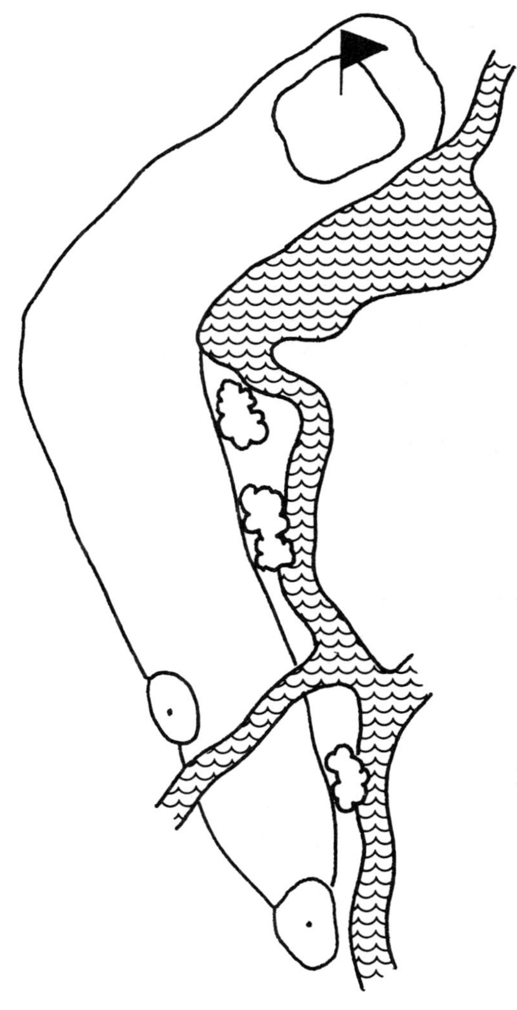

are looking for an enjoyable time, turn off Interstate 70 and drive to Meeker. I guarantee you will have a good time playing this interesting and attractive golf course.

MONTE VISTA COUNTRY CLUB

LOCATION: Monte Vista, Colorado. From Highway 160 near the west edge of town turn north on Dunham Street, and in a few blocks you will see the golf course.

TELEPHONE: 852-4906 and 852-9995

Golf has been played at the Monte Vista Country Club for over 50 years. The course is flat, easy to walk, and relatively short at 6019 yards for the two nines. Huge cottonwood and elm trees line most of the fairways. Although the course lacks a lot of hazards, most players will find all the challenge they are looking for on holes No. 2, 4, 7, and 9.

No. 2 is a lengthy, treelined par five at 535 yards that plays to a long, narrow, two-level green. The 4th hole is another lengthy one at 438 yards and par four. Trees again line the fairway, and we have another two-level green. No. 7 is interesting in that the teeing area sits over a large irrigation ditch that extends down the fairway's right side all the way to the green. The 7th green is also the toughest on the course because it is extremely large, with the right side elevated much higher than the lower left side. Favor the fairway's left side off the tee, then hope you get it close with your approach shot. This green can be a very touchy one to putt.

The 9th hole is a 188-yard par three. Really no fairway here, and your tee shot must clear a large cottonwood short of the green. This shot calls for a fairway wood or medium-long iron, depending on the extent of your golfing skills. Watch out for the long, thin sand trap to the right of the green.

This is a pleasant golf course, with well-maintained fairways and greens, and although it may not be as exciting as some, it is quite enjoyable and fun to play. The San Luis Valley is great outdoor country, so bring your fishing pole, because this area offers some of the best trout fishing in Colorado.

If you are interested in birds, other than on the golf course, visit the Alamosa-Monte Vista National Wildlife Refuge Complex. This is quite interesting and well worth your time.

MONTROSE GOLF CLUB

LOCATION: Montrose, Colorado. Go east of town on Highway 50 until you come to Hillcrest. Turn right on Hillcrest, and this road will lead you to the golf course in about a mile. A shopping center is located on the right at the intersection of Hillcrest and Highway 50.

TELEPHONE: 249-8551

The 22-year-old Montrose Golf Club is a mature and established course with well-cared-for greens and fairways. Good size trees, which always seem to be in the wrong place, line both sides of most of the fairways. A large spruce tree in the right rough indicates 125 yards from the green on each hole. The course is quite lengthy at 6600 yards for two nines and has several demanding and challenging holes. No. 4, 6, 8 and 9 could be a part of anyone's golf course, and the best of golfers will find par difficult to come by on any of them.

The lake on No. 6 is an especially difficult hazard. It forces most players to lay up short off the tee, then requires another fairway wood to the green. Out-of-bounds to the right causes further concern. In addition this 400-yard hole plays gradually uphill, which lengthens the hole considerably.

Water guards both corners of the dogleg on the 325-yard, uphill par four 4th hole. Play for position here and hit a lofted wood or long iron off the tee. The 8th hole is an extremely long uphill 425-yard par four that plays much longer than the indicated yardage. No. 9 is a long par three at 212 yards and because of its length and contour of the green is a tough finishing hole.

Put Montrose on your list of courses to play because it's one of the best nine-hole layouts in the State. Facilities here include a limited number of riding golf carts, pull carts, putting green, and a driving net. Snack bar items, beer, and soft drinks are available at the golf shop.

MT. MASSIVE GOLF CLUB

LOCATION: Leadville, Colorado. From the center of town go west on 6th to a dead end, turn right and follow this blacktop road for about 3 miles to the golf course.

TELEPHONE: 486-2176

At an elevation of 10,200 feet, Mt. Massive Golf Club claims to be the highest golf course in the world. I was pleasantly surprised to find such a fine course at this elevation. The greens are not of country club standards, but the fairways are lush and as good as any you will find in Colorado. Seven of the holes are heavily treelined with tall lodge pole pine, and accuracy is a must from tee to green. Five of the holes are doglegs and usually require a medium iron approach shot to get on in regulation. No condominiums line fairways here, and it is a welcome relief to experience the freedom of this beautiful setting.

Mt. Massive is relatively flat with gentle slopes, which makes for easy walking. It is not rare to see an occasional elk, deer, cougar cub, or even a curious brown bear. Rarely do you have to call ahead for tee times, and golfers play throughout the day since temperatures seldom exceed 80 degrees. Stop and play Mt. Massive. You will find it an enjoyable experience.

THE RANCH AT ROARING FORK

LOCATION: Carbondale, Colorado

This golf course is a true par three with par at 27. It is, however, a great golf course for improving your short game, and you hardly ever will have a problem getting on the course. You will find this short little course in excellent condition with good fairways and greens. Water is of some concern on five of the nine holes. Since it won't take long to play this golf course, you will have time for some trout fishing in the Roaring Fork. Good luck!

RIFLE CREEK GOLF CLUB

LOCATION: Rifle, Colorado. Go three miles north of Rifle on Colorado Highway 13. Turn right on Colorado Highway 325 at the Fireside Inn, and go three miles north where you will see the golf course on your right.

TELEPHONE: 625-1093

Rifle Creek was built in 1960 and is a mature well-maintained golf course with excellent fairways, greens, and plenty of trees. It is rather short at 5875 yards for the two nines, but par 72 is hard to come by for most players. The golfer faces a good variety of holes at Rifle Creek, and consequently it is an interesting course to play. This is another out-in-the-country golf course, which makes it all the more enjoyable.

My favorite holes are No. 1, 2, and 6. No. 1 is 346 yards long and par four. It plays level, bends a little left, has out-of-bounds close to the right side, and loosely spaced small evergreens crowd the fairway's left side. A huge cottonwood watches over the green from 20 yards out to the right front. No. 2 is really a good one. It is a par five at 477 yards and plays slightly downhill. Out-of-bounds is right, and both sides of the fairway are lined with widely spaced small evergreens. Most golfers will want to layup short of the stream cutting across the fairway immediately in front of and to the left of the green. Large cottonwoods guard the green's left and right side, and a small sand trap also defends to the green's right. Be satisfied to get on this green in three.

The trouble is all right on the 351-yard par four 6th, so favor the fairway's left side a little as you line up your drive from the elevated tee. Rifle Creek and large cottonwoods extend down the right side of this righthand dogleg and will not allow even the long hitter to go over the corner. Also a small fairway bunker awaits about 40 yards to the right front of the green.

Another nine holes and a new clubhouse are in the planning stages. They are scheduled to be completed in late 1985 or 1986. Facilities here now include a fully equipped pro shop, riding golf carts, pull carts, club rental, driving range, chipping green, and putting green. A snack bar serves lunch, sandwiches, beer, mixed and soft drinks.

This golf course is quite level, and a good one to walk. In addition to getting some exercise, walking gives you more time to enjoy the beautiful scenery of the area.

SALIDA GOLF CLUB

LOCATION: Salida, Colorado. From the main highway near the west edge of town, turn north on Holman Avenue at the green and white golf course sign. Go to the stop sign at the top of the hill and turn right on Poncha Blvd. Go to Grant Street and turn left. You will find the clubhouse on your left after a few blocks.

TELEPHONE: 539-6373

This is another golf course that has been around for almost 50 years. The view of the mountain peaks in all directions is spectacular. You will find the course flat, easy to walk, and with a mixture of old and new cottonwood trees lining some of the fairways. The greens and fairways are well maintained, and at 6360 yards for the two nines it is not a short, easy golf course. I particularly like the 1st, 3rd, 5th, and 8th holes. No. 1 is a lengthy par five at 566 yards, playing straightaway from tee to green. Several sizeable cottonwoods extend along the fairway's left side, while left and right front grass bunkers defend the green. This is a good long par five.

No. 3 is a 200-yard par three with a small pond threatening in the left rough about 30 yards short of the green. The 5th hole is a long par four at 408 yards. Again it plays straightaway, but two bunkers not visible from the tee guard the landing area. Several large cottonwoods surround this green and although they make an attractive setting for the green, they can easily spell trouble for your approach shot.

The 173-yard par three 8th is a tough one because the elevated table-top green on the other side of a lake is so difficult to hold. Actually, all of the holes here at Salida are interesting, and you will enjoy playing the entire course. Facilities in the attractive old log clubhouse include a bar serving beer, mixed drinks, sandwiches, and soft drinks. Course facilities include riding golf carts, pull carts, chipping green, and putting green.

STEAMBOAT GOLF CLUB

LOCATION: Steamboat Springs, Colorado. Five miles west of Steamboat Springs on Highway 40.

TELEPHONE: 879-4295

This golf course was built in 1966, but the many huge cottonwood trees growing here laid claim to the territory a long time before that. Steamboat is short at 5300 yards for two nines, and quite flat, making it an enjoyable course to walk. No doglegs or sand traps to bother you, but the streams, ponds, trees, narrow fairways, and out-of-bounds make it a tight and challenging layout.

I especially like the 2nd and 4th holes. No. 2 is a short par five at 472 yards, but the landing area off the tee is quite narrow with a pond to the left and out-of-bounds to the right. A large cottonwood tree guards the golfer's approach to the green from the fairway's right side. No. 4 is a 393-yard par four with a small stream running along the fairway's left side and out-of-bounds crowding the right side.

You will also find the two short, picturesque par threes quite demanding golf holes, both requiring pinpoint accuracy off the tee.

Course facilities include a fully equipped pro shop, driving range, putting and chipping greens, club rental, riding golf carts, and pull carts. If you are in the area, be sure to play the Steamboat Golf Club. It's a more than adequate challenge to any golfer.

WESTBANK RANCH GOLF AND COUNTRY CLUB

LOCATION: Glenwood Springs, Colorado. Go south of town on Colorado Highway 82 for about 3½ miles. Exit to the right on Road 154, then cross the river bridge and follow the Westbank signs to the clubhouse.

TELEPHONE: 945-7032

Westbank was first open for play in 1970, so it is not an old, mature golf course, but neither is it a new one. Par on this quite open layout is 70 for the two nines, and its length is a fairly respectable 5956 yards. Out-of-bounds left is of concern on the first five holes, and water comes into play on the final four. The fairways and greens are well taken care of and are in excellent, playable condition. Walking this course is not difficult, so hoist your clubs on your back and get some exercise.

All of the holes at Westbank are good ones, but I like No. 2, 6 and 9 the best. The 2nd hole is a 343-yard par four over a bumpy fairway, with out-of-bounds to the fairway's left edge. The rough on this side drops off severely from tee to green. The 6th hole plays 373-yards long and is a par four. It is quite level, doglegs left, and a lake hides behind the green. Out-of-bounds is left, so target your drive a little right of the spruce and aspen trees growing at the left side of the fairway.

No. 9 is a great finishing hole at 443 yards and par four. The problem is the lake in the right rough, and even the long hitter will probably have to go over water for his second shot. The fairway doglegs right at the end of the lake, with no way any player can cut this corner off the tee. Lots of breaking putts can be expected on this undulating green, which is also the largest one on the course.

Facilities at Westbank include a fully equipped pro shop, riding golf carts, pull carts, club rental, chipping and putting greens. At the clubhouse you can get lunch, sandwiches, beer, mixed and soft drinks. A full service restaurant is planned for 1984.

YAMPA VALLEY GOLF CLUB

LOCATION: Craig, Colorado. From Highway 40 in Craig turn south on Ranney Street. Go approximately 2 miles, turn left and go ¼ mile past the airport. At this point you will see a sign indicating the golf course off to the left.

TELEPHONE: 824-9952

This is one of my favorite nine-hole golf courses. At 5510 yards it's not long, but the many majestic old cottonwood trees thriving here make a beautiful setting. I can't tell you how tall these trees are, but it's almost impossible to hit over them with a pitching wedge! There are five doglegs on this course, and the huge cottonwoods are in control on all of them. In addition, several of the straightaway holes have a tree or two situated in the middle of the fairway. The grass in the fairways is lush, and the greens are in excellent condition. Breaking putts are not the exception here! This is another flat valley course and is an easy one to walk.

All the holes are good ones at Yampa Valley, but I think No. 5 and 6 are the best. The 389-yard par four 5th plays longer than indicated and is a sweeping dogleg to the left with plenty of trees guarding that side of the fairway. Shortly past the dogleg are three sizeable trees growing in the fairway's left center. Try to stay right of them off the tee. For most golfers your second shot will be a fairway wood or long iron to the green. If you like breaking putts you will like the 5th green, because I don't think a level spot is to be found. (see sketch pg. 303)

No. 6 is a short par five at 480 yards that doglegs left around a bend in the Yampa River. It's straight off the tee, but the river can come into play for your second shot if you try to reach the green in two. Best to play this hole down the fairway, pitching on with a short iron and hope to get it close for an easy putt. Watch out for the sand trap at the green's left side.

You will find a fully equipped pro shop at Yampa Valley, as well as a driving range, chipping and putting greens, golf carts, and club rental. Lunch, beer, mixed and soft drinks are served daily, while breakfast is available on weekends.

Yampa Valley No. 5
389 yards par four

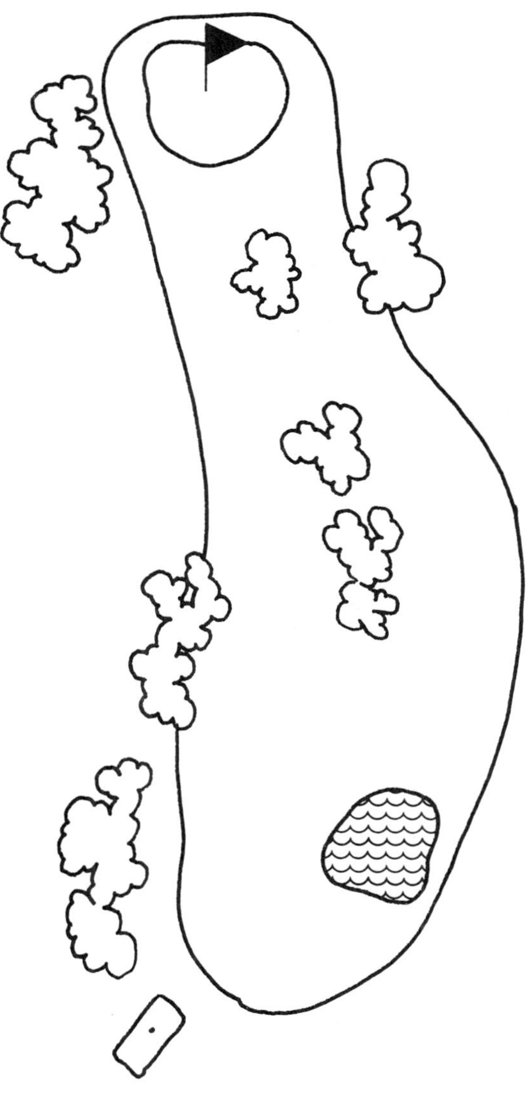

A new back nine is presently under construction and is scheduled for play in late 1984 or mid 1985. If you are anywhere close to Craig, Colorado don't miss playing this fine golf course. It's well worth your time.

CIMARRON HILLS GOLF CLUB

LOCATION: Colorado Springs, Colorado. From Academy Blvd. on the east side of the city go east on Palmer Park Blvd. for a little over 2 miles and you will see the golf course on the left. Take Tuskegee Place into the golf course.

TELEPHONE: 597-2637

Located on the far eastern edge of Colorado Springs, this golf course is probably overlooked by many visitors to the area. The course is long at 6767 yards for the two nines and par is 72. It is a combination of flat, wide-open fairways and several long, sloping hills. All of the greens are of good character, well maintained and trapped. Breaking putts are the rule. You will find the fairways in excellent condition, and work is presently under way to improve the quality of the rough. Several other projects are in the planning stages to further improve the character of this privately owned public golf course.

I like the 6th and 8th holes best, because they play up and downhill. Also the view from the 6th green and the 8th tee box is magnificent! Pikes Peak and the entire Rampart Range loom up to the west. You can see as far south as the Spanish Peaks!

The 362-yard par four 6th plays longer than indicated because it is uphill over a rather roomy fairway. Out-of-bounds and severe rough are left, a sizeable water reservoir sits about 40 yards to the right front of the green, and the green is well trapped with one to the right front and two at the left front. As you can see, plenty of opportunity for trouble awaits on this hole.

No. 8 is another tough one. It plays from an elevated tee down a fairway that doglegs left rather sharply. Several small evergreens guard the inside corner, and it will take a strong hit to clear them. Approaching the green will require at least a mid-iron for most golfers and a longer iron for others. The well-contoured green is trapped to the left front, and several grassy mounds around the edges add to its difficulty.

This fine golf course is worth playing for the challenge it presents while the marvelous view is thrown in for good measure at no extra charge. Give this one a try. I know you will enjoy it.

Facilities here include riding golf carts, pull carts, club rental, driving range, chipping and putting greens. Sandwiches, beer and soft drinks are available at the clubhouse.

CITY PARK MUNICIPAL GOLF COURSE (NORTH COURSE)

LOCATION: 3406 Thatcher Ave., Pueblo, Colorado

TELEPHONE: 561-4946

Par is 60 for the two nines, and the length is only 4162 yards, but you will find this well-established and mature nine-hole golf course of adequate challenge. Interesting terrain, plenty of trees, and several water hazards will help sharpen your short game. You will also find the course in excellent condition and quite exciting to play. Adequate practice, eating, and other clubhouse facilities are readily available as the North course is adjacent to the 18-hole City Park golf course.

COLORADO CITY GOLF CLUB

LOCATION: Colorado City, Colorado. Take Interstate 25 south of Pueblo for about 20 miles, then take Exit 74 to the right. Go about two miles or until you see the signs directing you to the golf course.

TELEPHONE: 676-3340

Colorado City is another out-of-the-way golf course that you absolutely must play. This quiet, peaceful valley with its rolling and sloping terrain makes an ideal setting for a golf course. The Greenhorn Mountains looming to the west only add to this scenic and comfortable part of Colorado. You will find the golf course in excellent condition, with well-maintained fairways, top-notch greens, and each hole offering a different challenge. As usual every hole is interesting, but I especially like No. 2, 4, and 7. No. 2 is a 363-yard par four that plays down a fairway that bends gently left and also kicks slightly right to left. A large cottonwood guards the outside corner at the 150-yard marker, and grassy rough is a small problem to the fairway's left side. The center or left center of the fairway is the place to be off the tee. Approach this green with caution, because it is surrounded by large cottonwoods on three sides and guarded by a drainage ditch to the left side and rear. The cottonwood on the right hangs over the green's right side.

Although not long, the 351-yard par four No. 4 is a dandy. It plays straight off the tee, then bends left about 130 yards from the green. Water to the front and right front of the green requires an accurate approach shot. The green is a little below the golfer as he surveys his shot from the fairway, but take enough club to clear the water.

No. 7 is the number 1 handicap, and it's a good one. At 565 yards and straightaway this par five calls for two long woods and an accurate short iron to reach the green in regulation. Your drive must clear a large lake, then negotiate a narrow fairway that also slopes somewhat right to left. No tree trouble on either side, but the thin grass and sandy rough can be a problem. Favor the fairway's right side off the tee. A good drive will get most golfers to the crest of the fairway. Your second shot is over a valley to the fairway beyond. Cottonwood trees guard the green's right side, and a large elm guards the left. This green has some personality and like most of the others is a touchy one to putt.

While in this area, take some time to visit the mountains to the west. It will be well worth your time, and you will see one of the most beautiful areas in the entire state of Colorado. A lot of people overlook this part of Colorado — don't be one of them!

Facilities at the golf course include riding golf carts, pull carts, club rental, driving range, chipping and putting greens. At the clubhouse you can get breakfast, lunch, sandwiches, dinner, beer, mixed and soft drinks. A swimming pool and tennis courts are also available.

LA JUNTA GOLF CLUB

LOCATION: La Junta, Colorado. Four miles north of La Junta off Highway 109.

TELEPHONE: 384-7133

Flat, well-maintained course with lush fairways and some of the best greens you will ever putt. These greens are small and demand accurate approach shots, but they are also quite level and possess very little break. Mature trees line most of the fairways, and the 439-yard par four 3rd and the 417-yard par four 7th will demand the best from any golfer. The rough is natural prairie and quite costly if you stray from the fairway. This course is seldom crowded, so give it a try when you are in the La Junta area. Be sure to visit the Koshari Indian Museum in town and Bent's Fort nearby. They are both fascinating. Facilities here include a pro shop and practice putting green. Soft drinks and beer are available at the clubhouse.

LIMON MUNICIPAL GOLF COURSE

LOCATION: Limon, Colorado. One mile south of Limon on Colorado Highway 71.

TELEPHONE: 775-9998

The Limon Municipal Golf Course, also known as the Tamarack Country Club, is an excellent nine holes of golf. The fairways are roomy, and the grass is thick, resulting in good clean lies. The greens are large with plenty of character, causing most putts to have a fair amount of break. The two lakes, several greenside bunkers, and the hilly terrain make this a golf course of adequate challenge. Par will not be within reach of most golfers. The facilities here are very good with a fine restaurant serving lunch, dinner, beer, and mixed drinks. The pro shop is well equipped, and practice facilities include a driving range, chipping green and putting green. You will remember the personality of this "out-on-the-prairie" golf course, especially holes No. 1 and 3. These two par fives will fight you all the way before yielding to par.

MEADOW CREEK GOLF COURSE

LOCATION: Colorado City, Colorado. West edge of town on the north side of the highway.

This golf course was not open for play in 1983. If you are in the area, you might want to check it out. I have never played the golf course, but have driven by and observed it. From all indications it appears to be an interesting layout, but will need some attention before opening the course for play again.

PATTY JEWETT

LOCATION:	Colorado Springs, Colorado. Take the Nevada Exit off Interstate 25 and turn east on Espanola. This road will lead you to the golf course.
TELEPHONE:	578-6825 Pro shop 578-6827 Starter

Par is 34 and the distance is 3006 yards from the middle tees on this interesting, old nine-hole golf course. Because the course is part of the total golfing complex at Patty Jewett, it is used primarily for those golfers only wanting to play nine holes. The play here is much like the eighteen-hole course in that the terrain, large trees, hazards, etc., are all similar. Check the eighteen hole section of this book for further information.

I especially like holes No. 1, 3 and 9. The 1st is a long 444-yard par four that plays straightaway over a fairway that slants just a little to the right. Avoid the large cottonwoods to the left off the tee and you should have an open, but long approach to the green. A large bunker, below and to the right, awaits at greenside.

At 360 yards No. 3 is not a long par four, but it is quite difficult. This fairway doglegs left and slopes sharply to the right, making for an extremely touchy tee shot. A medium-to-long iron might be the best shot here. Favor the left side and hope you don't kick right too much and find the drainage ditch along the fairway's right side.

The 411-yard par four 9th could be the finishing hole on anyone's golf course. It plays level and straight, but does bend a little left at the end on the other side of the drainage gulch. Trees line the fairway at the left early on, and are also to the right as you proceed towards the green. A well-hit drive will still leave a long approach shot to the green, which is not trapped but does have several depressed grass bunkers surrounding it. Going for the green or laying up short of the gulch is the big decision and challenge on this hole.

You will like playing this well-conditioned and mature golf course. If you come out as a single, the starter usually will be able to find a game for you.

ROCKY FORD GOLF CLUB

LOCATION: Rocky Ford, Colorado. From the center of town at the stop light, turn south on Main Street. This will lead you into the park and the golf course.

TELEPHONE: 254-7528

Rocky Ford needs to have considerable work done on the fairways before it will reach the fine standards of most of the golf courses in Colorado. Plans are to accomplish this as soon as funds become available. In the meantime one must be content to play golf on a well-laid-out course, with sub-par conditioned fairways lined with many large elm trees. You will find the greens here very good although quite small. No clubhouse facilities are available, but pull carts and golf clubs are for rent.

SPREADING ANTLERS GOLF CLUB

LOCATION: Lamar, Colorado. Go approximately one mile south of town on Highway 287. The golf course will be on your left.

TELEPHONE: 336-5274

Spreading Antlers is not long at 5901 yards for the two nines, but no easy holes await you on this 18-year-old golf course. Willow Creek, which is a rather sizeable drainage draw, comes into play on six of the nine holes. Any ball hit into Willow Creek is a sure goner. Local players have other names for this hazard!

Every hole at Spreading Antlers is interesting and exciting, but I like No. 1, 6 and 9 the best. A long iron or no more than a five wood is all the golfer can hit off the first tee or he will end up in Willow Creek. This forces a fairway wood second shot and a short iron third to get on the green in regulation. This 495-yard par five is not long, nor is it an easy one to par.

In my book, No. 6 is the toughest hole at Lamar. It is a 363-yard par four that plays from an elevated tee, over Willow Creek in the valley below, then uphill to the fairway which doglegs right. Plenty of trouble in both the left and right rough, and I wouldn't recommend trying to shorten this hole by attempting to cut the corner.

No. 9 is another right-hand dogleg at 360 yards and par four. A good drive should get most golfers to the dogleg, but you can almost count on an uphill lie at that point. Proper club selection is important for your approach to the green from this quite hilly fairway. Take one extra club for this shot.

Spreading Antlers is another well-cared-for golf course with excellent greens and fairways. Don't miss any opportunity to play it. This is a walkable course, but somewhat more hilly than others.

The golf course offers a fully equipped pro shop, riding golf carts, pull carts, rental clubs, driving range, chipping and putting greens. Clubhouse facilities include a bar serving sandwiches, beer, mixed and soft drinks.

TRINIDAD MUNICIPAL GOLF COURSE

LOCATION: Trinidad, Colorado. From Interstate 25 near the south end of town, take Exit 13-A to Country Club Drive. Go up the hill part way on Country Club Drive to Nolan Drive. Turn right on Nolan, and you will find yourself at the golf course.

TELEPHONE: 846-9954

The golf course at Trinidad is over 60 years old and is blessed with great natural terrain, hundreds of mature elm and cedar trees, and is always in excellent playing condition. This is not an easy golf course by any means, and any loosely hit shot from tee or fairway will end up in the trees or one of the several canyons running through the area. Every hole at Trinidad is a good one, and they are all different, which makes them quite interesting. Don't forget to ring the bell on No. 2 after your second shot!

It's not easy to pick out any "best" holes on this golf course since they are all challenging, but No. 4, 6, and 7 will give every golfer a run for his money. The 4th is a long par four at 435 yards, which in itself is plenty of trouble. Also, out-of-bounds and many large elm trees closely guard the fairway's left side, as well as another thick line of elm trees extending along the right side of the fairway. Two small sand traps guard the green's left side, and two more crowd the right side of the green. A further problem is the sharp drop-off behind the green.

No. 6 is another long par four at 439 yards and is also heavily treelined with cedars to the left and elms to the right. If you hook your tee shot into the cedars on the left, you can almost count on it being a goner in the deep canyon that extends along that side. Keep your ball in the fairway, and you might have a chance for par.

The 181-yard par three 7th is a good one. It plays from an elevated tee, over a valley to a green on the other side. This picturesque green is surrounded by elm and cedar trees and is deserving of its number 3 handicap rating.

A good job has been done here in relocating tee boxes for the back nine. As a result, the second nine is much more interesting to play than on many other nine-hole courses.

I have tried to stay away from rating golf courses, but Trinidad has to rank right up there with the best of them. I'm sure you will agree, so make every effort to play this fine course at your first opportunity.

Take a moment to observe the clubhouse, both inside and out. Built in 1922, it was considered an interesting and outstanding facility for its time.

Golf carts, pull carts, and golf clubs are available at the pro shop, while practice facilities include a chipping green and putting greens. At the clubhouse one can get sandwiches, beer, mixed and soft drinks.

WALSENBURG GOLF CLUB

LOCATION: Walsenburg Golf Club. The golf course is in Lathrop State Park, which is 3 miles west of town on Highway 160. Turn into the park and follow the signs.

TELEPHONE: 738-2730

Golf is played well into the month of November and beyond at Walsenburg because this course is laid out on the south side of gentle sloping terrain. Many medium size cedar trees loosely line all of the wide and inviting fairways. The condition of this golf course is superb. The greens are all slightly elevated, quite small, and all possessing subtle breaks. You will find the ball sitting up nicely on all the fairways.

I would call Walsenburg a "Holiday Course," because there are no sand traps or water hazards. Its length, 6395 yards for the two nines, makes up for this shortcoming to some extent. The scenery around here and in the distance is spectacular, and the fresh air is exhilarating. Excellent camping facilities lie near the golf course in Lathrop Park, so if you are a camper and a golfer, this might be just the place you are looking for.

Course facilities here include a pro shop, riding golf carts, pull carts, club rental, driving range, and a practice putting green. At the clubhouse one can obtain sandwiches, dinner, beer, mixed and soft drinks.

Don't drive by this golf course without playing it. You will also find it an enjoyable one to walk.

PRIVATE COUNTRY CLUB

COUNTRY CLUB	CITY
Bear Creek Golf Club	Jefferson County
Bookcliff Country Club	Grand Junction
Boulder Country Club	Boulder
Broadmoor Golf Club	Colorado Springs
Burlington Country Club	Burlington
Castle Pines Golf Club	Castle Rock
Cherry Hills Country Club	Englewood
Colorado Springs Country Club	Colorado Springs
Columbine Country Club	Littleton
Country Club of Colorado	Colorado Springs
Denver Country Club	Denver
Eaton Country Club	Eaton
Eisenhower Golf Club	Colorado Springs
Fitzsimons Golf Club	Aurora
Ft. Collins Country Club	Ft. Collins
Fox Acres Country Club	Red Feather
Fox Hill Country Club	Longmont
Gleneagle Country Club	Colorado Springs
Glenmoor of Cherry Hills	Cherry Hills Village
Greeley Country Club	Greeley
Green Gables Country Club	Denver
Heather Ridge Country Club	Denver
Hiwan Golf Club	Evergreen
Inverness Golf Club	Englewood
Kissing Camels Golf Club	Colorado Springs
Lakewood Country Club	Lakewood
Los Verdes Golf Club	Denver
Lowry Golf Club	Denver
Mechaneer Golf Club	Colorado Springs
Meridian Golf Club	Englewood
Perry Park Country Club	Colorado Springs
Peterson Field Golf Club	Colorado Springs
Pinehurst Country Club	Denver
Pinery Country Club	Parker
Plum Creek Golf Club	Castle Rock
Pueblo Country Club	Pueblo
Ranch Country Club	Denver

Rolling Hills Country Club	Golden
Shadow Hills Golf Club	Canon City
Southglenn Country Club	Littleton
Sterling Country Club	Sterling
Valley Country Club	Aurora
Willow Springs Country Club	Morrison
Woodmoor Country Club	Monument

You may purchase extra copies of this book from your local Colorado golf professional or book store. However, if not available there you may order direct from the publisher. Just send $8.95 per book plus $1.25 per book for postage and handling. Colorado residents please add 32 cents for state sales tax.

Total cost for out of state residents	$10.20
Total cost for in state residents	$10.52

Mail check or money order to:

COLORADO LEISURE SPORTS
P.O. Box 1953
Estes Park, Colorado 80517

Be sure to include return address.